Colonial and Imperial Banking History

T0360891

This book sheds new light on the role played by European banks in the economic colonization of much of the globe. Based on previously unused archival material, it examines the origins and development of imperial banking systems. Contributors utilize new developments and methodology in business history to explore a broad range of countries including Cuba, Brazil, Portugal, South Africa and Algeria.

The central topic of interest in this book is the institutional history of central, issuing and rediscounting banks. While much attention has been paid to the British, Dutch and French banks and financial institutions, this book is unique in its focus on colonial and overseas banking. Using a range of case studies, this volume highlights both the immense variety and the cohesion that defined colonial banking practices.

This book will be of interest to researchers concerned with international finance and banking and economic history.

Hubert Bonin is a researcher at the GREThA Research Institute, Bordeaux University, and at Sciences Po Bordeaux, Bordeaux, France.

Nuno Valério is Full Professor at the School of Economics and Management, Universidade de Lisboa, Portugal.

Banking, Money and International Finance

Colonial and Imperial Banking History

Edited by
Hubert Bonin and Nuno Valério

Routledge
Taylor & Francis Group

LONDON AND NEW YORK

First published 2016
by Routledge
2 Park Square, Milton Park, Abingdon, Oxon OX14 4RN

and by Routledge
711 Third Avenue, New York, NY 10017

First issued in paperback 2017

Routledge is an imprint of the Taylor & Francis Group, an informa business

British Library Cataloguing in Publication Data
A catalogue record for this book is available from the British Library

Library of Congress Cataloging in Publication Data
A catalog record has been requested for this book

ISBN 13: 978-1-138-49554-8 (pbk)
ISBN 13: 978-1-84893-582-2 (hbk)

Typeset in Times New Roman
by Deanta Global Publishing Services, Chennai, India

Contents

Illustrations

Contributors

Hubert Bonin is a researcher in modern economic history at *Sciences Po Bordeaux* and at the GREThA research centre at Bordeaux University. He is a specialist of the history of services companies (Suez Canal Company, colonial and overseas trading houses and their maritime affiliates) and of French banking history (regional banks, Paris deposit banks, corporate banks and investment banks), on which he has published several monographs and a number of handbooks. He is preparing a large history of French *Société générale* (from 1864 to the 1940s) in several volumes (the first published in 2006) and is developing histories of the French global economy of investment banks and of the action of French banks in eastern Asia and in Greece. As a specialist in business history, he has co-guided the research programs *Ford in Europe (1903–2003)* (published in 2003); *American Firms in Europe* (published in 2008); *Old Paternalism, New Paternalism, Post-Paternalism* (published in 2013); and *Investment Banking History* and *Imperial Banking History* (2014), and he is taking part in several programs in banking and business history along French, European or Asian perspectives, especially about investment banking, merchant and trade banking, economic patriotism, entrepreneurship and European business.

Piet Geljon studied economics and economic history at the Free University in Amsterdam. In 1964 he joined Nederlandse Overzee Bank, one of the predecessors of Bank Mees & Hope/MeesPierson, which was, through Fortis, ultimately absorbed into ABN AMRO. He worked in the economic and securities research departments and ended his career as an economic advisor to MeesPierson. He has published on capital and futures market developments and wrote the history of a private Dutch banking house and two Amsterdam securities firms. In 2005 he took his Ph.D. with a study on the general banks in the Netherlands and the securities business in the period 1860–1914. In collaboration with ABN AMRO Archives, Art & History Department he is now preparing a study on the history of Netherlands Bank of South Africa/Netherlands Overseas Bank (*Nederlandsche Bank voor Zuid-Afrika/Nederlandse Overzee Bank*).

Ton de Graaf studied modern and economic-social history at the University of Amsterdam. Since 1991 he is corporate historian at ABN AMRO Archives, Art & History Department. He has published about bank-historical, business-historical and regional-historical themes. He is chairman of the Association of Enterprise and History (Vereniging Bedrijf & Historie). In 2012 he took his Ph.D. at Utrecht University with a study on the Netherlands Trading Society, a predecessor of ABN AMRO Bank. He is now preparing a study on the history of United Savings Banks (*Verenigde Spaarbank*).

Carlos Gabriel Guimarães (MA, University Federal Fluminense; Ph.D., University of São Paulo; postdoctoral, University of Lisbon) is Professor Associate IV at the University Federal Fluminense, Rio de Janeiro, and Researcher 1 of the National Center for Scientific and Technological Development (CNPq). He is visiting research fellow at University of York/CEGBI (2014–2015). He was president of the Brazilian Association of Researchers in Economic History (ABPHE, 2005–2007), and he is associate member of the European Business History Association (EBHA) and others. He received the Scientist Award of Our State granted by the Research Foundation of the State of Rio de Janeiro (FAPERJ, 2009). His recent publications include *A Presença Inglesa nas Finanças e no Comércio no Brasil Imperial. Os casos da Sociedade Bancária Mauá MacGregor & Co. (1854–1866) e da firma inglesa Samuel Phillips & Co. (1808–1840)*, São Paulo, Alameda, 2013; *Ensaios de História Econômico Social: Séculos XIX e XX*, Niterói, EDUFF, 2012, p. 274; 'Contratos e contratadores do Atlântico sul na segunda metade do setecentos', *História, histórias*, I/2013, pp. 72–87; 'London and Brazilian Bank Limited (1862–1871)', in *Dicionário de História Empresarial Portuguesa, Séculos XIX e XX*, vol. I: *Instituições Bancárias*, first edition, Lisboa, Imprensa Nacional e Casa da Moeda, 2013, pp. 596–601; 'Finanças e Comércio no Brasil da primeira metade do século XIX: a atuação da firma inglesa Samuel Phillips & Co, 1808–1831', in Carvalho, José Murilo e Neves, Lucia B. P. das (eds), *Perspectivas da cidadania no Brasil Império*, Rio de Janeiro, Civilização Brasileira, 2011, p. 461–485; 'Os Bancos e a Históriografia Econômica: uma discussão historiográfica', in Martins, Monica L. (ed.), Encontros *entre a Economia e a História*, Rio de Janeiro, Multifoco, 2011, pp. 63–74.

Pablo Martín-Aceña is professor of economics and economic history at the University of Alcalá (Madrid). He has been visiting scholar at the Karl Marx University of Economics (Budapest), Harvard University (Boston, MA), Leuven University (Leuven, Belgium), El Colegio de Mexico (Mexico DF), Université Paris VII, *Institut de sciences politiques* (Paris), and the University of Cambridge. His research interest focuses mainly in monetary and financial history. His latest books in English are *The Economic Development in Spain Since 1870* (with J. Simpson), London, Edward Elgar (1995) and *Monetary Standards in the Periphery* (with Jaime Reis), London, MacMillan Press (2000). He edited the volumes *150 Years in the History of the Bank of Spain* (2006) and *A Century of History of the Spanish Financial System* (2011). He is former editor of the *Revista de Historia Económica* and former president of the Spanish Economic History Association.

Ines Roldán de Montaud is full research scientist in history at the Spanish National Research Council (CSIC – *Consejo Superior de Investigaciones*

Científicas-España) and has been an associate professor at the faculty of arts of the Universidad de Alcalá (Madrid) since 1997. She was a research scholar at the London School of Economics, 1992–1993. She is the author of several books, monographs and chapters and has published numerous research essays. Roldán de Montaud's publications include *La Restauración en Cuba: el fracaso de un proceso reformista* (CSIC, 2000); *La Banca de emisión en Cuba, 1856–1898* (Banco de España, 2004); *Las Cajas de Ahorros de las provincias de Ultramar, 1840–1848. Cuba y Puerto Rico* (FUNCAS, 2010); and, as editor, *Las Haciendas públicas en el Caribe hispano en el siglo XIX* (CSIC, 2008).

Samir Saul is a professor of international history at the Université de Montréal. He specializes in the history of modern France and the modern Arab world. He is the author of *La France et l'Egypte de 1882 à 1914: intérêts économiques et implications politiques* (Paris, 1997) and co-editor of *Méditerranée, Moyen-Orient: deux siècles de relations internationales* (Paris, 2003). He has published articles on the history of banking, insurance, oil and electricity. He is completing a book on French economic interests and the decolonization of North Africa.

Palmira Tjipilica, Angolan nationality, MA in history at the Universidade Nova de Lisboa (1995), has been professor at the University Agostinho Neto, Luanda, since 2003. Main publications include 'Economic activity in the Portuguese Colonial Empire: a factor analysis approach', *Économies et Sociétés*, series 'Histoire économique quantitative', AF, 39(9), 2008 (co-author); 'Idéaux républicains et régime des indigènes dans l'empire colonial portugais après l'instauration de le République en 1910', *Outre-Mers. Revue d'histoire*, second semester 2012 (co-author).

Nuno Valério, Portuguese nationality, Ph.D. in economics at the Technical University of Lisbon (1982), is full professor at the School of Economics and Management, Universidade de Lisboa, since 1989. Main publications include *Asian Imperial Banking History*, London, Pickering & Chatto, 2014 (co-editor); *Foreign Financial Institutions and National Financial Systems*, Warsaw, European Association for Banking and Financial History, 2013 (co-editor); *The Concise Economic History of Portugal. A Comprehensive Guide*, Lisboa, Almedina, 2011 (co-author); *History of the Portuguese Banking System* (2 volumes), Lisboa, Banco de Portugal, 2006–2010 (editor); *The Escudo, The Portuguese Currency Unit, 1911–2001*, Lisboa, Banco de Portugal, 2001; *Portuguese Historical Statistics* (2 volumes), Lisboa, Instituto Nacional de Estatística, 2001 (editor); *Growth and Stagnation in the Mediterranean World in the 19th and 20th Centuries*, Leuven, Leuven University Press, 1990 (co-editor).

Grietjie Verhoef is professor in accounting, economic and business history in the Department of Accountancy at the University of Johannesburg. She is the director of the South African Accounting History Centre. She has published widely on insurance and banking history as well as the history of South African conglomerates, with special reference to the rise of Afrikaner business in South Africa. She is engaged in research on the accountancy profession in South Africa in comparative perspective with other Commonwealth countries and with research into the reconstruction of colonial gross domestic product for the second half of the nineteenth century in South African colonies, as well as research into big business groups and family businesses in South Africa. She has published chapters in 12 books and 58 peer reviewed articles and delivered 60 international and national conference papers. She was recently president of the International Economic History Association.

Part I

Overall issues

1 Issues about European colonial banking

Varieties of cultures, models and histories

Hubert Bonin and Nuno Valério

One might suppose that banking history has come to a turning point. The accumulation of case studies has for many years offered the opportunity to understand the specific role of banks in long-term economic development. In recent times, the business history approach – both methodological and theoretical – has added new elements for a more specific evaluation of the Chandlerian paradigm – the couple 'strategy' and 'structure' – in this sector. There are many reasons to appreciate the effort that has been made to adapt a methodology, and a sort of *Weltanschauung* (some kind of a world-wide system), conceived for big industrial companies to financial institutions. However, some areas of banking history still need improvement, and that is the case for banks active in overseas territories either under European influence or still undergoing the move to development. This explains why this book chose to confront various histories on a geographical field (Africa, Latin America and the Caribbean, with a few in Asia) but also on a thematic field: colonial and imperial banking.

The book is the result of a workshop conducted as part of the World Economic History Association (WEHA) Congress held at the University of Stellenbosch, South Africa, in August 2012. It was chaired jointly by Professor Hubert Bonin (Sciences Po Bordeaux and GREThA-Bordeaux University, France), Professor Nuno Valério (Universidade de Lisboa, Portugal) and Professor Kazuhiko Yago (Waseda University, Japan). The theme of the workshop was *Imperial Banking: Imperial strategies of exporting finance modernisation (19th–20th centuries)*. This book is the second volume of the proceedings of this workshop; the first one was published by Pickering & Chatto in December 2014, earmarked to *Asian Imperial Banking History*. This one contains the papers presented at the workshop which were earmarked to colonial and imperial banking outside Asia, even though some chapters include Asia into their comparative and conceptual developments. But, although the original project was presented first as a workshop at the International Economic History Conference in South Africa, it has not of course kept the structure or the characteristics of the conference proceedings; the re-elaboration has been deep and very rigorous. All the chapters are largely the result of very fresh and recent research in many archives.

Targeting colonial, imperial or overseas banking history

The central topic analyzed in our book is part of the institutional history of central, issuing and rediscounting banks, as their role and initiative are strongly connected with the activities of the local banking sub-system in colonial areas. Indeed, we recognize that the topic is not original in general, because there are many remarkable books and articles about important British, Dutch or French banks and financial institutions that built their fortunes in the colonies, as an articulation of the national banking system in the motherland. But our collective publication strongly complements the legacy of the overall historiography about colonial and overseas banking. The original elements are the variety and the cohesion of the different case studies highlighted in the different chapters. The geographical extension of the book adds yet another element. Most of the continents are considered, and not only the most studied – Asia or South America. One of the predominant ideas is to enlarge the concept of 'imperial banks' to any relevant financial institution of Western Europe working in both colonies and parts of the different overseas empires, and even in independent entities like South Africa. The chapters evaluate not only the interaction – and its varieties in time and space – between the colonial or imperial banks and their financial background in Europe but also their specific performance, and such assessments are due to the deep archival research conducted by all the contributors to this book. This approach, given the long-term perspective in the collection of articles, enriches our understanding of colonial and banking histories and permits, at least in some cases, a consideration of the banking activities in the years following the end of the colonial period as well.

By the time European powers had imposed political control over most of Africa, the Pacific islands and a significant part of Asia, banking systems were already well established and formed a relevant part of the economic life of these colonizing powers.[1] Along with the somewhat raw forms of 'imperialism' and colonialism (army, police, customs, tax collection, mining exploitation, economy of plantation), the imperial banking system was also connected with softer forms of imperialism and colonialism, what may be called 'gentlemanly capitalism'.[2] It was only natural that banks became important instruments of economic exploration in the colonized territories. This book examines the origins and development of such 'imperial' banking systems and, where it occurred, their continuation after decolonization.

In that context, the qualification of 'imperial' is drawn for the phrase 'colonial empires', as it became usual to talk about imperial cultures and imperial economies to characterize histories about the colonial empires. It draws lessons from the recent breakthroughs in the knowledge of the 'imperial economic systems' and provides fodder for comparative ways of grappling with issues that contribute to the main theme established for the WEHA Congress: *Exploring the Roots of Development*.[3] But our conclusive chapter will dedicate its arguments to the very topics of the differentiation between imperial, colonial and transnational banking, indeed! Thus, colonial territories as 'imperial areas' were involved;

that is, the economies of port cities and trading hubs within dependent countries (for the overall book) or independent countries (South Africa after WWII). 'Colonial' or 'imperial' overseas strategies, practices and skills linked all these countries, where port cities formed key hubs for the deployment of banking institutions, together.

Recent developments in methodology, archive retrieval and approaching problematics have opened new ways for tackling the history of the banking business. Our book applies these methods to the specialized field of colonial and overseas territories; it draws lessons from the recent breakthroughs in the knowledge of the 'imperial economic systems' and fuels comparative ways of grappling with such issues, as well as the wider issues of 'international banking'.[4] It then highlights points of differentiation between them as they both belong, in a fashion, to multinational or transnational firms.[5] One important element of novelty might be that the chapters offer new paths thanks to case studies where risk management and creditworthiness have been deeply gauged, and where network analysis and the human resources factor have been taken into account, with clear evidence of the building of human resources constituencies around teams of expatriates, members of diasporas, and native business and political elites. The human factor is considered a key element also in evaluating the capabilities to respond with the highest skills and competences to very complex tasks in everyday banking activities, mainly when crises were to be faced. All these elements also contribute to a profile of some of the most relevant elements depicting the specific corporate culture of these banks and financial institutions, their specificity and their difference compared to the homeland banks.

At the same time, the 'varieties' of overseas capitalism demand specific approaches depending on area and territory; the differences between various models of overseas banking depend on the political and economic background of these overseas territories and the status of the institutions themselves (based overseas or in the metropolis, connected with the state or more independent), etc. Each participant thus provides his or her own definition and overview of what constituted 'overseas banks'. Some of the key points will be scrutinized in the following sections.

The geographical span of the enquiry covers several continents. A traditional approach deals with the bilateral links between Western Europe and the areas involved in colonial banking, trade, commodities and maritime flows; that is, for this book, the Caribbean islands, North Africa, sub-Saharan Africa and southern Africa. The contribution of the banking sector to 'imperialism' in this unequal relationship is to be gauged, therefore.

Institutional business history and overseas banking strategies

Extensive studies on the imperial deployment of European banks have appeared in several collective works, in particular *Banks as Multinationals*.[6] The interaction between European and Asian trading hubs goes back to imperial and colonial times,[7] with banking power given as much importance as overseas politics and commerce,[8] to the extent that one talked of 'paradise lost'.[9] Major banking institutions sprang up as part of this 'imperial' deployment, whether in the territories controlled by the Ottoman Empire[10] or within Japan's commercial hegemony.[11] Examined in another book (*Imperial Banking History*), Asia saw on its side the emergence of big 'imperial' banks from Western Europe,[12] Russia and Japan, which positioned themselves at the heart of the information, commercial paper and currency networks.[13] Though Asia had both official and 'informal'[14] empires, the 'imperial' bank was a very real entity, whatever the status of the territory it was active in.

We propose to study the institutional history of central, issuing and rediscounting banks as the cornerstone of the local banking subsystems overseas – and the case of Algeria is brought out. We assess, with the help of monographs and archives, the founding, maturing and performance of local banking systems overseas. We outline the strategies adopted by metropolitan private and public institutions or specific colonial bodies. We also highlight and compare the variety of connections between 'metropolitan' or 'mainland' territories and their overseas outlets. Case studies are confronted within the somewhat classical 'colonial' deployments (British, French, Dutch, etc.).

Skills portfolios constitute the centrepiece of the following chapters. The differentiation and convergence between the overseas banking services and the metropolitan banking and financial sectors will be outlined. The specificities of foreign banking practices will be determined: risk management, assessment of creditworthiness, collateralizing and pledges, etc. We will identify the techniques used to preserve the durability of businesses as well as their corporate culture. Finally, we shall trace the building of human resources from teams of expatriates, the diaspora and local elites.

Corporate banking was the catalyst for enhancing the convergence between metropolitan business forces active abroad and the banking sector within a 'consolidated' economic system in each imperial area. Banking in colonial port cities is to be seen as an original 'variety of capitalism' – it integrated connections between the colony and the metropolis, on one hand, and between the colony and the rest of the world, on the other. The connections between the metropolitan financial market and overseas banking have been analyzed with regard to investment banking, underwriting, etc. The integration of banking into the development of 'modernized' areas and overseas economic pockets and its contribution to the emergence of local forms of capitalist business and social groups will be outlined.

The collapse of several markets for metropolitan and foreign companies active overseas, along with the geo-economic rebuilding of the world frames for production and exchanges and the evolution of the relations with native entrepreneurs and with customers, could also be a centrepiece of 'imperial banking'. No stability at all predominated, either under the impulse of competition or because of the changes of the local productive systems – not to mention the disappearance or the resurgence of a market economy in the countries choosing the path of a centralized economy (for instance in China or in Vietnam and, to some extent, in India).

Geographical paths for colonial banking

Banking did not play any role in the first period of European colonization in America and the Far East between the sixteenth century and the early nineteenth century. However, by the early nineteenth century, banking had progressed sufficiently to become an important instrument of European colonial endeavours. There is no room to engage in a lengthy discussion here of the origins of banking systems or the roots of European imperialism. In spite of that, some aspects of the framework provided by these structures must be considered in order to examine whether it is possible to distinguish between different types of 'imperial' or 'colonial' banking in different European colonial powers.[15]

The Netherlands and Great Britain may be credited with the earliest development of banking systems. As both nations were already significant colonial powers in the early nineteenth century, it should come as no surprise that they created the earliest European colonial banks, during the first half of the nineteenth century. The fourth section deals with early Dutch and British colonial banks. France, Spain and Portugal were the other main European colonial powers at the beginning of the nineteenth century. At the time, these countries lacked banking systems that were as developed as those of the Netherlands and Great Britain, and the Iberian powers ended up losing most of their colonial possessions between 1810 and 1830. This explains why they only began to establish colonial banks by the mid-nineteenth century. These French, Spanish and Portuguese colonial banks of the mid-nineteenth century were somewhat different from the early Dutch and British ones. The fifth section deals with French, Spanish and Portuguese colonial banks of the mid-nineteenth century.

The progress of European 'imperialism' between the 1860s and 1880s inevitably led to further developments in the form of new types of banks designed specifically for colonial business, especially in Great Britain, France and Germany. The sixth section deals with this generation of British, French and German colonial banks that appeared in the second half of the nineteenth century. The late nineteenth century witnessed what became known as the scramble for Africa (and also the Pacific islands and Asian territories). Of course, this called for the formation of a new wave of colonial banks. The seventh and eighth sections deal with the colonial banks established in the late nineteenth century and early twentieth century. A few additional colonial banks were created during the interwar period, either as the consequence of the establishment of new colonies (especially under the League of Nations' regime of mandates) or as a result of the increased sophistication of economic life in the old colonies: the ninth section deals therefore with the main colonial banks established in the interwar period. The last sections provide an overview of this elementary survey of European colonial banks.

The early Dutch and British colonial banks

The first generation of European colonial banks comprised one Dutch bank, Bank of Java [*De Javasche Bank*], created in 1828 for the Dutch East Indies, which included at the time Java and parts of some neighbouring Indonesian islands (hence the name of the bank). It later came to include most of the Indonesian archipelago and western New Guinea, the exceptions being northern Borneo (British) and East Timor (Portuguese). This corresponds to present-day Indonesia. The British colonial empire was, on its side, equipped with several British 'chartered banks': Bank of Australasia, created in 1835 for Australia and New Zealand, and Colonial Bank, created in 1837 for the British West Indies and British Guiana. The British West Indies included the Bahamas, Barbados, Jamaica (with the Turks and Caicos Islands and the Cayman Islands as dependencies), Trinidad and Tobago, the Windward Islands (Grenada, Saint Lucia, Saint Vincent and the Grenadines, and Dominica), the Leeward Islands (Antigua, Barbuda, the British Virgin Islands, Montserrat, Saint Kitts, Nevis and Anguilla) and British Honduras (present-day Belize); British Guiana corresponded to present-day Guyana. Also established as levers to 'colonial banking' were the so-called presidency banks chartered by the British East India Company for different regions of British India during the first half of the nineteenth century – Bank of Calcutta, created in 1806 and renamed Bank of Bengal in 1809; Bank of Bombay, created in 1840; and Bank of Madras, created in 1843.

These banks were based on a solid British and Dutch experience that had already materialized into well-developed banking systems, including a proto-central bank, respectively Bank of England and Bank of the Netherlands [*De Nederlandsche Bank*]. The new colonial banks displayed a number of similarities with these proto-central banks: they were joint-stock banks performing issuing and commercial operations; and they were promoted by the government to provide short-term financing for public and private agents in a given territory. They enjoyed a rather successful evolution, although somewhat divergent in terms of their relationships with their respective governments. Bank of Java remained within the orbit of the Dutch government, later becoming the issuing bank of Indonesia in 1949 and being transformed into Bank Indonesia after its nationalization in 1953.[16]

The British 'chartered banks' drifted away from the orbit of the British government and, during the second half of the nineteenth century, gradually became similar to the freestanding banks mentioned later in the chapter. Colonial Bank ended up being acquired by the Barclays group and merged with Anglo-Egyptian Bank and National Bank of South Africa to form Barclays Bank (Dominion, Colonial and Overseas – DCO) in 1925.[17] National Bank of South Africa belonged to the local bank type mentioned later. It was created in 1888 as National Bank of the South African Republic [*De Nationale Bank der Zuid-Afrikaansche Republiek*] (Transvaal). It later absorbed several other local banks: in 1910, National Bank of the Orange River Colony, created in 1877 as National Bank of the Orange Free State [*De Nationale Bank van den Oranje Vrystaat*]; in 1912, Bank of Africa, created in 1879 to take over the operations in the Cape Colony of Indian Oriental Bank, which in 1873 had absorbed Eastern Province Bank, the second oldest local bank of the Cape Colony, created in 1838; and in 1914, Natal Bank, the oldest local bank of the Natal Colony, created in 1854. Bank of Australasia eventually merged in 1951 with Union Bank of Australia, a local bank created in 1837, to form today's ANZ Bank.[18] The Indian presidency banks merged in 1921 to form Imperial Bank of India, which was acquired in 1955 by the proto-central bank, Reserve Bank of India, created in 1935, to form a government-owned bank called State Bank of India.[19]

During the same period, the development of European societies overseas provided the basis for the formation of local banks in several British colonies. The earliest cases were those of Bank of Montreal, created in 1817 in Canada, which still survives today as one of the largest Canadian banks; the already-mentioned Union Bank of Australia, created in 1837 in Australia, which merged with the Bank of Australasia to form today's ANZ Bank; and Cape of Good Hope Bank, created in 1837 in South Africa (Cape Colony), which was absorbed in 2003 by Nedcor Bank. The latter has its roots in Dutch Bank and Credit Union for South Africa [*Nederlandsche Bank en Credietvereeniging voor Zuid-Afrika*], a free-standing Dutch bank created in 1888 to do business in the then independent South African Boer Republic (Transvaal).[20] A last institution was Union Bank, created in 1839 in India (Bengal), which collapsed in 1848. The first successful local bank in India was Allahabad Bank, created in 1865. Many other local banks were created in the following decades.

Other colonial empires did not experience the formation of banks during the first half of the nineteenth century, at least not successful ones. An interesting example of a failed experiment of this nature was the first Bank of Brazil [*Banco do Brasil*], a mixed case of a government-promoted bank and a local bank, created in 1809 by the Portuguese government when it was established in Rio de Janeiro after fleeing from the French occupation of the continental part of Portugal. This first Bank of Brazil was a long way from fulfilling the expectations of the Portuguese government, and it had to be liquidated two decades later by the government of Brazil, by then already an independent country.[21]

French, Spanish and Portuguese colonial banks of the mid-nineteenth century

By the mid-nineteenth century, the French, Spanish and Portuguese colonial empires had acquired their earliest successful colonial banks. These banks were of quite different types. Most French colonial banks of the first generation were created in the wake of the abolition of slavery in the French colonies in 1848. This was the case with *Banque de la Guadeloupe, Banque de la Martinique, Banque de la Guyane, Banque de La Réunion* and *Banque du Sénégal*.[22] The initial capital of these banks was formed from money deducted from the indemnities that the decree of 27 April 1848 paid to the former slave owners: it was made mandatory for one-eighth of all indemnities over 1,000 francs (corresponding to two slaves) to be paid in the form of shares in the equity of these banks, according to the Law of 11 July 1851 (Law of 1 July 1854, in the case of *Banque de la Guyane*). Thus, the former slave owners (mainly plantation owners) of each territory were forced to become shareholders of an organization that was supposed to provide them with credit for developing their businesses on a new footing.

For that purpose, these banks combined the operations of issuing, commercial, mortgage and agricultural investment banks. Each bank was supposed to operate only in the colony that gave it its name, as well as having its head office in the territory of that colony. As the would-be shareholders had not accepted their status voluntarily, the French government had to provide the initial impulse and exercised a great deal of control over the process. As was to be expected, the troubled economic evolution of each colony in the short term resulted in a great number of problems for each bank over the following decades, but in the end they managed to survive and to fulfil the role assigned to them in their initial design.

These banks remained within the direct orbit of the French government until the post-WWII years. In 1944 the government decided to put an end to the role of the *Banque de la Guadeloupe, Banque de la Martinique, Banque de la Guyane* and *Banque de La Réunion* as issuing banks, making this the task of the Central Fund of Overseas France [*Caisse centrale de la France d'Outre-Mer*]. Over the course of the following decade, these four banks became part of the *Crédit lyonnais* group. *Banque du Sénégal* had a different evolution. Another bank created in the 1850s in order to operate in a French colony was *Banque d'Algérie*. This was quite different from the banks that had been created for the plantation colonies, since its design was based on the model of *Banque de France*. Notice that Algeria was conceived as a settlement colony, although the European settlers always remained a minority among the Arab-Berber population. The ultimate consequence of this contradiction was the protracted war of independence between 1954 and 1962. Thus, it was simultaneously the sole banknote issuer in the territory and a commercial bank, without any interest in long-term operations. It remained faithful to this model throughout most of its evolution, in spite of some experiments with long-term credit in the late nineteenth century. It was only natural that it should eventually become a central bank, a transformation that took place after Algeria was granted independence in 1962.[23]

The Spanish colonial banks of the mid-nineteenth century belonged to the mixed government-promoted local bank type already mentioned in the case of the first Bank of Brazil. *Banco Español Filipino* was created in 1851, and *Banco Español de La Habana* was created in 1856. Both were issuing and commercial banks designed to foster the financial and economic development of the colony where they were established. *Banco Español Filipino* was rather successful, and its activity even survived the end of Spanish rule in 1898. During the period of American rule, it was renamed Bank of the Philippine Islands in 1912 and remained an issuing bank until the establishment of Central Bank of the Philippines [*Bangko Sentral ng Pilipinas*] in 1949. Nowadays, it is one of the country's main universal banks.[24] *Banco Español de La Habana* tended to become overly dependent on the Spanish government in Cuba because of the role it played in financing the government during the first nationalist revolt of 1868–1878. It changed its name to *Banco Español de la Isla de Cuba* in 1881, but did not change its links to the government, which increased during the second nationalist revolt beginning in 1895. As a result, it collapsed when Cuba fell to the United States of

America in 1898. A third Spanish colonial bank, *Banco Español de Puerto Rico*, was established in 1888, also operating as an issuing and commercial bank. It was able to avoid the pitfall of government dependence that destroyed the Cuban bank and survived, like the Philippine one, into the period of American rule as Bank of Puerto Rico.[25]

The Portuguese *Banco Nacional Ultramarino* was designed to perform the same operations as the French colonial banks of the plantation colonies. However, it had several quite distinctive features. Its creation in 1864 was the result of a joint venture between an entrepreneur (Francisco Chamiço) and the Portuguese government. It was formed as one single bank for the whole Portuguese colonial empire, not as a specific bank for each colony. At the time, the Portuguese colonial empire comprised six colonies: Cape Verde (including the coast of Guinea, which later became a separate colony), São Tomé and Príncipe, Angola, Mozambique, India and Macao (including East Timor, which later became a separate colony). And the bank combined its colonial role with its operations as an ordinary commercial bank in Portugal proper. This last detail proved crucial. On the one hand, it was positive, because it allowed the bank to more easily overcome the ups and downs resulting from the evolution of the colonial economy over the short term, which caused so many problems for the French and Spanish imperial banks. However, on the other hand, it absorbed most of the resources of the bank, giving rise to frequent critical appraisals of its activity, which was described as not really being that of a colonial bank.

British colonial and imperial banks: the varieties of models

Besides the case of HSBC itself, which will be considered in the conclusive chapter of the book, a second generation of British colonial banks was created during the third quarter of the nineteenth century. They were no longer government-promoted banks designed to operate in a given territory. They were commercial banks, created by private entrepreneurs in order to develop their business in colonial territories. This often meant that banks ended up performing both issuing operations and investment operations, in order to complement their core commercial business.

Chartered Bank of India, Australia & China, created in 1851, may be considered a transitional case. It was chartered by the British government, as its name implies, but it was formed at the initiative of a private entrepreneur (James Wilson), and, although it eventually became an issuing bank in Hong Kong and Shanghai, its core business was that of a commercial bank in India and China. After WWII, in 1957, it bought Eastern Bank, establishing its presence in the Middle East. Eastern Bank was a freestanding bank created in 1909, which had a network covering India, the Middle East and Malaysia, although this was somewhat weakened by the nationalization of its operations in Iraq (1964) and South Yemen (1969).

Standard Bank of Africa, created in 1862; Anglo-Egyptian Bank, created in 1864; and Hong Kong & Shanghai Banking Corporation, created in 1865, are the most important examples from this group of freestanding banks. Standard Bank of Africa, formed at the initiative of John Paterson, began its business in South Africa, but later expanded into the British colonies of southern, Central and East Africa. In 1879, it absorbed London and South African Bank, a similar freestanding bank created in 1861, and in 1920 it acquired African Banking Corporation, created in 1890 (see the eighth section). After WWII, it bought Bank of British West Africa, also created in 1890 (ibid.), establishing its presence in the British colonies of West Africa too. In 1969, Chartered Bank of India, Australia & China and Standard Bank of Africa merged, giving birth to the present-day Standard Chartered Bank.[26]

Egypt was then in the ambiguous situation of being an Ottoman province that was independent for all practical purposes – a situation further complicated from 1882 onwards by its becoming an informal British protectorate, which became formal (together with the severing of its ties to the Sublime Porte) in 1914. The British protectorate was formally ceased in 1922, but remained in practice until the immediate post-WWII years. Anglo-Egyptian Bank, formed as a joint venture of several London private bankers, had its first branch in Alexandria, but later extended its activity not only to Egypt in general, but also to other British Mediterranean possessions – Cyprus in 1878, Malta in 1881, Gibraltar in 1888, the British colony of Sudan on the eve of WWI and the newly created British mandate of Palestine immediately after WWI. In 1921, Barclays Bank acquired control of Anglo-Egyptian Bank, which merged with Colonial Bank and National Bank of South Africa to form Barclays Bank (DCO) in 1925. Parts of the former network of Anglo-Egyptian Bank were nationalized in the post-colonial era and gave birth to national banks. This was the case in 1956 with the Egyptian operations, which became Bank of Alexandria, and in 1970 with the Sudanese operations, which became Bank of Khartoum.

Challenging British colonial and imperial supremacy

Determined to restrain the hegemony of British thalassocracy, French banks were trying to get a share of the Far East business. The forerunner was *Comptoir d'escompte de Paris*, which opened branches in Shanghai and Calcutta in 1860 and expanded its overseas network during the following decades to Bombay, Hong Kong, Yokohama, Alexandria, Melbourne and Sydney, besides opening branches in French territories such as La Réunion and Saigon.[27] The expansion of the French colonial empire into Indochina from the 1860s onwards led to the formation in 1875 of *Banque de l'Indochine*, a consortium of several large French banks (the main ones being the Paribas [*Banque de Paris et des Pays-Bas*], and later on *Société générale*), created for the purpose of doing banking business in the East. This bank adopted a similar design to that of the second generation of British colonial banks. Its activity stretched from the French colonies of East Africa (French Somalia, present-day Djibouti) to the Pacific islands (French New Caledonia, French Polynesia and the Anglo-French Condominium of the New Hebrides, present-day Vanuatu), but it remained largely centred in the region that gave the bank its name, where the French colonies included

Vietnam, Laos and Cambodia, and in the newly opened ports along the Chinese coast.[28]

The profitability of the trade that was taking place in these new ports along the Chinese coast also attracted banking organizations from other Western European countries. The most important case was that of Germany. *Deutsche Bank* opened branches in Shanghai and Yokohama in 1872, but had to close them down three years later, because of the losses that it had incurred in the silver trade. In 1889, the German Asian Bank [*Deutsch-Asiatische Bank*] was created as a consortium of several large German banks (the main ones being *Disconto-Gesellschaft* and *Deutsche Bank*).[29] This organization, whose design was based on the model of *Banque de l'Indochine*, was a successful one, in spite of inevitable setbacks in the wake of the German defeats in the two world wars; it remained a separate branch of *Deutsche Bank* until 1988.

Colonial banks in the late nineteenth century and the early twentieth century

The partition of Africa and the Pacific islands, and the control of some further territories in Asia in the late nineteenth and early twentieth centuries, introduced new demands for colonial banking activity. Initially, these demands were partly met by the parallel banking activities of chartered companies involved in the process, such as the British South Africa Company in Zambezia, or the International African Association [*Association internationale africaine*] in the Zaïre basin. The British South Africa Company was created by Cecil Rhodes to administer the territories of the Zambezi basin, which he had succeeded in adding to the British colonial empire and which later became known as Rhodesia (present-day Zambia – formerly Northern Rhodesia – and Zimbabwe, formerly Southern Rhodesia). The International African Association was a formally nongovernment organization set up by King Léopold II of Belgium to explore and develop the African continent. Its Belgian branch came to administer a significant part of the Zaïre basin, which eventually became the so-called Congo Free State, a formally sovereign state personally owned by King Léopold II of Belgium. Its bankruptcy for all practical purposes forced Belgium to take over the Congo Free State as the Belgian Congo on the death of Léopold in 1908. However, the solution adopted necessarily involved both expanding the former colonial banks and creating new colonial banks.

The most important instances of the expansion of former colonial banks occurred in the French colonial empire. *Banque du Sénégal* was transformed in 1901 into *Banque de l'Afrique occidentale* (BAO), which then began to perform the same role as the old *Banque du Sénégal*, first in French West Africa, which comprised the colonies of Sénégal, Soudan (present-day Mali), Mauritania, Niger, Upper Volta (present-day Burkina Faso), Guinée, Côte d'Ivoire and Dahomey (present-day Bénin). Later on (after WWI), BAO extended its grip on French Equatorial Africa and in the French mandate territories of Togo and Cameroon. As might be expected, *Banque de l'Afrique occidentale* lay at the origin of the central banks established in 1962 in the former French colonies in West and Equatorial Africa, Central Bank of West African States [*Banque centrale des États de l'Afrique de l'Ouest*] and Bank of Central African States [*Banque des États de l'Afrique centrale*]. The Central Bank of West African States is the common central bank of the former members of French West Africa (except Mauritania, which abandoned the monetary union in 1973) and of Togo and Guinea-Bissau (which became a member of the monetary union in 1997). The activity of *Banque d'Algérie* was broadened in 1904 into the neighbouring protectorate of Tunisia, which only received a separate central bank after independence in 1958.[30] And several institutions scrambled all over North Africa to mix 'colonial banking' and commercial banking and develop an integrated trans-Mediterranean capitalist empire there.[31]

The Portuguese *Banco Nacional Ultramarino* also underwent a significant expansion, both as a consequence of the expansion of the Portuguese colonial empire into continental Africa (Guinea, Angola and Mozambique) and as a consequence of a strategy to imitate the business of the second generation of British and French colonial banks. However, the bulk of its new activities were performed not within an imperial framework but in Brazil.

Bank of British West Africa, created in 1890 by Alfred Jones and George Neville, was an example of a freestanding bank formed to satisfy the needs of the new British colonies in the western part of the continent. Its activity spread to Nigeria, Ghana, Sierra Leone and the Gambia (and, after WWI, also to Cameroon). Its history came to an end in 1965, as a consequence of its acquisition by Standard Bank of Africa. The African Banking Corporation, also created in 1890, was a consortium of several large British banks (the main ones being Lloyds, National Provincial and Westminster) that was set up for African business. It established part of its operations through the acquisition of local South African banks, such as Western Province Bank (created in 1847), Worcester Commercial Bank (created in 1850) and Kaffrarian Colonial Bank (created in 1862), but ended up being acquired by Standard Bank of Africa in 1920.

The State Bank of Morocco [*Banque d'État du Maroc*] was created in 1906 to support the consolidation of the submission of Morocco to the protectorate of European powers. It acted as the issuing bank for the part of Morocco under French protectorate[32] and eventually became the central bank of Morocco after independence in 1956, under the name of Bank of Morocco [*Bank Al-Maghrib*].[33]

Of course, new colonial powers had to create new colonial banks. The most important examples are those of *Banque du Congo belge*, created in 1909, and the German colonial banks: *Deutsch-Ostafrikanische Bank*, created in 1904 for German East Africa,[34] and *Deutsch-Westafrikanische Bank*, created in 1906 for Togoland[35] and Cameroon.[36] The designs of these Belgian and German colonial banks were based on the French model, except that, in the case of German banks, mortgage operations were not included among their functions. The German colonial banks disappeared when the German colonial empire was occupied by the winners of WWI. *Banque du Congo belge* duly extended its activity into

Rwanda and Burundi as those territories came under Belgian administration in the aftermath of the same war. It became the *Banque centrale du Congo belge et du Ruanda-Urundi* in 1951, and was divided into separate currency issuing boards for the different territories in which it acted in 1960, as a preparatory step for the creation of central banks after independence. However, commercial operations were kept separate from the issuing operations at the time, and this area of the bank's business has survived until now as *Banque commerciale du Congo.*[37]

New steps of colonial banking in the interwar period

The main colonial banks established during the interwar period were the French *Banque de Syrie*, the French *Banque de Madagascar* and the Portuguese *Banco de Angola*. *Banque de Syrie* was created in 1919 and became the issuing bank for the French mandate of Syria in 1920. In 1924, it was renamed *Banque de Syrie & du Grand Liban*. This situation continued until WWII. The separation of Syrian and Lebanese currencies took place after independence in 1948. *Banque de Syrie & du Grand Liban* became the Central Bank of Syria, and responsibility for Lebanese currency issue was assumed by a currency board until the formation of *Banque du Liban* in 1964. At the same time, commercial operations were conducted separately under the name of *Société nouvelle de la Banque de Syrie & du Liban.*[38]

Banque de Madagascar was created in 1925 as an issuing bank for the French colony of Madagascar, similar to the Bank of West Africa. It became *Banque de Madagascar & des Comores* in 1945, but currency issue in the two territories was split again when Madagascar became independent in 1960: *Banque de Madagascar & des Comores* became Central Bank of Madagascar [*Banky Foiben'i Madagasikara*], while currency issue in the Comoros became the responsibility of the Issuing Institute of the Comoros [*Institut d'émission des Comores*], which became *Banque centrale des Comores* in 1981.[39]

In 1926, *Banco de Angola* was created as a separate issuing and commercial bank for the Portuguese colony of Angola and was allowed to operate as a commercial bank in Portugal proper, just as *Banco Nacional Ultramarino* was. When decolonization came, issuing and commercial operations were handed to the national banks created in 1975 in the former Portuguese colonies in Africa from the local operations of *Banco Nacional Ultramarino* and *Banco de Angola*: *Banco Nacional da Guiné-Bissau*,[40] *Banco de Cabo Verde*, *Banco Nacional de São Tomé e Príncipe*, *Banco de Moçambique* and *Banco Nacional de Angola*. Moreover, *Banco Nacional Ultramarino* had to cease its activity in Portuguese India (in 1961) and Portuguese Timor (in 1975), as they were occupied by India and Indonesia, respectively. The remaining operations of *Banco de Angola* in Portugal proper were merged with those of two other small Portuguese banks during the 1970s. The remaining operations of *Banco Nacional Ultramarino* in Portugal proper were taken over in the 1990s by the government bank *Caixa Geral de Depósitos*. Thus, *Banco Nacional Ultramarino* remains today only as an issuing and commercial bank in Macao.[41]

The legacy of colonial and imperial banking

What is perhaps missing from our book is a study of the spillover of portfolios of skills, competencies and risks management by the 'developed' banking capitals of the times – of the 'capitals of capital', as Youssef Cassis said[42] – that is, London, Paris, Amsterdam and Berlin, before the upsurge of New York.[43] Expatriates and locally trained recruits did provide the port cities and hubs of trade and money exchanges with methods of analyzing risks, of gauging accounts and balance sheets, of collecting information and of assessing the risk of reputation. The managers piled up their own capital of experience and enriched the overall capital of experience of their bank group or of its affiliate(s) because they frequently moved from one branch to another, and sometimes from a country to another – as was the case at HSBC, Chartered, *Banque de l'Indochine*, Bank of London & South America (BOLSA) and Barclays DCO. This fostered a banking culture abroad, in the colonies, dominions or 'imperial territories', like Latin America or Chinese settlements; and this favoured some 'maturity'. Working in such marketplaces remained for a long time an 'adventure' because the business morale, accounting habits and fraud granted uncertainty. Confidence was at stake, whereas competition was often strong, despite cartel agreements and some solidarity among sound foreigners. And the succession of collapses is dire proof of this intrinsic fragility of colonial and imperial banking.

The apprenticeship did, however, resist the flow of history. First, the duration of so many institutions overseas forged a corporate culture and a banking culture that helped the port cities and other hubs of exchange to establish basic business cultures and, mainly, the culture of credit, even if the famous City phrase 'my word is my bond' had to be considered abroad with great attention. Second, while so many banks disappeared in the wake of decolonization or strategic redeployment by the mother houses, less preoccupied by Third World affiliates than by multinationalized networks, another group did stay faithful to their ex-colonial and ex-imperial offshoots. Barclays, Chartered (then Standard Chartered) and French *Société générale* maintained their corporate culture and store of experience and skills, despite wars, recessions, crises of commodities markets etc. Third, even when colonial banks were nationalized and their teams of expatriates flew back home, so many middle-level employees could have preserved the legacy, which helped the institutions to regain momentum, even if corruption, clannish political interference or bad risk management could have halted that revival.

Opening doors to the contribution of the case studies

Is it possible to say that different entrepreneurial and banking traditions in different European countries meant that European colonial banks took different forms? The discussion presented here suggests a positive answer to this question. Three main characteristics distinguish Continental imperial or colonial banking from British imperial or colonial banking. First, the links to the government are to be considered. Whereas most Continental colonial banks were to some extent government creations, most British colonial banks were entrepreneurial initiatives.

Of course, early British colonial banks were chartered, but this was partly just a consequence of the fact that a royal charter was needed for the creation of a limited liability joint-stock company in Britain until the Joint Stock Companies Act of 1844 and the Limited Liability Act of 1855.

Second, the range of operations was at stake. While most Continental colonial banks were universal banks, most British colonial banks restricted their activity to standard commercial operations. The following quotation from a French expert on the eve of the outbreak of WWI gives a clear idea of what it was considered that a colonial bank should be according to the Continental model:

> The role of colonial banks is particularly difficult and complex; each one in its own colonial territory, they have to gather the whole variety of qualities and forms of overall financial institutions of every kind existing in the big Metropolis, or they would not be able to provide the relevant services expected by the colonies.[44]

Third, the evolution of strategies, profiles and activities presented common and different paths, along colonial history, strategic opportunities, institutional choices by the national authorities and amalgamation processes. While Continental colonial banks often became central banks, British colonial banks tended to become part of present-day large banking conglomerates – and even the core of these conglomerates in the cases of ANZ Bank, Standard Chartered Bank and HSBC. Another significant element of British colonial banking that was almost completely absent from Continental colonial banking was the formation of local banks.

Of course, both models had different variants depending on the specific characteristics of both the colonial powers and their colonized territories.[45] The collapse of colonial banks as a consequence of the end of the colonial endeavours to which they were linked (as in the cases of the Spanish colony of Cuba in 1898 and the German colonies in Africa after WWI), the survival of colonial banks subject to a new imperial environment (as in the cases of the Spanish banks of the Philippines and Puerto Rico under American rule) and the separation of the issuing and commercial operations (the first being taken over by government-controlled organizations, the latter becoming private endeavours) of several Continental colonial banks after WWII (as in the case of the French overseas departments, Lebanon and Belgian colonies) are perhaps the most important of these variants. The geographical separation of colonial operations from the operations conducted in 'Portugal proper' by Portuguese colonial banks partly allowed for a similar process to occur in Portugal.[46]

Notes

1 See Peter J. Cain and Anthony G. Hopkins, 'The political economy of British expansion overseas', *Economic History Review*, 33/4, 1980, pp. 463–90.
2 Peter Cain and Anthony Hopkins, 'Gentlemanly capitalism and British expansion overseas: New imperialism, 1850–1945', *South African Journal of Economic History*, 7(1), 1992, pp. 182–215.

3 See Stanley Engerman, Philip Hoffman, Jean-Laurent Rosenthal and Kenneth Sokoloff, *Financial Intermediaries in Economic Development*, Cambridge, Cambridge University Press, 2003.
4 Rondo Cameron and Valery Bovykin (eds), *International Banking, 1870–1914*, Oxford, Oxford University Press, 1991.
5 See Geoffrey Jones (ed.), *Banks as Multinationals*, London, Routledge, 1990. Geoffrey Jones, *British Multinational Banking, 1830–1990*, Oxford, Clarendon Press, 1993. Richard Roberts, *Inside International Finance*, London, Orion Business Books, 1998.
6 Geoffrey Jones (ed.), *Banks as Multinationals*, op. cit. Also see Geoffrey Jones (ed.), *Multinational and International Banking*, Aldershot, Edward Elgar, 1992.
7 Simon Mollan, 'International correspondent networks: Asian and British banks in the twentieth century', in Shizuya Nishimura, Toshio Suzuki and Ranald Michie (eds), *The Origins of International Banking in Asia. The Nineteenth and Twentieth Centuries*, Oxford, Oxford University Press, 2012, pp. 217–29. Shizuya Nishimura, 'British international banks in Asia, 1870–1914: An introductory essay', ibid., pp. 55–85. Ranald Michie, 'The City of London as a centre for international banking: The Asian dimension in the nineteenth and twentieth centuries', ibid. pp. 13–54.
8 See Clarence Davis, 'Financing imperialism: British and American bankers as vectors of imperial expansion in China, 1908–1920', *Business History Review*, 56(2), 1982, pp. 236–64.
9 David Merrett, 'Paradise lost? British banks in Australia', in Geoffrey Jones (ed.), *Banks as Multinationals*, London, Routledge, 1990, pp. 62–84.
10 Christopher Clay, 'The Imperial Ottoman Bank in the alter nineteenth century: a multinational "national" bank?', in Geoffrey Jones (ed.), *Banks as Multinationals*, London, Routledge, 1990, pp. 142–59.
11 Norio Tamaki, 'The Yokohama Specie Bank: a multinational in the Japanese interest, 1879–1931', in Geoffrey Jones (ed.), *Banks as Multinationals*, London, Routledge, 1990, pp. 191–216. Makoto Kasuya, 'The overseas expansion of Japanese banks, 1880–2006', in Shizuya Nishimura, Toshio Suzuki and Ranald Michie (eds), *The Origins of International Banking*, op. cit., pp. 166–73.
12 Motoaki Akagawa, 'German banks in East Asia. The Deutsche Bank (1870–1875) and the Deutsch-Asiatische Bank (1888–1913)', *Keio Business Review*, The Society of Business and Commerce, Keio University, 45(1), 2009, pp. 1–20. Frank King, *The History of the Hong Kong and Shanghai Banking Corporation*, vol. 1. *The Hong Kong Bank in Late Imperial China, 1864–1902: On an Even Keel*, Cambridge, Cambridge University Press, 1987.
13 Simon Mollan, 'International correspondent networks: Asian and British banks in the twentieth century', in Shizuya Nishimura, Toshio Suzuki and Ranald Michie (eds), *The Origins of International Banking*, op. cit., pp. 217–29. Christopher Cook, 'The Hong Kong & Shanghai Banking Corporation on Lombard Street', in Frank King (ed.), *Eastern Banking: Essays in the History of the Hong Kong & Shanghai Banking Corporation*, London, Athlone Press, 1983, pp. 193–203. Olive Checkland, Shizuya Nishimura and Norio Tamaki (eds), *Pacific Banking (1859–1959). East Meets West*, London, MacMillan; New York, St Martin's Press, 1994.
14 Peter Duus, Ramon H. Myers and R. Mark Peattie (eds), *The Japanese Informal Empire in China, 1895–1937*, Princeton, NJ, Princeton University Press, 1989.
15 On the development of banking in Europe, see Hans Pohl and Gabriele Jachmich (eds), *Europäische Bankengeschichte*, Frankfurt, Fritz Knapp Verlag, 1993. R. Bogaert, G. Kurgan-Van Hentenrik and H. Van der Wee, *A History of European Banking*, Antwerp, Fons Mercator, 1994.
16 On the evolution of Bank of Java, see the website of Bank Indonesia.
17 On the evolution of Colonial Bank, see the website of Barclays Bank.
18 On the evolution of Bank of Australasia, see the website of ANZ Bank.
19 On the evolution of the presidency banks, see the website of the State Bank of India.

20 On the evolution of the banking system in South Africa, see G. Verhoef's chapter in this book (Chapter 5).

21 On the history of the first Bank of Brazil, see Afonso Arinos Melo Franco, *História do Banco do Brasil (Primeira Fase 1808–1835)*, São Paulo, Instituto de Economia da Associação Comercial, 1948.

22 Except for Senegal (see the fourth section, on the early Dutch and British colonial banks), all these territories are today French overseas departments [*départements*].

23 On the history of French colonial banks, see Hubert Bonin, 'Banques et outre-mer', in Claude Liauzu (ed.), *Dictionnaire de la colonisation française*, Paris, Larousse, 2007. Hubert Bonin, 'Les banques et l'Algérie coloniale: mise en valeur impériale ou exploitation impérialiste?', *Outre-Mers. Revue d'histoire*, June 2009, 97(362/363), pp. 213–26. Hubert Bonin, 'Compagnie algérienne', 'Banque de l'Algérie', 'Crédit foncier d'Algérie & de Tunisie', in Jeannine Verdès-Leroux (ed.), *L'Algérie et la France*, Paris, Robert Laffont-Bouquins, 2009. Hubert Bonin, 'Les banquiers', in Jean-Pierre Rioux (ed.), *Dictionnaire de la France coloniale*, Paris, Flammarion, 2007, pp. 563–8. On the history of the Bank of Algeria, see Samir Saul's chapter in this book (Chapter 7). Also, Samir Saul, 'La Banque d'État du Maroc et la monnaie sous le Protectorat', in Jacques Marseille (ed.), *La France et l'Outre-Mer. Un siècle de relations monétaires et financières*, Paris, Comité pour l'histoire économique et financière de la France, 1998, pp. 389–427.

24 On the history of *Banco Español Filipino*, see the website of the Bank of the Philippine Islands.

25 On the history of the colonial banks of the Spanish Caribbean possessions, see the chapter by Pablo Martín-Aceña and Ines Roldán de Montaud in this book (Chapter 2).

26 On the evolution of Standard Bank of Africa, see James-Archibald Henry and Harry-Arthus Siepmann, *The First Hundred Years of the Standard Bank*, Oxford, Oxford University Press, 1963. On the evolution of both Chartered Bank of India, Australia & China, and of Standard Bank of Africa, see the website of Standard Chartered Bank.

27 On the activities of CEP in India and Australia, see, respectively, Geoffroy de Lassus, *The History of BNP Paribas in India, 1860–2010*, Paris, BNP Paribas, 2010; Geoffroy de Lassus, *The History of BNP Paribas in Australia and New Zealand, 1881–2011*, Sydney, BNP Paribas Australia and New Zealand, 2011. Also, Hubert Bonin, 'Le Comptoir national d'escompte de Paris, une banque impériale (1848–1940)', *Revue française d'histoire d'outre-mer*, 78(293), 1991, pp. 477–97.

28 On the history of the *Banque de l'Indochine*, see Marc Meuleau, *Des pionniers en Extrême-Orient: Histoire de la Banque de l'Indochine, 1875–1975*, Paris, Fayard, 1990. Today, its activities have been swallowed by the *Crédit agricole-CACIB* group.

29 Motoaki Akagawa, 'German banks in East Asia. The Deutsche Bank (1870–75) and the Deutsch-Asiatische Bank (1889–1913)', *Keio Business Review*, 45(1), 2009, pp. 1–20.

30 See Hubert Bonin, 'L'outre-mer, marché pour la banque commerciale (1876–1985)?', in Jacques Marseille (ed.), *La France & l'outre-mer*, Paris, Comité pour l'histoire économique & financière de la France, 1998, pp. 437–83.

31 Hubert Bonin, *Un outre-mer bancaire méditerranéen. Histoire du Crédit foncier d'Algérie & de Tunisie (1880–1997)*, Paris, Publications de la Société française d'histoire d'outre-mer, 2004; reedition en 2010. Hubert Bonin, 'Une banque française maître d'oeuvre d'un outre-mer levantin: le Crédit foncier d'Algérie & de Tunisie, du Maghreb à la Méditerranée orientale (1919–1970)', *Outre-Mers. Revue d'histoire*, 91(342/343), 2004, pp. 239–72. Hubert Bonin, 'La Compagnie algérienne levier de la colonisation et prospère grâce à elle (1865–1939)', *Revue française d'histoire d'outre-mer*, 328/329, 2000, pp. 209–30. Hubert Bonin, 'Une histoire bancaire trans-méditerranéenne: la Compagnie algérienne, d'un ultime apogée au repli (1945–1970)', in Daniel Lefeuvre et al. (eds), *La Guerre d'Algérie au miroir des décolonisations*

françaises (En l'honneur de Charles-Robert Ageron), Publications de la Société française d'histoire d'outre-mer, 2000, pp. 151–76 (second edition in 2005).

32   In the part of Morocco under Spanish protectorate, and in the city of Tangiers under international administration, the circulation of money was guaranteed under the form of counter-stamped Spanish banknotes.

33   On the history of the State Bank of Morocco, see the website of the Bank of Morocco.

34   German East Africa included Tanganyika (now the continental part of Tanzania), Rwanda and Burundi.

35   Togoland included what is now Togo and Ghana's Volta Region.

36   Cameroon included what is now Cameroon and parts of the present-day states of Taraba, Adamawa and Borno of Nigeria. Between 1911 and 1914, it also included parts of the present-day Republic of Congo, the Central African Republic and Chad.

37   On the evolution of Bank of Belgian Congo, see the website of Commercial Bank of Congo.

38   On the history of Bank of Syria & Great Lebanon, see the website of Bank of Lebanon.

39   On the history of Bank of Madagascar, see the website of Central Bank of Madagascar.

40   National Bank of Guinea-Bissau disappeared in 1997, as the country became a member of the West African monetary union.

41   On the evolution of Portuguese *Banco Nacional Ultramarino* and *Banco de Angola*, see Ana Bela Nunes, Carlos Bastien, Nuno Valério, Rita Martins de Sousa and Sandra Domingos Costa, 'Banking in the Portuguese colonial empire (1864–1975)', *Économies et Sociétés*, series 'Histoire économique quantitative', AF, 44(9), 2011, pp. 1483–554.

42   Youssef Cassis, *Capitals of Capital. A History of International Financial Centers, 1780–2005*, Cambridge, Cambridge University Press, 2006. Youssef Cassis, *Les capitales du capital. Histoire des places financières internationales, 1780–2005*, Geneva, Slatkine & Pictet, 2005; Paris, Honoré Champion, 2008. Youssef Cassis and Éric Bussière (eds), *London and Paris as International Financial Centres in the Twentieth Century*, Oxford, Oxford University Press, 2005.

43   Steven Haffe and Jessica Lautin, *Capital of Capital. Money, Banking and Power in New York City, 1784–2012*, series 'Columbia Studies in the History of the US Capitalism', New York, Columbia University Press, 2013.

44   'Le rôle des banques coloniales est singulièrement difficile et complexe; elles doivent – chacune dans sa colonie – réunir toutes les qualités et toutes les formes différentes des établissements financiers de tous les genres qui existent dans les grands pays, sous peine de ne rendre à la colonie aucun service appréciable', Max David, *Étude sur la Banque de l'Indo-Chine*, Paris, Albin Michel, 1909.

45   René Mingot, *La question des banques coloniales*, Angers, Siraudeau, 1912; and Raul Carmo, *Bancos coloniales*, Lisbon, Bayard, 1914, provide interesting overviews of the colonial banks existing on the eve of the outbreak of WWI.

46   The editors sincerely thank the two referees of a first draft of the book proposal and have taken into account their pieces of criticism, through complements and addenda.

Part II

Colonial banking

From Latin America to Africa

2 Colonial banking: one model, two histories

Cuba and Puerto Rico before independence

Pablo Martín-Aceña and Ines Roldán de Montaud

Joint-stock banks with limited liability emerged in Cuba in the mid-nineteenth century – *Compañía de Almacenes de Regla* – which sowed the seed for the *Banco del Comercio: Banco Industrial, Crédito Territorial Cubano, Banco de San José* and *Banco Español de la Habana* were established in the 1850s, and came to join *Caja de Ahorros, Descuentos y Depósitos de la Habana*, which had been incorporated in 1841.[1] In Puerto Rico, the early part of the century saw various initiatives to set up financial institutions that ultimately failed.[2] The first bank, *Sociedad Anónima del Crédito Mercantil*, was not created until 1877. Afterwards came four more: *Banco Español de Puerto Rico*, the *Banco Territorial y Agrícola*, *Banco Popular* and the *Banco de Crédito y Ahorro Ponceño*. There were also six saving banks; the first, established in 1865 in San Juan, was followed by four others in Mayagüez, Ponce, San Germán and Humacao. On neither island, however, were there more than ten financial institutions. The largest were those which, in addition to operating as commercial banks, also enjoyed the privilege to issue banknotes, namely *Banco Español de la Habana*, founded in 1855, and *Banco Español de Puerto Rico*, established in 1888. Both handled more than half of their respective islands' financial resources, acted as government banks and played a dominant role in the economy of the territories they were based on.

In the first section of this chapter we offer a brief account of the establishment of the two banks. In the next we examine their financial performance and trace their similarities and their differences. The third section looks at the role played by the two banks during the war of independence. The chapter concludes with a brief section summarizing their main features and comparing their accomplishment as commercial and as issue banks.[3]

Two banks of issue: *Banco Español de la Habana* and *Banco Español de Puerto Rico*

The first attempts to open an issue institution in the island of Cuba harked back to the 1940s. None of the projects was approved because the government of Madrid doubted the convenience of introducing a regime of fiduciary money in the colony.[4] In Cuba, where the circulation of gold was abundant and was complemented by a significant volume of commercial paper, the authorities in the metropolis considered that there was no need for the establishment of an issue bank. What they thought was needed were financial institutions capable of providing long-term and mortgage credit to sugar and tobacco planters.[5]

As a result credit in the island remained, until the foundation of banks and saving banks, in the hands of a small number of private bankers and of commercial firms, which, exerting a near monopoly, met the financial requirements of the island's economy. They discounted bills of exchange, supplied short-term loans and made use of the well-known 'contratos de refacción' to provide for the financial needs of the landowners of the colony.[6] Located in the main port cities, from where the sugar production was exported, these merchant firms had solid financial links with British and American merchant credit institutions through which most the produce was sold in foreign markets.

Emerging colonial banking in Cuba

However, the rapid economic expansion of the island since the middle of the century led to the constitution of a series of joint-stock financial companies, and eventually to the establishment of the *Banco Español de la Habana*.[7] In 1854, a group formed by local merchants, planters and slave traders requested authorization in Madrid to open a bank of issue in the city of La Habana.[8] The timing coincided with a liberal atmosphere in the metropolis which led to the approval of less restrictive legislation for the establishment of issue banks and credit companies. Hence, on 6 February 1855, a royal decree authorized the constitution of a company with the name of *Banco Español de la Habana*.[9] The bank was to be incorporated with a nominal capital of 3 million pesos. The charter was granted for a period of 25 years, and the bank was bestowed with the monopoly of banknote issue for the entire territory of the colony. The issue ceiling was set at half the paid-up capital, although the issue could be raised insofar as the bank had in its safe-deposit box an equivalent amount in gold or silver bars. Later, under the pressure of the promoters who complained about the strict limitations for issuing, the legal amount of banknotes in circulation was raised and equated to the paid-up capital of the bank. As a commercial bank, it was authorized to undertake any kind of financial operation. It was not authorized, however, to loan against its own shares or to invest in public debt. The banknotes should be of a denomination equal to or above 50 pesos. This was a high nominal value at the time and made the notes almost only useful as a credit instrument to conduct large commercial transactions and to make large payments.

The internal organization adopted the model defined by the Peel Act of 1844 for Bank of England, so that *Banco Español de la Habana* was divided up into two departments: an issue department, and a commercial – or loans and discounts – department entrusted with the ordinary operations. The institution's director had to be a merchant resident of the city of La Habana and was to be appointed by the metropolitan government from a list of three members proposed by shareholders. The government also reserved for itself the appointments of the two sub-directors. Once authorized, the formation of the bank proceeded without delay. The subscription of capital was opened on 1 June 1855 and was closed on 6 October, when the 25 per cent of the capital was entirely paid. The rest had to be completed in one year. The first general assembly of shareholders took place in September, and the statutes and the by-laws were approved by royal decree on 7 January 1856.[10] Finally, *Banco Español de la Habana* was formally constituted on 9 April and opened its doors and began operating on the morning of 12 April.[11]

The capital funds to erect the bank came from within the economy of the island. As was the case in the foundation of all of the credit institutions established in the island during the 1850s and 1860s, Cuban savings – not resources from Spain – associated to form *Banco Español*. The commercial elite and the largest landowners of Cuba were among the major shareholders. Seventy of them controlled nearly half of the capital of the bank, and the rest was widely distributed among local merchants and professionals of the city of La Habana.[12] Although the bank was created entirely with private capital, its monopoly of issue, a privilege granted by the Crown, and the fact that the directors were appointed by the Madrid government gave it an unavoidable semi-official character, which eventually, as will be seen, determined its evolution and performance.

Colonial banking emerging in Puerto Rico

Banco Español de Puerto Rico was not founded until 1888, although the establishment of an issue financial institution in the colony had been attempted on numerous occasions.[13] In 1875 a group of merchants and landowners in San Juan hit on the idea of constituting a bank of issue with the compensation money that the Treasury was obliged to pay the owners of the slaves emancipated by the 1873 law.[14] Hence, they requested authorization from the metropolis to set up a credit institute which, as in Cuba, would have the privilege to issue banknotes. They believed that the new bank would provide the credit the economy needed and resolve the long-standing shortage of hard currency. The petition was unsuccessful, but the colony's businessmen did not give up their attempts to open a bank. However, instead of an issuing bank, which required government authorization, they decided to set up a deposit and discount company. Thus it was that, in 1877, *Sociedad Anónima de Crédito Mercantil* emerged.[15]

One year later, in 1878, a royal decree on issuing and discount banks in the colonies was passed. According to the new legislation, the Madrid government was given the exclusive authority to charter banks as well as to set the conditions for the establishment of new financial institutions. We refer to the Royal Decree of 16 August 1878, which allowed the creation of issuing banks in the colonies. It was passed 'to standardise the organisation of banks to facilitate their mutual relationships and transactions' and 'to fill, in short, a genuine void in overseas legislation'. It also indicated that 'there will be three institutions of this kind (issuing) and they will be called *Banco Español de la Isla de Cuba, Banco Español de Filipinas* and *Banco Español de Puerto Rico*'. Common standards were put in place for new incorporations: the term of existence was set at a maximum of 25 years, the share value at 500 pesos and the banknote issue limit equal to three times the paid-up capital. The royal decree listed the operations in which the banks could engage and imposed the formation of a reserve fund equal to 15 per cent of the paid-up capital. The decree attributed the appointment of governors to the Madrid authorities, and established their responsibilities and those of the boards of administration. Foreigners could be shareholders, but could not assume management positions. Banks operating in Cuba and the Philippines could continue to be governed by their old statutes, although managers and shareholders could apply, if approved by the general assembly, for the new legislation to be implemented.

After publication of this major legal provision, it was ten years before an issuing bank was founded in Puerto Rico – a time during which the managers and shareholders of Crédito Mercantil tried unsuccessfully to turn their discount society into an issuing bank. It was not until March 1887 that a decree by the Ministerio de Ultramar (Overseas Ministry) opened up a tender for the creation of a credit institution with an exclusive issuing privilege subject to the regulations set forth in the aforementioned 1878 decree.

Two proposals were presented: one signed by representatives of Crédito Mercantil and another by a small group of traders and bankers of the island. The Madrid government, having studied the specifications of both proposals, enacted the royal decree of 5 May 1888 awarding the tender to the former. According to the decree, *Banco Español de Puerto Rico*, born as a discount bank with the exclusive privilege to issue, was to have capital of 1.5 million pesos in Spanish silver currency. The financial life of the bank was 25 years. The limit on notes in circulation was set at an amount of three times the paid-up capital; one-third had to be secured by gold and silver and the other two-thirds by short-term securities. In exchange for the issuing privilege, the new institution was obliged to make up to 500,000 pesos available to the Treasury. Moreover, the government reserved the right to appoint the governor at its discretion and the sub-governor on proposal from the shareholders.

Diverse difficulties prevented the bank from being incorporated until early 1890. Two provisions hampered a speedy incorporation. First, the government stipulated that the concession be made to individuals signing the application but not as agents of Crédito Mercantil. This required them to raise capital that was independent of that committed to Mercantil. As the promoters of *Banco Español* did not have enough funds to incorporate the new society, they were forced to liquidate Crédito Mercantil. The second provision which held back the project's implementation was that capital had to be paid up in national or Spanish silver currency, rather than in Mexican silver pesos, which was the money currently employed on the island. This requirement proved a major stumbling block. According to the promoters, if they necessarily had to raise the capital in national currency, the bank would have a currency that was useless for market transactions.[16] Although the winners of the tender organized a campaign calling for the institution to be allowed to raise its capital in Mexican currency, the government failed to authorize this, because it was planning to make a monetary conversion to substitute the Mexican currency for a new national money. As a result, the full nominal capital of 1.5 million pesos could not be paid up, and the first instalment was instead limited to just 375,000 pesos.[17]

Another difficulty arose with the issuing privilege because, as for capital, the decree regulating the establishment of the bank required banknotes to be issued in national currency – precisely the one island traders used least. Moreover, the fact that capital, reserves, and banknotes were designated in national currency, whereas the bank had to operate in the market with Mexican or current currency, forced the bank to keep its books (balance sheets, profit and loss accounts) in both currencies until 1895, when the monetary conversion that unified the monetary system finally took place.

Comparisons between Cuba and Puerto Rico

Both similarities and differences, then, existed between the two issuers at the moment of their incorporation. The similarities are obvious. First, both were born as semi-official institutions, with the issue privilege granted to them by the metropolitan authorities, which in turn kept the power to appoint the director or governor, who was its official representative. Second, both were private banks formed with capital raised in each colony. Third, the two banks were established as commercial banks and not as government banks, and they could undertake all sorts of financial operations, from discounting and short-term credit to long-term financing. Each was established to promote the economy of the island and to diversify its currency structure. And fourth, when approved, both had a fixed expiry date of 25 years. In the case of the Cuban bank, when the term expired in 1881, the concession was renewed for a further 25 years, and at the same time its name was changed to *Banco Español de la Isla de Cuba*. The Puerto Rican bank was dissolved when it expired in 1913, and its assets and liabilities were transferred to a new entity.

The differences are notable as well. The years of creation are far apart: the Cuban bank in 1856 and the Puerto Rican bank more than three decades later. The size is also a major difference: compared to a nominal capital of 3 million pesos which were fully paid up from the start in the case of the bank of Cuba, the Puerto Rican bank was launched with half that amount, and began operations with only 375,000 pesos, 25 per cent of its nominal capital. At the time of their creation, the issue limits were also different: smaller in the Cuban case (equal to the paid-up capital) than for the Puerto Rican Bank (three times the paid-up capital). A further difference was that, until 1868, the structure of *Banco Español de la Habana* was split into two departments. However, many of the initial features of the Cuban bank disappeared in 1888, when the Puerto Rican institution was founded, since a significant number of amendments to its original charter were introduced in the Cuban bank to accommodate it to the royal decree of 1878.

One model, two histories of imperial banking

Although certain similarities existed when the two entities were founded, their institutional lives diverged. Despite their kinship, and the fact that both banks were operating in colonial territories that belonged to the same metropolis, the way they functioned and the way their operations were conducted offer a striking contrast. *Banco Español de la Habana* and *Banco Español de Puerto Rico* were subject to different economic and political vicissitudes and took different directions, becoming two colonial issuers with very little in common. Aside from the difference in their size and the differing duration of the period they operated under Spanish sovereignty, the major contrast between them was related to their financial involvement with the state. Whereas the Cuban bank, by force of circumstance – namely uprising and war in 1868 – maintained close links with the Public Treasury, the Puerto Rican institution remained distant from public powers. Constantly burdened by deficit, Cuba's Treasury resorted to the issuing bank for finance, which in turn impinged on its commercial activities and on its financial results. On the other hand, the Puerto Rican Treasury, with a small but healthy budget, had no need to turn to the bank of issue.[18] Its development was therefore less troubled, and it was able to obtain better results. The Cuban institution soon became a bank at the service of the government, whereas its Puerto Rican counterpart was able to maintain its commercial character from the beginning until the end of Spanish sovereignty over the island.

The specifics of the Cuban institution

During its first decade of existence, *Banco Español de la Habana* made rapid progress.[19] Its assets rose from 16 million pesos in 1857 to 20 million in 1867. In 1859, it increased its capital by 1 million pesos and was authorized to extend its issue capacity to twice paid-up capital. The 2 million pesos of notes in circulation in 1857 rose to 10.3 million in 1867. Current accounts followed a similar upward trend: from 3.9 million pesos in 1857 to 10.6 million in 1865, although they fell abruptly to 3.8 million in 1866. By that date, liabilities accounted for 70 per cent of the bank's total funds. Discounts and loans stood at around 35 per cent, one-third of the assets. Cash on hand accounted for a higher proportion, at 50 per cent of liabilities, a not uncommon percentage for the time, but nevertheless it also suggests that the bank had too many idle funds.

The relations of *Banco Español de la Habana* with the state grew closer after its establishment. In 1858, it made out its first loan to the Cuban government for 2 million pesos. The expansionist policy of the metropolis – with the expedition to Mexico, the annexation of Santo Domingo in 1863, and the war in the Pacific – increased the Treasury's requirements, as the Cuban budget was burdened with responsibility for financing the campaigns. The Treasury issued bonds worth 16 million pesos, which ended up in the bank's portfolio, reducing drastically the resources that the bank could assign to its commercial operations. In 1867 the bank was authorized to double its social capital to 8 million pesos, and hence its potential issue ceiling rose. In the same year, the volume of banknotes in circulation doubled as a consequence of a new Treasury bond issue of nearly 9 million pesos that was placed on the bank's issue department.

The October 1868 uprising led to war, which lasted until March 1878. The conflict brought hardship for the Cuban Treasury, and the resulting budgetary imbalances impinged on the bank's performance. The war increased the financial needs of the Treasury, which could not be covered with its ordinary yearly revenue. Therefore it systematically resorted to the Español de la Habana in a variety of ways. In 1869, the bank put into circulation a first issue of Treasury notes for the sum of 8 million pesos. In subsequent years the issues of Treasury notes continued, reaching 72 million in 1874, a large part of which found their way to the bank's balance sheet. Nevertheless, a logical result of these continuous issues was the rapid depreciation of the Treasury bills. In 1872 they had depreciated 20 per cent, and convertibility was suspended. The Treasury bills were declared legal tender, and the island's paper currency entered a period of *corso forzoso*. The bank's own banknotes, although different in nature, were in fact identical to those of the Treasury and became, de facto, inconvertible. In 1874 the gold value of the currency hit the floor, with a depreciation of 194 per cent. After 1875, the Cuban Treasury was forced to resort to the bank in other ways, such as short-term loans and advances. By December 1877, Treasury indebtedness – in the form of debt securities, loans to the Treasury secured by promissory notes and other state assets, all in all 59 million pesos – represented 66 per cent more than total assets of 90 million. This latter figure violated the statutes of the bank, which only allowed credits to the government for the equivalent of its paid-up capital. Moreover, the bank had notes in circulation for a value of more than eight times its capital, exceeding also the legal limit stipulated in its articles of association.

As the uprising went on, so the bank's financial situation deteriorated. Its commercial activities declined markedly. Discount operations, worth 24 million in 1874, fell to 14 million in 1878, and in the same period loans dropped from 6 million to 2.5 million. All in all, the bank's private portfolio fell from 7.6 million to 3.1 million pesos between these two dates. It is apparent that the involvement of the bank with the Treasury had force it to abandon its role as a commercial entity linked to the island economy. The evolution of the bank's total assets was driven by its relation with the Treasury, while the private portfolio (credit and investments to the private sector) hardly represented more than a mere fraction. The 15 years that followed before the outbreak of the second war of independence was a period of huge economic and financial difficulty for the both the island and the bank. The war debt added up to 200 million pesos, an imposing figure by itself, and the Treasury suffered a growing budgetary deficit which in some financial years was the equivalent to more than 25 per cent of its ordinary revenues.

Banco Español de la Habana was also in a poor and critical situation. The bank's managers demanded payment of all Treasury outstanding debt and guarantees on the continuity of the institution given that its franchise ended in 1881. It was also in the government's interest that the bank should continue in operation because it was an important component of the colonial administrative machinery, and the only institution which could support colonial policy. To pay off the debt, the Treasury floated new bonds secured by Cuba's customs revenues for 25 million pesos and handed 12.1 million of these bonds over to the bank. In return, the life of the institution was extended for a further 25 years, along with its issuing privilege. Moreover, some reforms were introduced after a royal decree of

28 January 1881 which set forth new statutes and changed the official name of the institution to that of *Banco Español de la Isla de Cuba*. Article 1 of the new by-law stated, 'As of 7 January 1881, when its creation period ends, *Banco Español de la Habana* shall be called *Banco Español de la Isla de Cuba* and shall be the institution authorised by the Royal Decree of 16 August 1878 for sole fiduciary circulation throughout the island.' The change was intended to adapt the name to the geographical extension of its activities and perhaps indicated a desire to revitalize the bank so that it could embark on a new era.

However, the reforms and the payments made by the Treasury to discharge part of its debt did not change the bank's fortunes. The balance sheets of those years reveal that the Español de la Isla de Cuba was a lifeless company, incapable of initiative, loaded with huge amount of uncollectable government assets and a weak liability structure. Between 1872 and 1892, when the war note issue was eliminated, the bank was forced to separate its accounts under two denominations, depending on whether it was operating in gold pesos or in ordinary pesos (non-convertible banknotes). In gold pesos, its total assets were worth 49 million in 1880; in 1895, the year the second armed conflict began, they had dropped to 21 million. Investments and credits hardly changed and stayed around 3 million gold pesos with a declining tendency. The largest account was that of the loan and advances made to the Cuban Treasury in banknotes during the war, which continued in circulation until the end of 1892.[20]

Paid-up capital remained unchanged despite the authorization given to the bank to increase it, and the reserve fund evaporated. The volume of current accounts at the beginning and the end of the period was the same, which suggests that the public had lost all its remaining confidence in the institution. The banknotes of *Banco Español de la Isla de Cuba*, which replaced those issued by *Banco Español de la Habana*, came into circulation slowly and with great difficulty, because the public refused to accept them. The market came to equate the paper of the new bank with the notes issued by the Treasury, whose gold depreciation reached an astonishing 225 per cent. By the mid-1890s it was obvious that *Banco Español de la Isla de Cuba* was at the mercy of a bankrupt Treasury. It could no longer fulfil its issuing role properly, nor did it have the available funds to meet the credit requirements of the private sector, promote new business activities or make new investments. The bank was a hostage of the government, a lifeless financial institution far removed from the purpose for which it was originally created.

During this first decade, the institution's shareholders did not do badly: net benefits increased, and the bank's shares prices remained above par. The institution obtained a high level of return, close to 15 per cent, and in some years, 1859 and 1867, even exceeded the 20 per cent mark.[21] These positive results permitted quite a generous annual distribution of dividends while establishing a reserve of 400,000 pesos, 10 per cent of the paid-up capital. The initial years after the uprising were also good, but as the conflict deepened, share prices collapsed, and dividends had to be paid at the expense of reserves. From 1879 to 1895 the evolution was even worse. Net profits during those years were half those of the preceding decade. In an attempt to maintain a semblance of normality, dividends were distributed, but this could only be done at the expense of running down the reserves and making no provision for non-performing assets and contingencies. This unorthodox approach demonstrates careless management and a failure to comply with the bank's statutes. The best gauge of the decline of the institution was the evolution share prices, which fell as much as to 40 per cent below par in 1895. This means that the market value of each title was not the nominal book value of 500 pesos but rather was 300 pesos.

The specifics of the Puerto Rican institution

The development of *Banco Español de Puerto Rico* stands in stark contrast to the situation described for its Cuban equivalent. The bank started out on 1 February 1890. A main difficulty from the outset was the monetary duality which characterized the island's economy, with two currencies in circulation: the ordinary peso, or Mexican peso, and the national peso. Both were silver coins with minimal differences in weight and sterling standard, and they shared the name of peso. In 1890 they were quoted at par or with a small discount of 0.95 on the ordinary peso. In the years to follow, the Mexican peso depreciated to 40 per cent the year of the monetary conversion, in 1895. The directors of the bank considered this a serious limitation for the institution's development, as it was only empowered to issue notes in 'money different from the circulating currency.' If the bank's prosperity were based primarily on the issuing privilege, its future looked, so they complained, rather uncertain.[22] Despite the fears of the bank's directors, in its first five years of existence, the institution was able to get off the ground and even bring in some good results. Total assets rose considerably during the first two years and then slowed down in 1893 as a result of the economic and monetary crisis that hit the United States and from which the island could not be immune. In Mexican currency, assets rose from 1.1 million pesos in 1890 to 3.3 million in 1894. The situation was similar for national currency, although turnover was lower. Overall, assets (in both Mexican and national currency) doubled to reach 5.3 million pesos in 1894.

The annual balance sheets of the bank reveal the purely commercial nature of the institution, which specialized in short-term operations from the outset without getting involved with the government or with long-term company financing. The bank's portfolio – which included discounts and credits secured by goods and securities – represented about 50 per cent of total assets. The high level of cash reserves (a non-remunerated asset) maintained during those years, 40 per cent of total assets in Mexican currency, and almost 30 per cent in national currency, reflects either the caution with which its administrators operated or the absence of good investment opportunities. Similar percentages have been recorded for *Banco Español de la Habana* in its early years.

The liability side of the balance sheets reveals the origin of the financial resources handled by the institution. Paid-up capital accounted for a small part, around 9 per cent, because the amount that shareholders were prepared to channel to the bank was the legal minimum (375,000 pesos). Borrowed funds were greater. The aforementioned difficulties were no obstacle for the bank to place a growing number of banknotes in the market, the issue of which reached the highest amount permitted by the articles of association in 1892. Notes in circulation were as much as 67 per cent of total liabilities in national currency. The other source of financing was current accounts and deposits, which rose from 987,000 pesos in 1890 to 2.2 million in 1894. These numbers led the managers to express unreserved satisfaction with the performance of the bank, claiming that it was proof of the general public confidence in the institution.

Apart from the 1893 crisis, *Banco Español de Puerto Rico* enjoyed a relatively calm existence. It was granted a tax-collection contract with the Royal Treasury, which gave it additional income. The opening of a branch in Mayaguez extended the radius of its activities outside the city of San Juan. By extending the island's financial supply and breaking the oligopoly of the banker-merchants, its financial operations were quickly able to bring down the cost of capital: market interest rates dropped from 11 per cent in 1890 to 7 per cent two years later. Shareholders also benefited from the bank's growth. The earnings of 71,000 pesos recorded in the first financial year rose to 179,000 in 1894. Net profits showed a similar upward trend. Between the first and last year of this five-year period, they more than doubled from 44,700 to 98,000 pesos. As a result of this buoyancy, the average return on equity of the Puerto Rican issuer stood at a handsome 23 per cent, permitting a generous distribution of dividends to its owners.

The institution's second five-year period was marked by two significant events. The first one was the replacement of the Mexican silver peso for the so-called provincial silver peso, a new silver coin minted in Spain, with the consequent disappearance of monetary duality. The second event was the American invasion of the island and the subsequent end of Spanish sovereignty in August 1898. A royal decree of 6 December 1895 stipulated the creation of 'a special (provincial) currency' to replace the Mexican peso.[23] The new coin was of size and sterling standard identical to the five-peseta silver coin. The exchange ratio was set at 95 per cent; in other words, every Mexican peso was worth 95 cents of the new currency. To undertake the conversion from one system to the other an 'exchange paper note' was provisionally provided to enable the swift collection of the Mexican currency. Thus, in exchange for cash handed in, the public received one half in the new specially minted pesos and the other in exchange notes. The 'exchange paper note' could then be redeemed in cash very shortly afterwards. In fact, the circulation of 'exchange notes' ended three months after the day when collection of the Mexican currency finished in San Juan. Despite its apparent complexity, the operation went ahead quickly and smoothly. In total, nearly 16 million pesos, both old and new coins, crossed the ocean without incident. The Exchange Decree dates from 6 December 1895, and by 27 February 1896, the operation had been implemented. By 1896 the old currency had disappeared from circulation and with it, the previous duality. With the new unit of account, the Spanish or provincial peso became the ordinary peso that appeared on the bank's books.

For *Banco Español de Puerto Rico*, the exchange put an end to what had been considered a financial anomaly: that its capital and banknotes expressed in a currency that was not in circulation. In the 1895 report, it was stated that the exchange had corrected the anomaly, turning the bank into a real issuing entity in such a way that its banknotes 'were an effective and genuine representation of the currency circulating in the country.' It was expected that monetary unification would bring with it 'new blood'. Business in the island would expand, and the volume of banknotes would increase and would circulate beyond the limits of the city of San Juan. The figures for 1896 and 1897 suggest that the management's hopes were realized, for in both financial years, turnover rose substantially. Notes in circulation increased from 1.2 million in 1895 to 1.8 million in 1896 and to 2.2 million in 1897. Total assets also increased. Moreover, in 1896, shareholders increased paid-up capital, raising it to 750,000 pesos. Earnings and profits also exhibited an upward trend: the former, which in 1894 had stood at 179,000 pesos, rose to 307,000 in 1897; the latter increased from 98,000 to 178,000 pesos during the same period. These were the years in which *Banco Español de Puerto Rico* obtained its highest returns on equity, an average of about 30 per cent.

The banks and the war of independence

The contrast between the Cuban and Puerto Rican institutions is at its clearest in the differing roles they played during the final years of Spanish sovereignty over the islands. In Cuba, the bank was once again called upon to contribute to the financial needs of the Treasury to confront the pro-independence uprising. The result was an irreversible decline in its fortunes. In Puerto Rico, the war was short – three months – and the mark left on the bank accounts was the consequence of the deterioration in the island's economic situation.

In Cuba, the revolution broke out in February 1895. The war, which lasted for five years, had devastating effects on the economy and the island's Treasury. The ordinary budget deficit soared to the point where it accounted for around one-half of revenues. The conflict also implied increased military spending, which the metropolis decided should be funded by the colony's Treasury. Extraordinary loans were approved, new Cuban Treasury debt was issued and cash advances were agreed with *Banco de España* and *Banque de Paris & des Pays-Bas* (Paribas). The Treasury also resorted to *Banco Español de la Isla de Cuba*.[24]

In these turbulent years at the turn of the century, absorbed as it was in the Treasury's credit needs, the bank had virtually no links with the private sector. On the occasion, *Banco Español*, which had had so many operations and profits during the first war, could only look on powerlessly as private bankers inherited its business. Current accounts and gold deposits diminished, and the bank's results were poorer than they had ever been. With the sinking of the *Maine* and the subsequent declaration of war by the United States, the situation snowballed. The Cuban coastal blockade virtually paralyzed commercial activity. Customs revenues disappeared. Unemployment rose, and the scarcity and soaring prices of all kinds of goods generated a subsistence crisis. The value of the banknotes slumped, losing what little worth they still had as a means of payment. In April

1898, 100 nominal pesos were worth no more than 35 pesos; in the month of September the peso's value was even lower.

The bank's balance-sheets changes between 1895 and 1898 are the best way to understand what happened. Total assets rose from 21.2 million to 41.2 million pesos due exclusively to new loans and advances made to the Treasury. In return, the bank received silver Treasury notes. Discounts and credit to the private sector showed very little change, and cash reserves were reduced to a minimum. On the liabilities side, the banknotes in circulation dropped to a trifle: indeed, the institution ceased to act as issuing entity – its very raison d'être. In 1897 and 1898 net profits stood at 0.3 million and 0.4 million, respectively: testimonial amounts that were apparently distributed without earmarking any part to the reserve fund. The most illustrative indicator of the bank's poor situation, however, is the quotations of its shares in the last year of the war, with a devaluation of 60 per cent below par. In 1898, for all practical purposes, *Banco Español de la Isla de Cuba* was a walking corpse.

In Puerto Rico, the outbreak of war with the United States in spring 1898 interrupted the Treasury's history of budget equilibriums. With insufficient resources to face up to new expenditure, it had to resort to exceptional means: special taxes, advances from the Overseas Ministry and funds raised through a national subscription. Unlike Cuba, however, the Puerto Rican bank was not called on to finance the war. The conflict lasted just a few months, leaving little time to encumber it with the resulting financial burdens.

Nevertheless, the bank's existence was still affected. The annual report for 1897 (published in February 1898) described what happened:

> To expect Banco Español to escape from the effects of these circumstances would probably have been impossible; it can therefore come as no surprise that the limitation on operations observed in the commercial sphere from early 1897 or even in late 1896, has been reflected to some extent in the paralysis, albeit transitory, of the upward year-on-year trend recorded to date in what we might call the backbone accounts, of the bank's utilities.

The 1898 report alluded, with a degree of dramaticism, to the 'rude test' to which the entity had been subjected by the effect of the war and its unavoidable consequences for the island's economic order. According to its writers, the worst moments were not actually during the war itself, but were caused by the uncertainty that followed it, after the signing of the preliminary articles of peace with Washington, which led to moments of panic, withdrawal of money and conversion of banknotes. The bank found itself forced to limit loans and shorten loan terms, with the resulting decline in its business.

The abnormality caused by the war led gross earnings for 1898 to drop 30 per cent in relation to the 1897 figure. Profits also fell from 178,000 to 136,000 pesos. The bank's rate of return also suffered: whereas in the two-year period from 1895 to 1896 it had reached its peak of 30 per cent, in 1897 it dropped to 24 per cent and in 1898 to around 18 per cent, albeit still an acceptable result. These were the worst years for *Banco Español de Puerto Rico*, but they were not disastrous in the way they were for its Cuban counterpart. When sovereignty was handed over, the institution of San Juan may have been more lethargic as it awaited the outcome of events, but it was not dead like *Banco Español de la Isla de Cuba*.

Conclusion

What conclusions can be drawn from this comparison of *Banco Español de la Habana* and *Banco Español de Puerto Rico* during Spanish sovereignty? How did they differ and in what aspects were they similar? Which of the two best performed its role as bank of issue, and what was their contribution to the development of the financial systems of their corresponding territories? What can be said about their profitability as private institutions?

Both the Cuban and Puerto Rican institutions were the biggest banks on their respective islands. The former far surpassed all others operating in Cuba: its 8 million pesos of paid-up capital was the equivalent to the resources of all the other financial institutions put together. *Banco Español de Puerto Rico* also managed the equivalent to half of the total banking resources available in the colony.[25] Their origins have much in common: both were founded in response to the pressure exerted by businessmen, keen to have an institution that could break the monopoly of the merchant-bankers. The two banks also enlarged and diversified the means of payment in the islands by adding to the existing coinage the paper money they put into circulation. Finally, *Banco Español de la Habana* and *Banco Español de Puerto Rico* were private joint-stock companies, and the only of their kind in the two colonies.

The date of foundation is a first difference. *Banco Español de la Habana* was established in the mid-1850s, when most other Caribbean colonial financial institutions were erected in the British, French and Dutch possessions. The creation of *Banco Español de Puerto Rico* met, however, with more obstacles, and its establishment was delayed for nearly three decades, until 1888, when the last of many projects was eventually approved by the Spanish government. A second difference is in the size of the two banks, easily explained in turn by the size of the economy and population of the two colonies. Cuba's economy and population being much larger than those of Puerto Rico, the banks' size should cause no surprise.

Comparing the profitability of the two banks, as measured by their rate of return, for the Cuban banking institutions, the return on equity remained at high levels during the initial decades, around 15 per cent, but then fell abruptly to 7 per cent in the 1880s and even further in the 1890s, when it dropped to a low of 5 per cent. It should be borne in mind, however, that these estimates, at least during the two last decades, are more apparent than real, given that no amount was deducted from gross profit for reserves, nor was provision made for non-performing assets, contravening not only the statutes of the bank but also fair accounting practice. For *Banco Español de Puerto Rico* the estimated return on equity for the nine years under Spanish sovereignty was, on average, 22 per cent, and only in the final year of 1898 dropped below that percentage to 15 per cent, although the similar caveat made for the Cuban bank applies to the Puerto Rican institution. Hence, if the comparison of the two banks is restricted to the period in which both were operating, it can be asserted that the Puerto Rican bank was more profitable than the Cuban bank.

But the real difference between *Banco Español de Cuba* and *Banco Español de Puerto Rico*, however, lies in their relationship to the public treasuries of their respective territories. Few years after its incorporation, the Cuban bank began to establish close links with the Treasury of the island. After the 1868 uprising its commercial character weakened, and it became more and more a bank at the mercy of the government's financial needs. With the war of independence, all bank operations were tied to cover the financial requirements of the Treasury, which ultimately left it utterly discredited, bankrupt and ruined; if not legally, at least technically. The Puerto Rican issuer never became a bank of or for the government. Its operations always remained in the private trading sphere; it was above all a commercial bank.

The history of the two Spanish colonial banks of issue in the Caribbean offers more differences than similarities. Both operated under the same legislation and had similar statutes and resembling names. Both were chartered by the Madrid government. Both were private companies with capital raised in the respective islands. Both were aimed to solve the lack of means of payment and to break the oligopoly of the merchant-bankers. Both were supposedly established to contribute to the development of the islands. However, as has been seen, as commercial banks they performed quite differently. They also followed different paths as banks of issue. In short, *Banco Español de la Habana* and *Banco Español de Puerto Rico* – two colonial institutions born out of similar banking model – traced two different banking histories.

Notes

1 Studies on Cuba's financial system are partial and incomplete. Key works include those by José A. Pulido, *Banco Español de la Habana*, La Habana, Museo Numismático, Banco Nacional de Cuba, 1980. Manuel Moreno Fraginals and José A. Pulido, *Cuba a través de su moneda*, La Habana, Banco Nacional de Cuba (undated). Alejandro García Álvarez, 'Metamorfosis de una institución financiera: El Banco Español de la Isla de Cuba,' *Tiempos de América*, 2, 1998, pp. 117–35. Susan Fernández, *Encumbered Cuba. Capital Markets and Revolt, 1878–1895*, Gainesville, University Press of Florida, 2002. Inés Roldán de Montaud, *La banca de emisión en Cuba (1856–1898)*, Madrid, Banco de España, series 'Estudios de Historia Económica, 44,' 2004. Inés Roldán de Montaud, 'El Banco Español de la isla de Cuba (1856–1898): Historia de un emisor colonial,' *Revista de la Historia de la Economía y de la Empresa* (BBVA), 6, 2012, pp. 181–216. Francisco Comín, Ángel Pascual and Inés Roldán de Montaud, *Las cajas de ahorros de las provincias de ultramar, 1840–1898: Cuba y Puerto Rico*, Madrid, Fundación de las Cajas de Ahorros, 2010.
2 About Puerto Rico, the number of studies is limited. The most complete are those by Annie Santiago de Curet, *Crédito, moneda y bancos en Puerto Rico durante el siglo XIX*, Río Piedras, Editorial de la Universidad de Puerto Rico, 1989. And Francisco Comín, Ángel Pascual and Inés Roldán de Montaud, op. cit., 2010. Earlier works are: Biagio Di Venuti, *Money and Banking in Puerto Rico*, Río Piedras, University of Puerto

Rico Press, 1950. Ángel Sanz, *Reseña histórica de la banca en Puerto Rico*, Santurce, Puerto Rico, Departamento de Instrucción Pública, 1967.

3 This work is part of research project MICINN HAR 2009-07103 (Spain), *Diccionario biográfico español de ministros de Ultramar*, and ANR, GLOBIBER (France), *Le renoevau impérial des États ibériques: une globalisation originale?* It is also part of the project MICINN ECO 2009-08791 (Spain), *Financial Crises: Past, Present and Future*. Financial support from the Spanish Ministry of Science and Innovation is gratefully acknowledged.

4 Inés Roldán de Montaud, op. cit., 2004, pp. 18–20.

5 Vicente Vázquez Queipo, *Informe fiscal sobre el fomento de la población blanca en la isla de Cuba y emancipación progresiva de la esclava; con una breve reseña de las reformas y modificaciones que para conseguirlo convendría establecer en la legislación y constitución coloniales*, Madrid, Imprenta de J. Martín Alegría, 1845. Manuel Moreno Fraginals, *El ingenio: Complejo económico social cubano del azúcar*, La Habana, Editorial de Ciencias Sociales, 1978.

6 Roland Ely, *Cuando reinaba su majestad el azúcar. Estudio histórico-sociológico de una tragedia latinoamericana: el monocultivo en Cuba*, Buenos Aires, Editorial Sudamericana, 1963. José Ramón García López, 'Los comerciantes banqueros en el sistema bancario cubano, 1880–1910,' in Consuelo Naranjo, Puig Samper, Miguel A. y García Mora and Luis Miguel (eds), *La nación soñada: Cuba, Puerto Rico y Filipinas ante el 98*, Madrid, Doce Calles, 1996, pp. 267–92.

7 There is an account of these institutions in Carlos Tablada and Galia Castelló, *La historia de la banca en Cuba del siglo XIX al XX*, Tomo I, *La colonia*, La Habana, Editorial de Ciencias Sociales, 2007.

8 Archivo Histórico Nacional (AHN), Ultramar, leg. 47, document 7, 26 December 1854.

9 The royal decree in Joaquín Rodríguez San Pedro, *Legislación ultramarina concordada y anotada*, Madrid, Imprenta de Viota, Cubas y Vicente, 1865–1869, 16 volumes; here: vol. V, 1868, pp. 449–51.

10 The statutes and by-laws, in Joaquín Rodríguez San Pedro, op. cit., 1868, vol. V, pp. 451–68.

11 Archivo Nacional de Cuba, Gobierno Superior Civil, leg. 1189, núm. 46590. Contrary to what is generally written (Julio Le Riverend, *Historia económica de Cuba*, La Habana, Instituto Cubano del Libro, 1974. Gabriel Tortella, 'Desarrollo de la industria azucarera y la guerra de Cuba,' *Moneda y Crédito*, 91, 1964, pp. 131–63. Annie Santiago de Curet, op. cit., 1989, the bank did not receive public capital, and neither was the transformation of Real Caja de Descuentos.

12 A list of the main shareholders, in Roldán de Montaud, op. cit., 2004, p. 32.

13 Federico Asenjo, *comercio de la isla y la influencia que en él ha de ejercer el Banco Español de Puerto Rico*, Puerto Rico, Imprenta Militar, 1862. Annie Santiago de Curet, op. cit., 1989, pp. 156–64. Manuel Paniagua, *Informe relativo al Banco Español de Puerto Rico, luego Banco de Puerto Rico*, San Juan, Cantero, Fernández & Co., 1925.

14 Similar procedures were used to establish banks in other European colonies in the Caribbean. See Pierre Denizet, *Les banques coloniales*, Paris, A. Pedone, 1899. Albert S. J. Baster, *Imperial Banks*, London, P. S. King & Son, 1929. Keith Le Cheminant, *Colonial and Foreign Banking Systems*, London, George Routledge & Sons, 1931.

15 Annie Santiago de Curet, op. cit., 1989, pp. 156–64. *Informe relativo al Banco Español de Puerto Rico, luego Banco de Puerto Rico*, 1925.

16 On the monetary issue, Astrid Cubano, 'Comercio, moneda y política en Puerto Rico a finales del siglo XIX: una perspectiva socioeconómica,' in Luis E. González Vales (ed.), *1898: Enfoques y perspectivas*, San Juan, First Book, 1997, pp. 209–20. Alberto Sabio Alcutén, 'Un rasgo de la política monetaria en tiempo de guerra: El canje de moneda en Cuba y Puerto Rico, 1895–1898,' *Tiempos de América*, 3/4, 1990, pp. 3–18.

17 Annie Santiago de Curet, op. cit., 1989, pp. 156–60. In 1896 the shareholders made a second payment to make up the 750,000 pesos.

18 A comparison of the Cuban and Puerto Rican Treasuries can be found in Inés Roldán de Montaud, 'Las Haciendas públicas de Cuba y Puerto Rico desde el grito de la independencia hasta el final de la colonia,' in Inés Roldán de Montaud (ed.), *Las Haciendas públicas en el Caribe hispano durante el siglo XIX*, Madrid, Consejo Superior de Investigaciones Científicas, 2008.

19 The following is taken from Inés Roldan de Montaud, op. cit., 2004.

20 See Inés Roldán de Montaud, op. cit., 2004, pp. 116–25 and 137–50.

21 The return on equity has been calculated as the ratio between net profits and paid-up capital.

22 The historical account of the bank is taken from the annual reports; the figures given in the text all proceed from the balance sheets and income statements published with the reports. See Banco Español de Puerto Rico (1888–1898), *Memorias anuales*, 1890, pp. 6–7.

23 Legislation on the exchange, in *Gaceta de Madrid*, 8 December 1895. Details and a good explanation can be found in Alberto Sabio Alcutén, op. cit., 1999. References to 'the provincial silver currency for the island of Puerto Rico' are also made in *Moneda y numismática en Puerto Rico*, available online at www.angelfire.com/ri/caguax/ monedaprov and www.suagm.edu/une/portal_de_biblioteca/numismatica_historia.

24 A detailed study on the financing of the war in Cuba, in Inés Roldán de Montaud, 'Guerra y finanzas en la crisis de fin de siglo: 1895–1900,' *Hispania. Revista Española de Historia*, LVII, 2(196), 1997, pp. 611–75. For Banco Español de la Isla de Cuba's role during the war, see Inés Roldán de Montaud, op. cit., 2004, chapter IX.

25 The information is taken from Inés Roldán de Montaud, op. cit., 2004, p. 119. Annie Santiago de Curet, op. cit., 1989.

3 Foreign direct investment in imperial Brazil and the activities of British and Portuguese banks

Colonial banking versus imperial banking?

Carlos Gabriel Guimarães

This chapter[1] analyzes an instance of foreign direct investment (FDI) in Brazil during the Imperial period – specifically the organization and activities of two English banks, London & Brazilian Bank and Brazilian & Portuguese Bank (later called the English Bank of Rio de Janeiro), during the period 1862 to 1870. Measuring the presence of FDI in nineteenth-century Latin America is not a simple undertaking, because the historical sources are often unreliable. For instance, it can be challenging to distinguish what was invested in private portfolios from what was invested in public portfolios (i.e., public debt securities). Such difficulties notwithstanding, Albert Fishlow calculated that European assets in the region grew from $1.8 billion in 1855 to $6.4 billion in 1870, surging to $35.8 billion in 1914. As Fishlow noted, 'changes in the stock of assets before 1914 approximate flows of foreign investment.'[2]

In the case of Brazil, Maria Barbara Levy and Flávio Saes have called attention to the fact that although at mid-century 'the greater share of capital exports from industrialized countries was directed to titles of public debt, starting in the 1880s investment in the private sphere (direct and from portfolios) was reaching the magnitude of that in the public portfolios.'[3] However, if we look at the same data from M. de Paiva Abreu that those authors used, we can observe a rising trend of foreign capital in direct investments starting as early as 1860 reflected in the growth from £1.3 million in 1840 to £7.5 million in 1865, or an increase of 580 per cent.[4]

Although direct British investment in Brazil took many forms, from banks to railroads and insurance agencies, it was frequently organized until 1920[5] into 'free-standing companies'. This concept has been defined by Mira Wilkins as enterprises domiciled abroad, managed by British migrants who had been born and brought up in Britain but who resided overseas; such enterprises might not have a British head office or a British parent company. The individual Briton who settled abroad did not create a foreign direct investment, since there remained no obligation to anyone in Britain, whereas the expatriate who went abroad for years, who considered himself British and who then returned home, retaining an interest in his overseas business, became thereby on his return a foreign investor. In those instances where the expatriate tapped British capital markets, establishing a company or companies in England or Scotland, the British company became the foreign direct investor.[6]

But the emergence of this particular foreign-capital enterprise must also be understood within the dynamic context of institutional changes unfolding by the 1850s and 1860s in industrialized countries and about to occur in peripheral regions across the globe – a process that intensified with the Great Depression in the latter part of the nineteenth century (1873–1895).[7] These transformations facilitated an increase in novel organizational structures of FDI, principally through the development of anonymous limited-liability companies (called in Portuguese *Sociedades Anônimas de Responsabilidade Limitada, S/A Limitada*).[8]

During the Brazilian Empire (1822–1889), the increasing presence of foreign capital was related to the Imperial state's political stability after 1850,[9] and to the adoption of contractionary metals-based[10] monetary policies (see Table A3.6). These factors provided the macroeconomic conditions that could foster the establishment of new direct investment, particularly British investment, in such areas as banks and railroads.[11]

Actively participating in the Commercial Plaza in the city of Rio de Janeiro[12] since the 1820s and 1830s, English businessman Edward Johnston, principal director and manager of the firm Edward Johnston & Co., and Portuguese businessmen João José dos Reis (Count of Saint Salvador of Matosinhos) and Rodrigo Pereira Felício (Count of Saint Mamede)[13] organized their 'overseas banks' in association with bankers and entrepreneurs in London.[14] Johnston founded the London & Brazilian Bank Limited, and Reis and Felício founded the Brazilian & Portuguese Bank, which was renamed English Bank of Rio de Janeiro in 1867. The rise of these international institutions raises several key questions: What was the principal motive for creating banks in London with branches in Brazil? What types of enterprises and strategies did they pursue in the Brazilian marketplace? And what was the reaction of colonial banks to these new English ones, the type of which was more that of an 'imperial bank' active in a foreign colony?

The 1860 Barriers Act and circumstances favouring FDI

The historiography of the Brazilian economy has long emphasized the significance of Law no. 1.083, of 2 August 1860, which restored to the Bank of Brazil the monopoly on issuing paper currency.[15] This law, mono-metallist in its economic and political essence, reintroduced a monetary regime rooted in precious metal – specifically gold, 'with free and unlimited coinage so long as exchange value is fixed between metal and money.'[16] This law, characterized in the historiography as the Barriers Act (*Lei dos Entraves*), not only reintroduced the gold standard that had been instituted in Brazil once before, during the monetary reforms of 1846,[17] but also brought about an end to the liberal banking and lending practices espoused by Bernardo de Souza Franco (future Viscount of Souza Franco), finance minister in the ninth Cabinet. This likely pleased the Cabinet's president of the Counsel of Ministers, Pedro de Araujo Lima, recently the Marquis of Olinda,[18] who endorsed more conservative philosophies.[19] Analyzing the effects of the new economic policies implemented by Angelo Moniz da Silva Ferraz (Baron of Ururuguaiana), finance minister and president of the 11th Cabinet, we verified that in the period 1859–1860 to 1861–1862 'stock of currency fell 15 percent, prices decreased by 8.5 percent, and the value of currency increased from 25 pence/*mil réis* to 26.5 pence/*mil réis*.'[20]

The Barriers Act was deeply restrictive with respect not only to the activities of existent banks and banking houses but to the creation of new ones. The principal features distinguishing a banking house from a bank were its lower volume of capitalization and different organizational structure. A banking house was also regarded as a commercial, not anonymous, corporation, and it had fewer legal responsibilities than banks that were structured as limited liability companies (LLCs). Between 1851 and 1860, 16 Brazilian banks had opened in the city of Rio de Janeiro, 10 of them appearing between 1857 and 1860. But after passage of the Act, from 1861 to 1863, only five new banks were opened in the principal financial and commercial centre of the Brazilian Empire, and two of these were of English origin – London & Brazilian Bank Limited and Brazilian & Portuguese Bank Limited. Further detrimental effects of the Barriers Act can be traced in the startling number of bankruptcies of commercial houses in Rio's financial district, reaching 105 individual cases in 1862 alone. To put this number in perspective, in 1858, one year after the crisis of 1857, a total of 90 commercial houses became insolvent.[21] At the same time the new legislation was constraining the expansion of Brazilian banks in diverse ways, it enhanced the appeal of the Brazilian market to English banks because of the ease in converting currencies.

The development of this locus of English capital investment with the rise of novel forms of business in the sectors of finance and infrastructure (railroads etc.) became tightly interwoven with export activities.[22] Concerning this British presence in the 1860s, Geoffrey Jones highlighted,

> During the 1860s in British company legislation held foster a speculative boom in the promotion of overseas bank. In 1862, Parliament codified two previous company acts 1857 and 1858, which had introduced unrestricted creation of limited liability joint stock companies, including banking companies, and as result there was a spurt of enthusiasm for organization joint stock banks, both for domestic or overseas purpose.[23]

Brazil's first English bank: London & Brazilian Bank Limited

London & Brazilian Bank (LBB) was created in London on 13 May 1862, and incorporated four days later.[24] According to its Memorandum of Association, a document that was also translated into Portuguese, the bank was an anonymous LLC boasting nominal capital of £1 million which was divided into 10,000 shares of £100 each.[25]

Among the signatories to the Memorandum of Association was Edward Johnston, director and organizer of one of the largest coffee export firms in

Brazil, Edward Johnston & Co.[26]; his name lay alongside those of an illustrious selection of London's private bankers (see Table 3.1). That original memorandum includes a list of 320 shareholders, among the largest of which were directors Henry Louis Bischoffsheim, Edward Moon and John Bloxan Elin, with 500, 200 and 200 shares, respectively. Although the majority of shareholders was British, there were such notable exceptions as Robert A. Brenam, local agent of the Ottoman Bank (20 shares), New York businessman Watts Sherman (50 shares)[27] and Rio de Janeiro businessman João Baptista Lopes Gonçalves[28] (20 shares). But perhaps the most surprising member of this group was the Brazilian Francisco de Sales Torres Homem, who succeeded De Souza Franco as finance minister and devised the package of conservative policies that became the Barriers Act (20 shares).[29]

LBB was authorized to conduct business in Brazil, more specifically in the city of Rio de Janeiro, by decree no. 2.979 of 02 October 1862. Comparing the text of this decree with the bank's Memorandum of Association, two points call our attention: the nature of the LLC and the question of emitting debt. Brazil's mercantile legislation (the Brazilian Commercial Code) did not yet contain provisions for a limited liability company.[30] A legal document produced by the

Table 3.1 The directors of London & Brazilian Bank Limited (1862)

Name and address	Profession	Shares held
James Alexander, 10 Kings Arms Yard, London	—	50
Henry Louis Bischoffsheim, 10 Angel Court, London	Banker (Merchant Bank in London and Paris – Bischoffshein & Goldschmidt)	50
John White Cater, 11 Mining Lane, London	Commerce (Merchant Bank: Robert Benson & Co.)	50
Philip Charles Cavan, 29 Finsbury Circus, London	Businessman	50
Pascoe Charles Glyn, 62 Gresham House, Old Broad Street, London	Banker (Private Bank: Glyn, Halifax, Mills & Co.)	50
Edward Johnston, 4–6 Great St Helen's, London	Businessman (Trading Firm – Edward Johnston, Son & Co. – London; Edward Johnston & Co. – Rio de Janeiro/Brazil)	50
John Bloxan Elin, 34 Abchurch Lane, London	Businessman (esquire; director of The Alliance Bank of London and Liverpool*)	50
Edward Moon, Liverpool	Businessman	50
William Freer Schönfeld, Aldborough, Boroughbridge	Banker (Accepting House: Meyer & Schönfeld)	50

Source: BRASIL, Colleção das Leis do Império do Brasil 1862, op. cit., p. 325.
AHMOP. O Banco de Londres e do Brasil Sociedade Anônima (London and Brazilian Bank Limited), Memorandum de Associação e Artigos de Associação 1862. Guimaraes, op. cit., 1862.

Note
* *The London Review and Weekly Journal of Politics, Art & Society*, 4, London, January–June, 1862, VII.

Finance Section of the State Council gave permission to the English bank to open in Brazil but articulated that it would have to operate within the rules of the Brazilian empire:

> 4. The company of London and Brazilian Bank is organized in conformity with the legislation by which are regulated banking establishments in Great Britain, in the category of Anonymous Society [LLC]; being thus the responsibility of its members limited to the value of the shares that each may possess: but it is subject to the laws of the Empire, in anything that could have application to the activities it may undertake here.'[31]

The Finance Section's determination further emphasized that, with respect to such functions as currency exchange, credit and deposits, this new type of bank would have to act according to the rules that then defined a Brazilian commercial bank.

> It is our determination that the Imperial Government would provide a genuine service to the industries of Brazil by permitting the founding of the *London and Brazilian Bank* in the capital of the Empire, under the following conditions: 1. That this bank, beyond the basic operations of exchange, will expressly limit itself only to those which are permitted to the banks of deposits and credit issuance created within the Empire by authorisation of the Imperial Government. 2. That the company *London and Brazilian Bank* as well as any other establishments of the same form, founded by joint stock companies, will submit itself to the dictates of the laws and regulations that reign in Brazil now and those that may reign in the future.[32]

LBB opened for business in Brazil on the first day of February 1863. Its address, as advertised in a notice in the newspaper *Jornal do Commercio* on 20 January that year, was number 49 on the Rua da Direita (a thoroughfare in downtown Rio presently known as First of March). The offices were led by John Saunders, comptroller; Thomas Jones Tenet, manager; and Joseph Levi Montefiori, chief cashier.[33]

Even with all the complexity of analyzing historical data that was not recorded according to a consistent accounting standard, we can observe that the balance of assets from the first full year of operations (with subsequent years shown in Table A3.7) includes a remarkable increase of 100 per cent over time in cash loans and notes of credit and growth of 40 per cent in promissory notes. Cash on hand decreased by 19 per cent, while LBB's account at the Bank of Brazil increased by 40 per cent. With respect to liabilities, the capitalization of LBB grew by one-half from £1 million to £1.5 million, and deposits increased by over 100 per cent. The bank was rewarded for such impressive expansion and overall growth with the Imperial government's permission to open branches in the states of Pernambuco (decreed 1 September 1863) and Rio Grande do Sul (decreed 1 December 1863). Still in 1864, LBB announced the possibility of withdrawals, through the emission of letters of credit (bills of exchange), at the following national and international locations:

- Branches of London & Brazilian Bank:
- Pernambuco
- Rio Grande do Sul
- Lisbon
- Porto
- London, through London & Brazilian Bank
- Paris, through Bischoffsheim-Goldschmidt & Co.
- Hamburg, through J. H. Schroeder & Co.
- Montevideo and Buenos Aires, through London, Buenos Aires & River Plate Bank
- New York, through Aymar & Co.[34]

The 1864 annual report, prepared for shareholders by the directors in London, demonstrated how LBB's capital had grown through the issue of more than 5,000 new shares at £100 each; 2,800 of these were purchased by 'shareholders of the Anglo-Portuguese Bank, which has merged (*fez fuzão*) with the London & Brazilian, and 200 were sold at a premium.'[35] Details of that merger were not included in the report. Nonetheless, the burgeoning capitalization of LBB – and the ensuing impacts on the bank's profits and dividends – likely derived more from the number of branches opening in Brazil and Portugal than from this one consolidation, however notable it was.[36]

Portugal's recent experience of political and economic stability had been a critical precondition for the founding of branches there. Nuno Valério observes that, following the resolution of a political crisis involving the government and the Bank of Portugal, which had dragged on since the early 1850s (punctuated by the adoption of the gold standard in 1854, placed into law in 1857), finally 'normality was restored to monetary policy in Portugal in accord with the philosophies and practices then dominant.'[37] According to David Justino, this stability resulted in the institution of 'two discrete systems of emission: one based in the south, under control of the Bank of Portugal, and a competing network in the north.'[38]

Another important factor for the creation of bank branches (LBB) in Portugal was the financing of public debt in that nation. Rui Ramos suggests that the serious problem of deficits in Portugal's commercial balance, related to the 'agricultural crisis (1854–1857) and the gnawing epidemics that accompanied the scarcity of foodstuffs,' had spurred growth in public debt – surging '11% in 1857 and 12% in 1858.'[39] The only apparent 'solution' had been to further deepen the level of public debt, both internal and external. Thus the notes of external debt became assets for various foreign investors as well as some Portuguese, too.[40] Prominent among the latter were enterprising members of Brazil's Portuguese immigrant community: 'Those stalkers of lucre, as Oliveira Martins nicknamed them, due to their avidity for investing in notes of credit. They were the very lungs pumping the oxygen of credit into Portugal's Regeneration' during the 1850s and 1860s.[41]

Funds invested by 'Brazilians' (Portuguese living in Brazil) were remitted to banks situated in the City of London, typically in two forms: letters of exchange (withdrawals at 30 or 40 days), or cash (gold and silver coins).[42] LBB, aware that on the whole Brazil conducted far more business with England than Portugal, was immediately attracted to these 'remittances from immigrants in Brazil'[43] and decided to open a branch in Portugal in 1863. Figure 3.1 shows a schematic demonstrating the flow of capital linking these businessmen and their partners with institutions in Rio de Janeiro, Lisbon and London.

The creation of Brazilian & Portuguese Bank in Brazil (1863)

Brazilian & Portuguese Bank (BPB) was authorized to engage in business in Brazil through decree no. 3212, of 28 December 1863.[44] As with the approval process for the statutes of LBB, the Imperial government was careful to frame certain rules and conditions with explicit reference to the Barriers Act. It demanded

1. That this bank, beyond the basic operations of exchange, will expressly limit itself only to those activities which are permitted to the banks of deposits and credit issuance created within the Brazilian Empire by authorization of the Power of the Executive, and recorded into law in Paragraph 3, article 1 of Decree no. 2711 of 9 December 1860 [the Barriers Act] [...]. 2. That the company *Brazilian and Portuguese Bank* will submit itself to the dictates of the laws and regulations that reign in Brazil now and those that may reign in the future, regarding the establishments of the same type, that were founded by joint stock companies.[45]

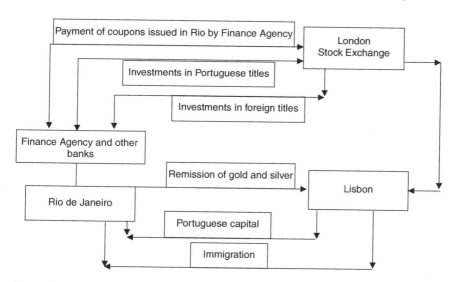

Figure 3.1 The Circuit of Capital: Portugal–Brazil–England.

Source: António Lopes Vieira, *Os Transportes Públicos de Lisboa entre 1830 e 1910*, Lisboa, 1982, p. 188, in: Rui Ramos, *O Sistema Fontista. Portugal Contemporâneo (1851–1910)*, volume II, Lisboa, Alfa, 1989, p. 130.

BPB began with nominal capital of £1 million, divided into 50,000 shares at £20 each.[46] Its main office was in London, at 13 St Helen's Place, and its Brazilian branch resided in the financial district of Rio de Janeiro at 63 Rua da Direita. Among its principal stockholders were some of the most important businessmen in London and Portuguese businessmen of commerce import and export of Rio de Janeiro. The London bank's first board of directors was composed of William Bevan, George Thomas Brooking, Arthur Bernard White, James McGrouter, Frederick Rodewald and John Knowles.[47] Although his name was not included in a period list of signatories (Table 3.2), John Knowles was a partner in the English firm of Knowles & Foster, one of the largest companies operating in both Brazil and Portugal.[48]

The Brazilian branch was directed by Portuguese businessmen João José dos Reis (Count of Saint Salvador do Matozinho) and Rodrigo Pereira Felício (Count of Saint Mamede), along with José Carlos Mayrink and Thomaz March Ewbank. José Reis and Pereira Felício were based in Rio's Commercial Plaza, and each had diverse linkages to businesses in Porto (Portugal), while Mayrink was the director of the first Commercial Bank of Rio de Janeiro.[49] Ewbank was a partner in the firm Ewbank Schmidt & Co.[50] The BPB statutes declared that members of the bank's board in Rio, 'each of them, when they might be in London, will have the *ex officio* right to participate with those Directors.'[51] However, the subordination of the Brazilian branch to the English main office was inscribed explicitly in the document: members of the Brazilian board would be 'nominated from time to time' (article 110) by the executives in England, and would have to answer directly to them (article 113).[52]

The bank commenced operations in 1864, and its first balance sheet in Brazil reflected loans in promissory notes with guarantees and in secured current accounts

Table 3.2 Signatories to Statutes of Brazilian & Portuguese Bank (1863)

Name and Address	Profession	# Shares Held
William Bevan, 2 Laurence Pountney Hill, London	Businessman	300
George Thomas Brooking, 64 Old Broad Street, London	Businessman	250
James McGrouter, 3 Crosby Square, London	Businessman	300
Arthur Bernard White, 9 Broad Street Buildings, London	Businessman	300
João José dos Reis, 22 Hannover Square, Middlesex/Praia dos Mineiros, 15 Rua da Direita, Rio de Janeiro, Brazil1	Foreign businessman[1]	300
Frederick Youle, 155 Fenchurch Street, London	Businessman	100
Frederick Rodewald, Wimbledon Common, County of Surrey	Businessman	500

Source: BRASIL, Colleção das Leis do Império do Brasil de 1863, op. cit, p. 431.

Note
1   Almanak Administrativo Mercantil e Industrial da Corte e Província do Rio de Janeiro para o anno de 1865, Rio de Janeiro, Eduardo e Henrique Lammert, 1865.

with guarantees from third-party warrantors (Table A3.8). One intriguing account in the assets column was an investment in an interest called Policies of Public Debt, in the substantial amount of 601 *contos de réis* (often abbreviated to *contos*) – an example of the remittances from 'Portuguese Brazilians' back to Portugal and beyond to other foreign banks. The liabilities included a type of deposit called 'current account with interest,' a form of savings plan that was common to Brazilian banks but not utilized at the time by typical London-based English banks (such deposits were recorded by LBB as well). This account, in the sum of 4,865 *contos*, was the largest deposit account by far for the reporting period ending June 1864 and represented 81 per cent of BPB's deposits.

In September that year, Brazil experienced a crisis in its financial sector. The Antonio Alves Souto & Co. Banking House, an institution at the heart of Rio's Commercial Plaza, went bankrupt. The weakened banking sector was soon sent reeling deeper into instability with the expansion of Brazil's war with Paraguay, an expensive and psychologically demanding conflict for the nation (and indeed much of the Southern Cone). The repercussions of that war for English banks in Brazil, and the solutions the bankers devised to navigate them, are addressed in the next section.

The Souto Crisis (1864) and the war with Paraguay (1864–1870): reactions and strategies from the English banks

The commercial and financial predicament of late 1864, which came to be known as the Souto Crisis due to the insolvency of the Souto banking house that heralded it, really represented the culmination of deeper problems that had been brewing in Rio's Commercial Plaza since at least 1860.[53] In the face of such insecurity in the financial sector, the Society of Plaza Underwriters, a corporation dedicated to protecting the interests of high commerce – i.e. the largest national and international banking, import-export and supply firms headquartered in Rio de Janeiro[54] – quickly organized a special task force. On 12 September 1864, its leader, Society president and banker José Joaquim de Lima e Silva (Viscount, later Count of Tocantins), formally directed an appeal to the Emperor to intervene.[55]

The Imperial government's chief executive, liberal statesman Zacarias de Goes e Vasconcelos, responded promptly with a series of measures. Notable among these were decree no. 3306 of 13 September 1864, which authorized Bank of Brazil to elevate its emission to triple the available funds; the decree no. 3307 of 14 September 1864, establishing mandatory issuing of notes by Bank of Brazil; and the decree no. 3308 of 17 September 1864. The latter included five articles creating extraordinary dispositions, among them the directive to regulate insolvencies of banks and banking houses at a term of 60 days, backdated to take effect on 9 September.[56]

The bank involvement and expansionist policies were reflections of the magnitude of the crisis. As a result of events from September 1864 through March 1865, there were 95 bankruptcies 'with a total loss of 115,000 *contos*, more than all the money circulating in Brazil at the time, which was somewhat more than 100,000 *contos*.'[57] During September many national banks and banking houses, including Souto & Co., resorted to discounts and bonds provided by Bank of Brazil because of panicked runs on their customer accounts (Table 3.3).[58] The English banks also turned to the Bank of Brazil, but received lower levels of assistance.

The political and economic context grew even more complicated after December 1864, when international tensions among Brazil, Argentina, Uruguay and Paraguay triggered military actions. The so-called Paraguayan War pitted the triple alliance of Brazil, Argentina and Uruguay against Paraguay. It was initiated on 11 November 1864, when Paraguayan forces captured the Brazilian steamship *Marquês de Olinda*, and lasted until the death of Paraguay's leader Solano López on 1 March 1870. At nearly six years, it was the lengthiest conflict on the American continents, and it brought fundamental challenges to the Imperial government.[59] Noted Brazilian writer and statesman Joaquim Nabuco observed that the war 'divided the waters,' bringing the Empire itself to a crisis point.[60]

Certainly the war was very expensive. According to calculations made by Pelaez and Suzigan, total expenditures reached 614,000 *contos de réis*[61] and 'generated a deficit of 387,397 *contos*, or 6.5 percent of all revenue.'[62] Principal sources of financing were domestic and foreign loans, and the levying of various taxes (Table 3.4). Brazil's borrowing included

> a foreign type-74 loan in 1865 in the value of £6,693,000 with liquidity of £5,000,000 (around 49,000 *contos*), at a rate of 5 percent with a 30-year term. There was also an internal loan of 27,000 *contos*, and the issuance of treasury notes (at 6% annually) in the sum of 171,000 *contos* during the war. The rest of the amount, roughly 120,000 *contos*, was issued as paper currency.[63]

Table 3.3 Amounts furnished by the Bank of Brazil, 10–30 September 1864

Institution	Discount (contos de réis)	Bond (contos de réis)
Rural & Hipotecário Bank	1.240:000$000	4.630:000$000
Mauá, MacGregor & Co. Bank	5.246:440$136	—
London & Brazilian Bank	382:766$240	500:000$000
Brazilian & Portuguese Bank	—	1.013:300$000
Gomes & Filhos	3.222:239$512	1.934:000$000
Bahia, Irmãos & Co.	8.207:831$061	1.804:600$000
Montenegro, Lima & Co.	2.108:507$274	1.088:000$000
Oliveira & Bello	22:250$000	—
D'Illion & Marques Braga	682:349$604	—
Portinho & Moniz	850:895$569	63:000$000
Silva Pinto, Melo & Co.	337:458$220	—
João Baptista Vianna Drummond	254:233$971	—
Manoel Gomes de Carvalho	183:343$282	—
Lallemant & Co.	347:884$570	—

Source: Brasil. Ministério da Justiça, Comissão de Inquérito sobre as causas da crise na praça do Rio de Janeiro de 1864, op. cit., p. 204.

Table 3.4 Financing the Paraguayan War (1822 values, in 1,000s of *contos*)

	Customs duties	Export fees	Provincial contributions	Other tributes	Total income
1864/5	5.9	1.7	1.6	0.4	9.6
1865/6	4.7	1.6	1.3	0.4	8.0
1866/7	4.7	1.4	1.5	0.2	7.8
1867/8*	4.1	1.8	2.0	0.1	8.0
1868/9	4.4	1.9	1.9	0.5	8.7
1869/70	5.3	1.8	2.3	0.1	9.5

Source: Nogueira, op. cit., p. 379.

Note
* Starting in 1867, 15% of the import-export tax was required to be paid in gold.

During the middle of the war, funding got a boost from an 1867 requirement that 15 per cent of all import-export taxes were to be remitted in gold, as well as from an increase in the obligatory payment of tributes to the central government from Brazil's provinces. Dênio Nogueira found that 'the latter source of income displayed the highest growth rates, increasing from 15 percent of total income to 25 percent between 1864 and 1869.'[64]

LBB was impacted by the economic crisis, as its period balance sheets and London directors' reports demonstrate. Declines in the bank's activities were felt as early as 1865 and intensified in 1867 with the new state measures to generate revenue for the war. On the asset side, in 1865, loans (notes and current accounts) and cash on hand reached a high of 18.189:898$370 Rs and 1.621:567$020 Rs, respectively, but these numbers would decline from 1866 through 1870. Loans in 1866 came to 14.883:992$970 (−18.2 per cent), and by 1870 had plummeted to 5.417:313$980 (−71 per cent). Similarly, cash on hand fell, albeit with a slight bounce, going from 1.244:017$620 Rs (−15 per cent) in 1866 to 1:969:257$740 Rs (+20 per cent) in 1867, finishing down at 607:530$110 (−66 per cent) in 1870. However, it is important to note the presence of two new accounts among the assets. One, in 1865, referred to a one-time deposit of 500:000$000 Rs made by LBB to Bank of Brazil. The other was listed from 1866 to 1870 and described guarantees for current accounts and sundry values, although the actual amount declined over time. It had started in 1866 with the substantial sum of 11.826:642$820 Rs.

In liabilities, there was an increase in capitalization in 1867. One-time deposits were made as well as deposits with different terms and interest structures (with notices of 3, 6, 10, 30 or 60 days). Even while this was contrary to what seemed to be mandated in the bank's statutes regarding the payment of interest for deposits, this diversified strategy indicates how LBB was maneuvering to grow its deposits during the financial crisis. In 1865 the deposits (LBB of London and branches, plus notes payable) came to 1.830:137$890 Rs. The following year deposits (LBB of London and branches, plus notes payable) grew dramatically by a factor of 9, to 10:869:260$287. Most of this came from the interest-paying deposits and notes payable, with a marked decline in holdings in the London office and the branches.

LBB directors, concerned with how the situation in Brazil might generate negative consequences in Great Britain, sought to fortify their position by merging with the Bank of Mauá, MacGregor & Co., one of Brazil's most important commercial banks.[65] To LBB's branches in London, Rio, Lisbon and Portugal were joined Bank of Mauá, MacGregor in Rio de Janeiro and Bank Mauá & Co. in Montevideo, São Pedro do Rio Grande do Sul and elsewhere. This new overseas bank was named London, Brazilian and Mauá Bank Limited (LBMB) and authorized to function by Brazil's government through decree no. 3,587 of 20 December 1865. Its board was composed of Mauá himself and LBB directors (Table 3.5), who hoped to continue all the previous activities of their various institutions on a more secure footing.

LBMB was launched with an impressive capitalization, estimated at £5 million. This was three times the capital of LBB and twice that of Mauá, MacGregor & Co. and all its affiliates. Potentially LBMB could have been a competitor even to the formidable Bank of Brazil, yet it failed to prosper. In light of the precarious financial circumstances it was imperative for the new board to unify and cooperate, but it was riven by internal suspicions and distrust. Directors from LBB began to perceive that some Mauá enterprises in both Rio de Janeiro and Montevideo[66] were not as successful as they had first appeared.[67] For his part the Baron of Mauá grew deeply concerned about exposure to the financial instability in London, which had recently brought about the bankruptcy of English investment bank Overend Gurney & Co. and resulted in the LBB raising fees on deductions and withdrawals.[68] According to Geoffrey Jones, citing A. S. Baster, 'many of these banks were fragile speculative enterprises which did not survive the major British banking

Table 3.5 Board of directors of London, Brazilian and Mauá Bank Limited

Names, addresses and occupations of the directors	*Shares held*
Irineo Evangelista de Souza, Baron of Mauá. Banker. Rio de Janeiro	100
Henri Louis Bischoffshein, 10 Angel Court, London. Banker (Merchant Bank: Bischoffshein & Goldschimidt). Businessman	100
Philip Charles Cavan, 16 Leadenhall Street, London. Businessman	100
Pascoe Charles Glyn, 67 Lombard Street, London. Banker (Private Bank-Glyn, Mills Currie & Co.*)	100
Edward Johnston, 6 Great St Helen's. Businessman: Edward Johnston & Co.	100
Edward Moon, 3 Cook Street, Liverpool. Businessman	100
William Freer Schönfeld, 22 Sussex Square, London. Banker (Accepting House: Meyer & Schönfeld), Esquire**	100
Total shares	700

Source: Guimaraes, 2012, op. cit, chapter 4, Table 15.

Notes
* This resulted from the merger of Glyn, Mills & Co. with Currie & Co. in 1864.
** Esquire is a term of nobility just under that of knight.

crisis in 1866, with the failure of the leading London discount house, Overend Gurney.'[69]

Meanwhile, BPB was weathering the crisis in a manner different from that of LBB.[70] In 1865 (Table A3.8), there was an increase in loans; promissory note accounts and guaranteed current accounts were up 5 per cent and 322 per cent, respectively. Cash on hand was up dramatically, from 182 *contos* in 1864 to 1,290 the next year, a growth of 708 per cent. In the liabilities column, deposits had doubled, and the sundry balances account grew by 456 per cent. Unfortunately we do not have the reports that might explain these 'extraordinary' increases in BPB's assets and liabilities in 1865. The picture changed in 1866 as there were some marked declines, such as a 43 per cent fall in loans. Notes payable were up 20 per cent. The assets do show a new account, current account guarantees, at the impressive amount of 2,792 *contos*. In liabilities there was a sharp decrease in deposits from 12,736 *contos* to 4,788 *contos*, which – along with the fall in sundry balances – indicates the effect of the Paraguayan War on bank depositors.

That same year, BPB's board of directors in London appealed to Brazil's Ministry of Finance to institute two changes to the statutes that had been approved at the recent shareholders' meeting in that city. The requests, which were approved, changed the corporation's name to the English Bank of Rio de Janeiro (EBRJ) and altered the regulations for determining directors of the bank in Rio 'because we believe it fitting to trust the leadership of this business to a local directorship, be it a commission or one manager.'[71] The government's favorable decision was quickly communicated to stockholders, along with the good news of official approval for opening a branch in Pernambuco state, and as of 21 December 1866 BPB became EBRJ.[72] In response to the modified statute on board membership, João José dos Reis, Rodrigo Pereira Felício and José Carlos Mayrink promptly retired from it. Within the year they formed their own banking, Commercial Bank of Rio de Janeiro.[73] The years 1865 and 1866 saw a period of tumult for the BPB branch in Porto. Loans, accounts payable and receivable, cash on hand, capital from London, all surged and fell with distressing unpredictability until the bank shuttered in June 1866.[74]

By contrast, the newly reorganized EBRJ endured a rough first year but ultimately found some stability. It suffered general declines in its balance sheet in 1867, but then entered a period of growth from 1868 through 1870. Its loan accounts, promissory notes, and guaranteed current accounts increased, as did pledges to current accounts. Cash on hand slipped downward in 1868 but grew over the next two years (20 per cent in 1869 and around 100 per cent in 1870). As to liabilities, the accounts of fixed-term deposits with notices and accounts payable increased steadily after 1867, reaching a rate of 50 per cent from 1869 to 1870. There was also a special reserve account maintained against damages in liquidation vouchers, which, although they represented relatively small sums, reflected the bank's preoccupation with the possibility of such circumstances. But it not only maintained its footing, it actually expanded in 1870 with the authorization of a new affiliate in the bustling city of Santos (São Paulo state).

The light at the end of the tunnel for these English banks, and indeed for the entire economies of Brazil and Portugal, came with the end of the Paraguayan War early in 1870. In its 1869 official report to LBB shareholders, the board of directors both reminisced and looked forward, affirming

> The directorship earnestly hoped that the shareholders would not continue to sacrifice their interests by selling their shares for a pittance, as some had done. We judged it fair and proper to assure that those shares were worth more than the market's asking price. The elements of prosperity for any bank are its actual condition and the strength of its credit; those shares convey the fortitude of LBB in these very same elements. It was only natural that their value would rise significantly with the cessation of the Paraguayan War, which seems finally well at hand. And in any case Brazil is a country blessed with many resources that offer fertile ground for profitable banking operations, especially if we can rely on the government honorably fulfilling its commitments.[75]

Conclusion

LBB and BPB/EBRJ were forms of FDI in Brazil, constituted as commercial deposit and credit banks that privileged short-term transactions with import-export businesses. They expressed the strategy of British business to exert actual influence in a country which, still a mixed Portuguese colony (an 'empire'), was also gaining in economic independence, before its full political autonomy. Such foreign banks gathered British and Brazilian-Portuguese investors, traders and bankers: they could be seen as 'colonial banks' from the point of view of Portuguese side or moreover as 'imperial banks' from the point of view of mixed transatlantic business. British thalassocracy experienced there one supplementary form of its 'imperial banking' modus operandi.

Given the macroeconomic and political contexts of Brazil and Portugal, and the significant factor of inexpensive credit in the city of London, the growth of these banks was frankly vertiginous compared to the contemporary profile of national banks and banking houses. However, with the insolvency of the Antônio José Alves do Souto & Co. Banking House in Rio de Janeiro's Commercial Plaza in 1864, and the rapidly ensuing Paraguayan War – both of which impacted the Brazilian and Portuguese economies – the two banks reacted and were affected differently. LBB experienced difficulties and reorganized towards the end of the crisis years, while BPB (after 1867, EBRJ) grew.

It should also be emphasized that the English banks were able to adapt to their new Brazilian habitat, engaging in practices uncommon to London such as the interest-paying deposits – a form of interest-paying current account that was routinely offered by Brazilian banks. This case demonstrates that 'foreign' banks could assimilate to business practices in the milieu where they operated, much as the writings of Maria Barbara Levy suggest. Nonetheless, while both a recuperation and a broad-based expansion of English banks in Brazil were optimistically anticipated by directors and investors in the years following the Paraguayan War, reality would not live up to their hopes.

Notes

1 An early version of this text entitled 'The London & Brazilian Bank: Comparing its capital-operation systems in Portugal and Brazil,' at the *XXIX Encontro da APHES*. I thank my students from undergraduate research: Luana Donin, Mateus Bertolino and Antonio Kerstenetzky.

2 Albert Fishlow, 'Lições do passado: mercados de capitais durante o século XIX e o período entre guerras,' in Albert Fishlow (ed.), *Desenvolvimento no Brasil e na América Latina: uma perspectiva histórica* (translated by Claudio Walter Abramo), São Paulo, Paz e Terra, 2004, p. 270. The data were found in Table 1, p. 272.

3 Maria Barbara Levy, 'Dívida externa brasileira 1850–1913: empréstimos públicos e privados,' *História Econômica & História de Empresas*, IV(1), 2001, p. 50. Levy returns to the study of foreign capital in the Brazilian banking system in Maria Barbara Levy, 'The banking system and foreign capital in Brazil,' in Rondo Cameron and Valeryi Bovykin (eds), *International Banking 1870–1914*, New York/Oxford, Oxford University Press, 1991, pp. 351–70. See also Karl Erish Born, *International Banking in the 19th and 20th Century*, London, Berg Publishers, 1984.

4 Marcelo de Paiva Abreu, 'A dívida pública externa do Brasil, 1824–1931,' *Estudos Econômicos*, 15(2), 1985, pp. 167–89; here p. 168.

5 Tamás Zsmrecsányi, 'A French free-standing company in Brazil's sugar industry: The case of the *Société des sucreries brésiliennes*, 1907–1920,' in Maria Wilkins and Harm Schröter (eds), *The Free-Standing Companies in the World Economy, 1830–1996*, Oxford, Oxford University Press, 1998, pp. 279–90.

6 Mira Wilkins, 'The free-standing company, 1870–1914: An important type of British foreign direct investment,' *The Economic History Review*, New Series, 41(2), May 1988, pp. 259–82; here p. 262. This concept was further explored in Mira Wilkins, 'The free-standing company revisited,' in Mira Wilkins and Harm Schröter (eds), *The Free-Standing Companies, op. cit.*, pp. 3–64. On other concepts such as 'investment groups' or 'multinational firms' see Stanley Chapman, 'British free-standing companies and investment groups in India and the Far East,' in Mira Wilkins and Harm Schröter (eds). *The Free-Standing Companies, op. cit.*, pp. 202–17. Geoffrey Jones, *British Multinational Banking, 1830–1990*, Oxford, Clarendon Press, 1993.

7 Charles Kindleberger and Robert Aliber, *Manias, Panics, and Crashes: A History of Financial Crises*, sixth edition, New York, Palgrave-MacMillan, 2011.

8 On the interplay of institutional change and foreign investment see David Landes, *Prometeu Desacorrentado. Transformação Tecnológica e Desenvolvimento Industrial na Europa Ocidental desde 1750 até a nossa época* (translated by Vera Ribeiro and revised by Cesar Benjamim), Rio de Janeiro, Nova Fronteira, 1994 (chapter 4, 'Eliminando a defasagem'). Lance Davis and Robert Gallman, *Evolving Financial Markets and International Capital Flow. Britain, the Americas and Australia, 1865–1914*, Cambridge, Cambridge University Press, 2001.

9 On the consolidation of the Brazilian Imperial State, see José Murilo de José Murilo de Carvalho, *A Construção da Ordem: a elite política imperial; Teatro de Sombras: a política imperial*, second edition, Rio de Janeiro, UFRJ/Relume Dumará, 1996. Ilmar H. de Mattos, *O Tempo Saquarema*, São Paulo, HUCITEC, 1987.

10 For more on metals in Brazil and the quantitative theory of currency, see Pierre Vilar, *Ouro e Moeda na História (1420–1920)* (translated by Philomena Gebran), Rio de

Janeiro, Paz e Terra, 1980. Arilda Magna Campanharo Teixeira, *Determinantes e Armadilhas da política monetária brasileira no II Império*, Niterói, masters dissertation (Economy), University Federal Fluminense, 1991.

11 The history of foreign enterprises in Brazil is explored by Ana Célia Castro, *As Empresas Estrangeiras no Brasil, 1860–1913*, Rio de Janeiro, Zahar, 1979. On foreign banks in Latin America, see Gail Triner, *Banking and Economic Development: Brazil, 1889–1930*, New York, Palgrave, 2000. André Villela and Ignacio Briones, 'European bank penetration during the first wave of globalisation: Lessons from Brazil and Chile, 1878–1913,' *European Review of Economic History*, 10, 2006, pp. 329–59.

12 The city of Rio de Janeiro was the capital of the Empire of Brazil, and also known as the Neutral Municipality of the Court.

13 Jorge Fernandes Alves, *O 'Brasileiro' Oitocentista e o seu papel social*, available online at http://ler.letras.up.pt/uploads/ficheiros/6391.pdf, p. 276.

14 The creation of commercial and investment banks in 1860s London is examined in Michael Collins, *Banks and Industrial Finance in Britain, 1800–1939*, Cambridge, Cambridge University Press, 1991. Larry Neal and Lance Davis, 'The evolution of the structure and performance of the London Stock Exchange in the first global financial market, 1812–1914,' *European Review of Economic History*, 10, 2006, pp. 279–300. Concerning 'overseas bank' operations in colonies of French and English empires see Stuart Jones, 'The apogee of the imperial banks in South Africa: Standard and Barclays, 1919–1939,' *The English Historical Review*, 103(409), October 1988, pp. 892–916. Hubert Bonin, 'French overseas banking as an imperial system: A background for Asian developments,' available online at www.hubertbonin.com.

15 Carlos Manuel Pelaez and Wilson Suzigan, *História Monetária do Brasil*, second edition, Brasília, UNB, 1981. Denio Nogueira, *Raízes de uma Nação*, Rio de Janeiro, Forense Universitária, 1988. Maria Barbara Levy, *História da Bolsa de Valores do Rio de Janeiro*, Rio de Janeiro, IBMEC, 1977.

16 The generalized use of gold as a monetary base is traced by Barry Eichengreen, *A Globalização do capital: Uma História do Sistema Monetário Internacional* (translated by Sérgio Blum), São Paulo, edition 34, 2000.

17 Carlos Manuel Pelaez and Wilson Suzigan, *História Monetária*, op. cit., pp. 64–9.

18 President of the Conservative cabinet (from 5 April 1857 to 12 December 1858), who succeeded the previous Conservative cabinet under the presidency of Marquis of Caxias (from 9 March 1856 to 5 April 1857). Regarding the Conservative Party, see Jeffrey D. Needell, *The Party of Order: The Conservatives, the State, and Slavery in the Brazilian Monarchy, 1831–1871*, Stanford, Stanford University Press, 2006.

19 Carlos Gabriel Guimaraes, *A presença inglesa nas Finanças e no Comércio no Brasil Imperial: os casos da Sociedade Bancária Mauá, MacGregor & Co. (1854–1866) e da firma inglesa Samuel Phillips & Co. (1808–1840)*, São Paulo, Editora Alameda, 2012. Carlos Manuel Pelaez and Wilson Suzigan, op. cit.

20 Nogeira, op. cit., p. 373. According to this author the valorization of the *mil réis* derived also from Brazil's recent foreign loan (type 90) of an amount equivalent to 1,373,000 *lira* at a rate of 4.5 per cent and term of 30 years, with an immediate discount on its face of 10 per cent. Brazil's period foreign borrowing is analyzed in Paulo Roberto de Almeida, *A Formação da Diplomacia Econômica no Brasil: as relações econômicas internacionais no Império*, São Paulo, SENAC; Brasília, FUNAG, 2001 (especially chapter 11).

21 Carlos Gabriel Guimaraes, op. cit., p. 199.

22 Ana Célia Castro, *As Empresas Estrangeiras*, op. cit., p. 12.

23 Geoffrey Jones. *British Multinational Banking, 1830–1990*, Oxford, Oxford University Press, 1993, p. 23.

24 Important works on the London & Brazilian Bank include David Joslin, *A Century of Banking in Latin America*, London, Oxford University Press, 1963 (especially chapter 4, 'British banking in Brazil 1863–1880'). Richard Graham, *Grã-Bretanha e o início da*

modernização no Brasil 1850–1914 (translation by Roberto Machado de Almeida), São Paulo, Brasiliense, 1973. Geoffrey Jones, *British Multinational Banking, 1830–1990*, Oxford, Oxford University Press, 1993.

25 AHMOP, *O Banco de Londres e do Brasil Sociedade Anônima* (London & Brazilian Bank Limited). Memorandum of Association and Articles of Association. Incorporated 17 May 1862. The orthography of the era has been maintained.

26 For more on Johnston's career see Edward Johnston & Co., *Rio de Janeiro 1842. Um Século de Café* (London, Rio de Janeiro, Santos, Paranaguá, 1942). Robert Greenhill, 'Edward Johnston: 150 anos em Café,' in Edmar Bacha and Robert Greenhill (eds), *Marcelino Martins & E. Johsnton. 150 anos de café*, São Paulo, 1992, pp. 135–72. Carlos Gabriel Guimarães, 'The British presence in the Brazilian Empire: the British firm Edward Johnston & Co. and export trade (1842–1852)' (forthcoming).

27 Watts Sherman, the father of William Watts Sherman, was a partner of the banking firm Duncan, Sherman & Co. of New York and the treasurer of Newport Casino.

28 Gonçalves, who bore an honorary distinction from the government, worked as Brazilian agent for a Portuguese wine company (Alto Douro Company) and cosigner of the Commissions House of Imports and Exports. *Almanak Administrativo, Mercantil e Industrial da Corte e Provincia do Rio de Janeiro para o anno de 1862. Decimo nono anno (segunda serie XIV)*, Rio de Janeiro, Eduardo & Henrique Lemmert, 1862, p. 489 and 517, available online at http://brazil.crl.edu/bsd/bsd/almanak/al1862/00000001.html.

29 AHMOP, *O Banco de Londres e do Brasil*, Memorando de Associação.

30 A limited society's members would be responsible in the case of insolvency or liquidation up to the amount stipulated in the contract. BRASIL, *Código Commercial do Imperio do Brasil*. Annotated with all the Brazilian legislation that refers to it. Commentary by Sallustiano Orlando de Araujo Costa, second edition, Rio de Janeiro, Eduardo and Henrique Laemmert, 1869.

31 No. 714. Resolution of 27 September 1862. In Brasil, Conselho de Estado, *Consultas da Secção de Fazenda do Conselho de Estado*, vol. 5, Rio de Janeiro, Typ. Nacional, 1860–1865, p. 309. The State Council, sometimes regarded as the head of Brazilian government itself in this era, is analyzed by Carvalho, op. cit., pp. 327–58. Maria Fernanda V. Martins, *A velha arte de governar: um estudo sobre política e elites a partir do Conselho de Estado (1842–1889)*, Rio e Janeiro, Arquivo nacional, 2007.

32 Ibid.

33 London & Brazilian Bank Limited, 'Declarações,' *Jornal do Commercio*, 20 January 1863, p. 1, column 6.

34 London & Brazilian Bank Limited, 'Declarações,' *Jornal do Commercio*, 20 March 1864.

35 *Assembleia Annual do London and Brazilian Bank Limited*. Correspondencia Commercial. Lisboa, 29 January 1864. See António Lopes Vieira, 'A política da Especulação – uma introdução aos investimentos britânicos e franceses nos caminhos-de-ferro portugueses. Análise Social,' XXIV(101/102), 1988 (20e 3), p. 731. *The Banker's Magazine, Journal of the Money Market and Commercial Digest*, xxiii, January–December 1863, London, Groombridge & Sons, 1863, pp. 54, 451–2 and 535–7.

36 *Assembleia Annual do London and Brazilian Bank Limited*. Correspondencia Commercial, Lisboa, 29 January 1864.

37 Nuno Valerio and Ana Bela Nunes, 'Moeda e bancos,' in Pedro Lains and Álvaro Ferreira da Silva (eds), *História Económica de Portugal, 1700–2000*, II, O Século XIX., second edition, Lisboa, ICS/UL, 2005, p. 290.

38 Davi Justino, *A Formação do Espaço Económico Nacional. Portugal 1810–1913*, II, Lisboa, Vega, 1986, p. 216.

39 Rui Ramos, 'A crise agrícola,' in: *Portugal Contemporâneo (1851–1910)*, II, Lisboa, Alfa, 1990, p. 137. On the impact of the agricultural crisis on prices see Justino, op. cit.,

chapter 8. For more on Portugal's public debt more broadly, see Maria Eugénia Mata, *As finanças Públicas Portuguesas da Regeneração à Primeira Guerra Mundial*, 1985, Ph.D. Dissertation (Economy), Instituto Superior de Economia da Universidade Técnica de Lisboa.

40 Rui Ramos, op. cit., p. 133.
41 Ibid., p. 133.
42 Ibid., p. 135.
43 Davi Justino, op. cit., p. 84.
44 The legal proceedings were similar to those authorizing LBB. Guimaraes, op. cit.
45 BRASIL, Colleção das Leis do Império do Brasil de 1863, tomo XXVI, parte II, Rio de Janeiro, Typographia Nacional, 1863, pp. 429–30. The ruling can also be found in PORTUGAL, AHMOP, Brazilian and Portuguese Bank Limited, Porto, 1863–1866.
46 BRASIL, Colleção das Leis, 1863, op. cit., p. 431
47 Artigo 84 dos Estatutos, ibid., p. 444.
48 BRASIL, Colleção das Leis do Império do Brasil de 1863, op. cit., p. 435. More on Knowles & Foster can be found in Stanley Chapmen, *Merchant Enterprise in Britain. From the Industrial Revolution to World War I*, Cambridge, Cambridge University Press, 1993, p. 243. Geoffrey Jones, *Merchants to Multinational: British Trading Companies in the Nineteenth and Twentieth Centuries*, Oxford, Oxford University Press, 2004, p. 28 and 43.
49 He was also 'Veador' and 'Camareiro-Mor' (Chamberlain) of Imperial House of Brazil. Guimaraes, op. cit., 2012.
50 *Almanack Administrativo*, op. cit., p. 501. This was not the American traveler Thomas Ewbank, author of the book *Life in Brazil: Or, a Journal of a Visit to the Land of the Cocoa and the Palm* (published in the US and Great Britain in 1856, with a Portuguese edition in 1973).
51 BRASIL, Colleção das Leis do Império do Brasil de 1863, op. cit., pp. 435–6.
52 Ibid.
53 Details and analysis of the Souto Crisis can be found in Sebastião Ferreira Soares, *Esboço ou primeiros traços da crise commercial da cidade do Rio de Janeiro em 10 de setembro de 1864*, Rio de Janeiro, Laemmert, 1864. Ana Maria Ribeiro de Andrade, 'Souto & Cia,' in Maria Barbara Levy (ed.), *Anais da 1ª Conferência Internacional de História de Empresas*, Rio de Janeiro, Div. Gráfica da UFRJ, 1991. Guimaraes, 2012, op. cit., chapter 4. Carlos Manuel Pelaez and Wilson Suzigan, op. cit., pp. 104–15. André Arruda Villela, *The Political Economy of Money and Banking in Imperial Brazil, 1850–1870*, London, Ph.D. dissertation (Economic History), London School of Economics and Political Science, 1999 (chapter 4).
54 The Society of Plaza Underwriters reorganized into the Commercial Association of Rio de Janeiro in 1867. See Eugene Ridings, *Business Interest Groups in Nineteenth-Century Brazil*, Cambridge, Cambridge University Press, 1994. Herculano Gomes Mathias, *Comércio, 173 anos de desenvolvimento: história da Associação Comercial do Rio de Janeiro, (1820–1993)*, Rio de Janeiro, Expressão e Cultura, 1993.
55 BRASIL, Ministério da Justiça, *Commissão de Inquérito sobre as causas da crise na praça do Rio de Janeiro. Relatório da commissão encarregada pelo governo imperial por avisos do 1º de outubro a 28 de dezembro de 1864 de preceder a um inquerito sobre as causas principaes e acidentaes da crise do mês de setembro de 1864*, Rio de Janeiro, Typ. Nacional, 1865. Documentos anexos ao Relatorio da commissão de Inquerito [...], series A, p. 4.
56 BRASIL, Ministério da Justiça, *Commissão de Inquérito sobre as causas da crise na praça do Rio de Janeiro,1864. Relatório da commissão encarregada pelo governo imperial por avisos do 1º de outubro e 28 de dezembro de 1864 de proceder um inquérito sobre as causas principaes e accidentaes das crise no mes de setembro de 1864*, Rio de Janeiro, Typ. Nacional, 1865, p. 4; (Representações), pp. 11–33.
57 Nogueira, op. cit., p. 377.

58 On the experience of the banking crisis for Bank Mauá, MacGregor & Co. and the Bank Rural & Hipotecário, see Guimaraes, 2012, op. cit. Carlos Gabriel Guimaraes, 'A Guerra do Paraguai e a atividade bancária no Rio de Janeiro no período 1865–1870: o caso Banco Rural e Hipotecário do Rio de Janeiro,' *HEERA*, 1, 2007, pp. 1–27.
59 On the Paraguayan War, see Wilma Peres Costa, *A espada de Dâmocles: o exército, a Guerra do Paraguai e a crise do Império*, São Paulo, HUCITEC/Ed. da UNICAMP, 1996. Maria Eduarda C. Magalhães Marques (ed.), *A Guerra do Paraguai: 130 anos depois*, Rio de Janeiro, Relume Dumará, 1995. Ricardo Sales, *A guerra do Paraguai: escravidão e cidadania na formação do exército*, Rio de Janeiro, Paz e Terra, 1990.
60 Joaquim Nabuco, *Um Estadista do Império. Nabuco de Araújo, sua vida, suas opiniões, sua época*, Rio de Janeiro, Garnier, 1897/98, 3 volumes, pp. 189–90.
61 Carlos Manuel Pelaez and Wilson Suzigan, op. cit., p. 114.
62 Mircea Buescu, *História Administrativa do Brasil. Organização e Administração do Ministério da Fazenda no Império*, Coordenação de Vicente Tapajós, Brasília, FUNCEP, 1984, p. 93.
63 Nogueira, op. cit., p. 378.
64 Ibid., p. 380.
65 Guimaraes, 2012, op. cit., chapter 4.
66 Ibid.
67 David Joslin, *A century of Banking in Latin America*, London, Oxford University Press, 1963, pp. 71–2. Unfortunately the *Jornal do Commercio* newspaper did not carry information on the 1867 Shareholders Meeting.
68 Ibid.
69 A. S. J. Baster, *The Imperial Banks*, London, King, 1929, pp. 126–9. Geoffrey Jones. *British Multinational Banking, 1830–1990*, Oxford, Oxford University Press, 1993, p. 23.
70 Guimaraes, 2011, op. cit.
71 Brasil, Ministério da Fazenda, Proposta e Relatório apresentados a Assemblea Geral. Primeira Sessão da Décima Terceira Legislatura, Rio de Janeiro, Typographia nacional, 1867, p. 21.
72 *The Banker's Magazine, Journal of the Money Market and Commercial Digest*, XXVII, January–December 1867, London, Groombridge & Sons, 1867, p. 688.
73 Established through decree no. 3,632 of 6 April 1866, this Commercial Bank of Rio de Janeiro was the second institution to conduct business under that name. The first had been founded in 1838 and closed in 1853. Interestingly, José Carlos Maywrink, businessman and nobleman related to the Imperial family, was involved in both banks. However, in the second Commercial Bank, his colleagues Reis and Felício owned more shares than he did.
74 Further research may bring to light a more detailed account of the bank's final years and what occurred after it closed.
75 Assembleia Annual do London and Brazilian Bank Limited. Jornal do Commercio. Correspondencia Commercial. Lisbon, 19 February 1869.

Appendices

Table A3.6 Brazilian Fiscal, Monetary and Exchange Policies, 1860–1870

| | Index (1822=100) | | Exchange rate (1,000 réis /£1) | Fiscal Policy (1,000s of réis) Income | | | | Expenditure | | | Balance (+ or −) |
	Cash in circulation	Prices		Total	Type Customs duties	Export taxes	Provincial contribution	Total	Type Military	Debt service	
1859/60	1,053	600.0	9.57	43.2	27.2	5.6	8.3	52.6	22.2	5.2	−1.9
1860/1	985.9	578.1	9.30	49.2	30.0	7.3	7.1	52.4	19.4	5.2	−1.5
1861/2	891.3	549.2	9.39	51.4	31.4	8.2	9.4	53.0	18.9	5.3	−2.6
1862/3	958.7	568.1	9.06	47.0	27.4	8.3	8.9	57.0	19.8	5.4	−10.0
1863/4	1,016	495.5	8.81	51.7	30.8	9.1	9.5	56.5	21.2	5.2	−4.8
1864/5	1,204	580.4	8.97	55.7	34.5	9.7	9.3	83.3	40.6	5.1	−27.6
1865/6	1,392	703.4	9.60	56.1	33.4	11	9.3	121.9	80.3	8.9	−65.8
1866/7	1,479	800.7	9.90	62.4	37.6	10.8	11.7	120.9	72.1	10.4	−58.5
1867/8	1,627	873.6	10.70	69.7	35.9	15.4	17.1	166.0	98.8	11.2	−96.3
1868/9	1,982	1,035	14.11	83.5	45.3	18.6	19.4	150.9	81.3	14.8	−67.4
1869/70	2,371	988.3	12.76	92.9	52.4	17.8	22.3	141.6	76.8	13.1	−48.5

Source: NOGUEIRA, op. cit., pp. 332, 375.

Notes

1 Since 1828, the fiscal year began in July.
2 In 1846, with Monetary Reform, the government depreciated the official exchange rate to 27 d/*mil réis* or 8$889/£1.
3 Starting in 1833, 50% of customs duties were collected in gold.
4 Starting in 1837, 100% of customs duties were collected in gold, as were export taxes.
5 Starting in 1853, the export tax was reduced 5% *ad valorem*.

Table A3.7 Balances of London & Brazilian Bank, 1863–1870 (in June of each year)

	1863	1864	1865	1866	1867	1868	1869	1870
Total capital*	—	—	13.333:333$330	13.333:333$330	13.333:333$330	13.333:333$330	13.333:333$330	13.333:333$330
Capital in cash	—	—	2.711:111$110	8.711:111$110	8.133:333$330	8.333:333$330	8.133:333$330	8.133:333$330
ASSETS								
Capital at branches and agencies	—	2.400:000$000	2.400:000$000	2.400:000$000	2.977:777$780	2.977:777$780	2.977:777$780	2.977:777$780
London & Brazilian Bank, London and local affiliates	—	445:235$260	—	703:654$080	—	—	—	—
Accounts payable	423:686$480	912:309$720	1.137:041$790	453:242$860	150:408$410	322:365$040	259:690$410	45:183$570
Promissory notes & accounts	3.172:134$800	4.476:390$790	4.162:845$010	2.993:841$670	2.752:176$290	1.615:846$150	1.144:243$190	739:845$870
Loans & guaranteed current accounts	4.166:641$420	9.004:161$860	12.890:011$570	10.636:858$440	6.023:488$410	4.978:893$070	5.332:248$770	4.632:284$540
Guarantees for current accounts & sundry values	—	—	—	11.826:642$820	5.330:886$580	1.638:613$490	1.422:420$010	972:841$330
Cash on hand	1.121:732$630	913:394$140	1.621:567$020	1.244:017$620	1.969:257$620	1.603:957$740	520:139$130	607:530$110
Buildings, furniture, office equipment	10:181$390	16:991$500	214:928$000	314:707$390	351:346$030	335:000$000	333:620$000	49:000$000
Deposits in current accounts:								
Cash account at Bank of Brazil and others	238:502$510	335:270$630	—	—	—	—	—	—
Demand deposit at Bank of Brazil	—	—	500:000$000	—	—	—	—	—
Foreign gold coins	—	27:899$160	—	—	—	—	—	—
TOTAL	9.132:879$230	18.561:623$060	22.926:393$390	30.572:964$880	19.555:341$000	13.472:453$270	11.990:139$290	10.024:763$220

(continued)

Table A3.7 (Continued)

	1863	1864	1865	1866	1867	1868	1869	1870
LIABILITIES								
Capital	3.111:111$110	4.622:222$220	4.622:222$220	4.622:222$220	5.200:000$000	5.200:000$000	5.200:000$000	5.200:000$000
London & Brazilian Bank, London and local affiliates	549:668$070	1.192:812$130	1.497:584$450	451:011$700	1.174:049$930	645:456$770	585:754$630	52:969$750
Deposits:								
*Current account	—	—	—	—	—	281:274$110	191:173$280	70:490$670
*With notice of 3, 6, or 10 days	—	—	—	2.081:896$450	2.778:727$590	1.800:915$250	671:545$970	674:017$380
*With notice of 30 or 60 dias	—	—	—	379:407$260	547:177$810	311:369$560	460:880$690	225:624$360
*With determined term	—	—	—	6.104:468$740	1.147:145$970	1.809:111$860	1.406:321$330	659:376$200
Guarantees for current accounts & sundry values	—	—	—	14.708:466$820	8.696:568$680	3.468:793$720	3.474:463$390	2.990:061$120
Notes to pay	274:580$040	606:863$130	332:553$530	2.231:503$990	611:671$020	5:630$000	—	—
Current accounts, deposits & other values	5.197:520$010	12.139:725$580	16.474:036$190	—	—	—	—	—
TOTAL	9.132:879$230	18.561:623$060	22.926:393$390	30.572:964$880	19.555:341$000	13.472:453$270	11.990:139$290	10.024:763$220

Source: Commercio, Balanço do London and Brazilian Bank, *Jornal do Commercio*, 1863–1870.

Note

* Does not include capital from the London & Brazilian Mauá Bank, which was authorized by official decree but did not get off the ground.

Table A3.8 Balances of the Brazilian & Portuguese Bank of Rio de Janeiro (1864–1866) and the English Bank of Rio de Janeiro (1867–1870) (in June of each year)

	1864[1]	1865	1866[3]	1867[2]	1868	1869	1870
Down payments to make*	4.444:444$444	4.444:444$444	4.444:444$444	4.444:444$444	4.444:444$444	4.444:444$444	4.444:444$444
Account balance	681:535$740	—	—	—	—	—	—
Brazilian & Portuguese bank Limited, London and local affiliates	—	2.479:244$450	—	—	—	—	—
ASSETS							
Promissory notes	7.160:027$562	7.575:732$061	4.314:403$937	5.102:354$015	4.761:668$024	3.414:566$025	5.543:795$873
Bonded notes and current accounts	566:733$902	1.828:107$237	2.240:618$441	2.765:607$562	2.837:652$133	2.903:205$029	3.400:816$757
Deposits with free withdrawals	600:037$685						
Guarantees for current accounts, loans and credits			2.792:385$529	2.081:295$980	2.743:218$820	5.200:465$125	4.376:655$600
Shares of public debt and other titles	601:481$020						
Titles in liquidation	—	—	211:113$428	81:927$715	73:259$965	22:756$100	15:511$680
Accounts payable	—	—	196:563$917	159:549$658	207:184$296	304:341$053	987:072$480
Sundry account balances	1.378:946$432	4.393:061$343	280:852$220	324:184$731	797:714$470	1.144:175$070	433:547$486
Building, furniture, office equipment	35:141$857	23:846$487	31:008$074	24:908$641	149:702$720		
Cash on hand	182:229$990	1.290:806$792	2.133:269$412	966:519$863	749:234$267	958:023$930	1.802:825$226
TOTAL	15.049:097$612	22.636:726$834	16.674:659$432	15.950:792$609	16.764:073$139	18.389:976$776	21.004:669$516
LIABILITIES							
Capital	8.888:888$888	8.888:888$888	8.888:888$888	8.888:888$888	8.888:888$888	8.888:888$888	8.888:888$888
Balance of sundry interest-bearing current accounts	4.865:461$153	5.328:350$375	—	—	—	—	—
Deposits — Current accounts	211:230$696	4.109:285$450	2.974:438$008	3.080:264$127	2.135:484$988	1.714:802$115	2.064:631$539
Balance of notes payable with funds received as interest/fees							

(continued)

Table A3.8 (Continued)

	1864[1]	1865	1866[3]	1867[2]	1868	1869	1870
Balance of commercial titles and others	1.058:783$091	—	—	—	—	—	—
All guarantees of credit and current accounts	302:344$444	—	—	—	—	—	—
Deposits in securities, etc.	—	2.387:134$760	—	—	—	—	—
Fixed-term deposits with notice, by note	—	—	1.717:074$870	1.524:958$895	2.153:817$290	996:854$785	4.630:763$774
Notes payable	—	—	—	26:181$590	188:005$851	382:610$171	422:510$845
Deposited notes	—	—	96:999$720	189:821$670	148:556$470	481:186$530	63:245$490
Titles in bonds and deposits	—	—	—	1.891:474$310	2.594:662$350	4.719:278$595	4.313:410$110
Total	5.937:819$384	12.736:605$226	4.788:512$598	6.712:700$592	—	—	—
Special reserve against damages in case of bankruptcy	—	—	—	—	35:297$780	10:000$000	10:000$000
Balances of sundry accounts	221:871$840	1.009:943$920	301:872$137	243:655$349	619:365$622	1.196:355$692	611:218$900
Guarantee	517$500	1:288$800	—	—	—	—	—
TOTAL	15.049:097$612	22.636:726$834	16.674:659$132	15.950:792$609	16.764:079$139	18.389:976$776	21.004:669$516

Source: Commercio, Balanço do Brazilian and Portuguese, *Jornal do Commercio*, 1864–1870

Notes

* Capital held by the Brazilian & Portuguese Bank.
1 General balance of operations carried out in Rio de Janeiro in the semester of 1 March to 31 August, 1864.
2 Starting in 1867, the English Bank of Rio de Janeiro Limited had capital of £500.000.
3 An account is missing from the records for 1866, so the sum is incomplete.

4 Dutch colonial and imperial banking

Different ways of entry and exit

Piet Geljon and Ton de Graaf

This chapter begins with an overview of the phenomenon of overseas banking, followed by a brief introduction to Dutch overseas banking. We then look at the three Dutch banks that were active in overseas banking: *Nederlandsche Handel-Maatschappij* in the Dutch East Indies/Indonesia between 1880 and 1960; *Nederlandsche Bank voor Zuid-Afrika* in South Africa from 1888; and *Hollandsche Bank voor Zuid-Amerika/Hollandsche Bank-Unie* in South America. All three banks were established in the nineteenth and early twentieth centuries; but the motivation for their creation was different in each case. For various reasons, the overseas operations all ceased in the period 1960–2008. The chapter ends with a number of concluding remarks.

Imperial banking and Dutch overseas policy

Overseas banking has a long history. It mainly took the form of banks with a head office in one (mother) country and a branch network operating in another country, the latter being a colony or other territory with special relations with the mother country and mostly situated far away from it.[1] With the very poor communications of earlier times, the management of a business on another continent was problematic, and conflicts often arose between the head office and the workers in the field. Mira Wilkins called this type of organization, which existed not only in the banking sector, but also in agriculture and mining, a free-standing company.[2] Writing from a British point of view and only with regard to banking, one of the first authors on this subject, A. J. Baster, made a distinction between imperial banks, which operated within the British Empire, and international banks working in other territories.[3] Otherwise the phrase 'overseas bank' is generally used.

The origins of overseas banking lie in Great Britain in the second quarter of the nineteenth century.[4] Apart from the Provincial Bank of Ireland (London, 1825), the first overseas bank was the Bank of Australasia (London, 1835). It was followed by institutions for Canada, the West Indies and – curiously – the Ionian Isles.[5] Later, London-based banking operations were started in other overseas territories. The Chartered Bank of India, Australia & China (1853) was intended to have a broad sphere of activity, including Japan and the Dutch East Indies. According to the strict definition, Hongkong & Shanghai Banking Corporation (1865) was not an overseas bank, because it was based in Hong Kong; nevertheless, because of its substantially British character, it is usually thought of as an overseas bank. South Africa's first overseas banks appeared in the early 1860s and included Standard Bank of British South Africa (1862), later renamed Standard Bank of South Africa. A number of institutions began operating in South America and Mexico at about the same time.

All these banks were independent institutions operating under a royal charter or later on as limited liability companies. They were engaged in financing international trade, but also developed local banking businesses, attracting deposits and granting credits. As most of these territories had no central bank, the overseas banks were allowed to issue their own banknotes. Many of these ventures did not survive the hardships and financial troubles of their host countries, but quite a number developed into respectable banks in London. Their head offices looked after the credit policy, the liquidity and the staff policy. In a later phase, overseas banks were established as subsidiaries or affiliates of banks in the mother country, but also as subsidiaries or affiliates of other entities, such as shipping companies or trading houses. Governments also stepped in, as in the case of the Imperial Bank of Persia (1889). In countries other than Great Britain – Germany, France and Portugal – governments encouraged their emerging banking systems to expand overseas, or even took the lead. Germany's *Deutsche Übersee Bank* (1886, later on *Deutsche Überseeische Bank*) is an example.[6]

The heyday of overseas banking was in the early twentieth century. In 1913, there were 31 British overseas banks with more than 1,300 branches all over the world, while other European countries also had banks with branch networks in their overseas territories. After WWI, a period of decline set in. War and depression took their toll, trade and foreign exchange restrictions hampered their operations and the general banks began to expand overseas. Some overseas banks failed outright, while mergers and takeovers also caused the number of overseas banks to decline. The first moves were amalgamations of banks operating in the same area, for example in Australia and South Africa. In South America, a new element appeared with the involvement of a clearing bank. In 1918, Lloyds Bank acquired the capital of one of the institutions there, merging it with another bank into the Bank of London and South America (BOLSA), which ultimately became the only British bank on that continent. Meanwhile, Barclays Bank had also entered the field with Barclays DCO (Dominion, Colonial and Overseas). By 1940, a total of 15 independent overseas banks remained.

WWII and the decolonization process that followed further undermined the position of overseas banks. Opposition to foreign banks, always latent in many countries, now came into the open, resulting in nationalization by governments or in acquisition of the banks by local shareholders. From the 1970s, the consolidation process intensified, and practically all overseas banks became part of big multinational banking groups. That pattern was seen throughout the sector, not only in British overseas banks. The only names that still echo the long and often dramatic history of overseas banking are Standard Chartered Bank and HSBC.

Against the international background described above, let us now turn to Dutch overseas banking. With its large overseas possessions – particularly in the Dutch East Indies (present-day Indonesia) but also in the Caribbean region – the Netherlands followed the general pattern already outlined, but also displayed some distinctive characteristics. It was, of course, quite natural that banks should be established in the Dutch colonies, and from the 1860s the first colonial banks came into being. However, the Dutch started banking operations in various other areas as well. After the independence of the South African Republic (Transvaal, 1881) feelings of kinship with the Boer population and economic prospects led to the creation of two Dutch banks in that country. A few decades later (around 1920), Dutch commercial banks expanded in other areas, one of which was South America. There were differences not only in the ways in which banking activities in these various regions started but also in the ways they ended: by nationalization after political conflicts; by agreed separation of the business; and by a takeover by another bank. Developments in the various regions referred to above are described in the following sections.

Dutch colonial banking: Indonesia

Until 1798, certain parts of the Dutch East Indies (now Indonesia) were con-trolled by the *Verenigde Oostindische Compagnie* (Dutch East India Company, or VOC, founded in 1602). Although the VOC was primarily a trading company, it also exercised colonial authority, employed its own soldiers and sailors, con-ducted trade and founded colonies. Following the VOC's insolvency in 1798, the Batavian Republic (the Netherlands) took over government of the Dutch East Indies. When Napoleonic France blockaded Britain, the British seized the Dutch colonies, because the Batavian Republic in 1811 was an ally of France. Dutch authority was restored in 1814, however.

Colonial schemes of banking expansion

Willem I became Dutch king in 1815 and quickly set about reasserting Dutch control over its East Indian possessions and promoting trade with the region. Trade with the Far East had recovered after the period of French hegemony, to the point where it even exceeded that seen at the height of the VOC era. However, much of it was by this time controlled by the British and the Americans. Important figures in the Dutch East Indies as well as King Willem I feared that British and American involve-ment could eventually undermine Dutch political power in the colony. The king was determined to prevent that happening and therefore backed the formation of a new company, for political as much as commercial reasons. So it was that, on the initiative of King Willem I, that *Nederlandsche Handel-Maatschappij* (Netherlands Trading Society, or NHM) was established in The Hague in March 1824. The com-pany's role was to encourage, facilitate and drive Dutch import-export trade with the East Indies. The company's object was defined very broadly, so that NHM could take over some of the activities previously carried out by VOC.[7]

At the outset, the geographical sphere of activity defined for the new company covered a large part of the world. It became clear that this was over-ambitious. Following heavy trading losses, King Willem I decided to intervene in 1827. He assumed the right to appoint the company's president and directors, and the sphere of activity was restricted to the Dutch East Indies. In 1826, an East Indian branch of the company, called *De Factorij* (the Factory) opened in Batavia (modern Jakarta).

From 1830, the 'cultivation system' was introduced to the Dutch East Indies, and NHM was given an important role in its administration. Under the system, the East Indian government obliged the local communities to cultivate certain produce – coffee, sugar, indigo and later also tea – and to give a proportion of their produce to the authorities. Within the system, NHM acted as the Dutch government's banker, commission agent and shipping agent. Transportation of the produce to the Netherlands and its sale in Amsterdam and Rotterdam were also overseen by NHM. One drawback for NHM was that it was obliged to extend credit to the Dutch state. By the late 1830s, the state owed NHM so much that parliament had to be informed and responded by bringing the practice to a halt. From the early 1850s, NHM began financing plantations in the Dutch East Indies. The finance schemes took the form of harvest cash advances, mortgage loans and capital participations. In 1858, an agency was established in Singapore to support activities in the Dutch East Indies.

Other banks were active in the Dutch East Indies during the nineteenth century. In 1828, *Javasche Bank* was founded in Batavia: the bank of issue, which developed into more of a commercial bank from the late nineteenth century. In 1857, again in Batavia, *Nederlandsch-Indische Escompto Maatschappij* (Dutch East Indian Escompto Company)[8] was set up. That was followed in 1863 by *Nederlandsch-Indische Handelsbank* (Netherlands India Commercial Bank), which was based in Amsterdam with its main agency in Batavia. Although these banks were to some extent active in the same fields as NHM, each of them had its own fields of specialization as well. With a view to maintaining the direction of this paper, it was decided that this section should focus exclusively on NHM, the biggest and most influential commercial bank of the Dutch East Indies.

Until approximately 1870, NHM was not a true bank in the current sense of the word. Before that date, a large proportion of its profits came from the commission earned on state commodity trading. Gradually, however, the state adopted a more liberal policy towards the Dutch East Indies, leading ultimately to, amongst other things, liquidation of the cultivation system. That deprived NHM of an important source of revenue, resulting in smaller dividends and declining profitability. A new direction was needed. NHM was already involved in providing credit to the state and others, such as sugar refiners, plantations in the Dutch East Indies and business associates in Japan. So the upscaling of its banking activities was an obvious choice.

In 1880, the banker Balthazar Heldring joined NHM's board: a carefully considered appointment that reflected the intention to change direction and to withdraw from commodity trade. That withdrawal was not in fact fully realized: NHM continued trading in and selling the produce of its own plantations and business associates and trading on behalf of the state. From 1880, the policy emphasis was mainly on plantation finance, such as credits on consigned produce (consignment credits), participation in plantation ventures, plantation start-ups and the issue of shares in plantation companies. The policy was pursued cautiously. NHM's own plantation enterprise was thoroughly reorganized from 1879, enabling it to endure the 1884 sugar crisis with relative ease. That was not the case everywhere: various financial institutions and plantations got into serious difficulties or even failed. Alongside cultivation activities, *De Factorij* began developing a foreign exchange business. Although it had previously been active in foreign exchange, it was only after 1880 that it became a major line of business. Other activities included securities transactions, telegraphic transfers, the issue of documentary credits and the financing of Dutch East Indian imports. The diversification into banking was mainly through *De Factorij* and the Singapore agency. NHM had a third group of activities, which were linked to its *crédit mobilier* role: participating in the foundation of industrial companies and shipping lines, building and operating railways, mining, operating its own port and bunker station on Sumatra and so forth. Such activities focused mainly on the Dutch East Indies or represented a 'national' interest, or both, according to the board. Around the turn of the century, NHM also tried to set up a bank in South Africa.

NHM was therefore a very varied undertaking. As well as being a trading company, it was a bank, an investment bank and a venture capital company. In other words, it had all the characteristics of a *crédit mobilier*. NHM had a position and role unlike any other Dutch bank. Around 1900, NHM became involved in banking within the Netherlands as well. By about 1914, it had already established itself as one of the country's five biggest banks. However, by the turn of the century, the competition had recovered from the damage caused by the sugar crisis. In the Dutch East Indies, NHM's main competitors in the early twentieth century were *Nederlandsch-Indische Handelsbank* (NIHB), *Nederlandsch-Indische Escompto Maatschappij* (NIEM) and, in particular, Javasche Bank. The presence of these rivals had the effect of squeezing margins in banking and exchange activities. Competition for NHM's new issues business in this area was nullified in 1912 by a cartel agreement with NIHB and NIEM. Because *De Factorij* did not want to be dependent on Javasche Bank in an emergency, part of NHM's capital was set aside to serve as a buffer in times of crisis. After 1900, new agencies were established in the Dutch East Indies and South East Asia.

The same period saw an increase in the number of sugar companies owned by NHM. The company was able to safely build up its involvement in sugar growing, because the 1902 Brussels Convention brought stability to cane sugar prices. The expansion of plantation activities also reflected the board's belief in a multi-track policy, as opposed to reliance on banking. NHM also acted as a guardian of 'national interests' in the Dutch East Indies. The role brought considerable financial benefit: income from the sale of the company's port and bunker station ultimately made a healthy contribution to profits in 1914. In 1916, the multi-track policy continued to bear fruit. The element of the company's portfolio that was regarded as fundamental to NHM's financial health was its plantation business. If the banking business was to gain in significance, it would have to be as a complement to the plantation and trading businesses, rather than as an alternative to them. In 1916, the banking business in the Netherlands was considerably expanded by an alliance with *Geldersche Credietvereeniging* (Gelders Credit Union), which was eventually taken over in 1936.

In the period 1900 to 1916, NHM found itself facing increasing competition in the Dutch East Indies, and the situation only intensified after WWI. Besides new Dutch banks, Chinese, Japanese and American competitors established footholds in the Dutch East Indies. The Great Depression that began in 1929 hit NHM harder than Nederlandsch-Indische Handelsbank and Nederlandsch-Indische Escompto-Maatschappij. NHM's losses were higher, and the bank had to close more branches during the Depression than the two other banks. The disproportionate difficulties that affected NHM were due to the interlinked nature of its banking and plantation activities. Following the 1884 sugar crisis, Nederlandsch-Indische Handelsbank had created a subsidiary – *Nederlandsch-Indische Landbouw Maatschappij* (Dutch East Indian Agricultural Company, or NILM) – in order to separate its banking and plantation activities and thus reduce the impact of the crisis for both NIHB and NILM. While global market prices for plantation produce were strong, NHM's multi-track policy was successful.

Colonial banking crossing economic and war crisis

Nevertheless, after the 1929 crisis, the weakness of the policy was revealed: if one part of the business got into difficulty, it was liable to bring the other down with it. NHM's plantation activities were not any harder hit than those of other similar organizations. NHM was quite willing and able – with its East Indian banking business and its business in the Netherlands – to make major cutbacks in its East Indian plantation business. However, NHM's proposals for rationalization and output reduction were felt by some competitors to be going too far, and NHM was pressed into accepting less effective compromise arrangements.

Heavy losses incurred by the plantation business necessitated drastic, across-the-board reorganization of NHM in 1934. The company's capital was cut by three-quarters (from ƒ80 million to ƒ20 million), and new shares to the value of ƒ15 million were issued shortly afterwards. Reorganization brought the book value of the plantation business back into line with its economic value. Drastic cuts in costs were made in both the Netherlands and the Dutch East Indies, thus bringing expenditure back under control. The crisis of 1934 was the biggest in the history of NHM. However, no one on the executive board or the supervisory board ever questioned the multi-track policy. During the 1930s, the Netherlands remained in recession for longer than other European countries; the economy began to recover only once the government left the gold standard and devalued the guilder in September 1936.

Following devaluation, both the plantation business and the banking business in the Dutch East Indies finally returned to profitability. The structural overproduction of sugar was addressed by slimming down the production, and the product became competitive on the export market once more. In purely economic terms, prospects for recovery and growth in the Netherlands and in Asia looked good. However, the political situation was far from stable in either Europe or Asia. In May 1940, the Netherlands was invaded and occupied by Germany. NHM responded by moving its registered office to Batavia and then, in 1942, to Paramaribo in Suriname. During the war, the company's Dutch and overseas businesses were separated.

The banking business in Asia was closed following the Japanese invasion of February 1942. In the Dutch East Indies, the banking branches went into liquidation, but the liquidation was never completed, meaning that operations could relatively easily be resumed after the liberation in August 1945. During the years of Japanese occupation, management of the plantations was quickly taken over by the invaders. Production consequently fell, and some of the businesses either ceased operating or took on other roles. Japanese occupation of the Dutch East Indies had much more far-reaching consequences for NHM personnel in that region than German occupation of the Netherlands had for the company's staff in its homeland. In the Dutch East Indies, the European staff were interned or sent to work as forced labourers on railway construction projects, both of which implied very harsh conditions. Consequently, 104 of the company's Asian personnel lost their lives during the war, compared with 19 in the Netherlands.

Colonial banking facing anti-colonial mindsets and institutions

Post-war recovery in the Dutch East Indies did not go smoothly, partly because NHM had lost a number of key managerial personnel. Many plantations had also suffered extensive damage and – crucially – Indonesia had declared independence on 17 August 1945. As a result, Japanese capitulation did not end warfare in the area; it merely ushered in a new phase of conflict, as the Netherlands sought to restore its authority. The Dutch military offensives of 1947 and 1948 brought many plantations back under Dutch control, but at a high price, because of the scorched-earth tactics adopted by the retreating Indonesians. Despite the political uncertainty – Indonesia gained independence in December 1949 – the board decided to restore the damaged plantations. The company remained wedded to the multi-track policy, with a banking business, a plantation business and a venture capital business – through which NHM participated in attractive-looking ventures and companies, including Dutch aeroplane manufacturer Fokker – all operating side by side.

From 1950, however, independent operations in Indonesia became increasingly difficult, partly because of tensions between the Netherlands and Indonesia over New Guinea. The island had remained under Dutch control following Indonesia's independence, but the new nation refused to recognise Dutch sovereignty. Business activities were further complicated and profitability adversely affected by various new regulations imposed by the Indonesian government. Because the transfer of profits to the Netherlands was also made difficult, it was decided that some of the earnings should be used to restore the plantations. Not only was the situation on the production side very different after the war – the cost of production rose several hundred per cent – but the post-war market for plantation produce was also quite changed, as decolonization led to the disappearance of traditional export markets. NHM's struggles in Indonesia were brought to an end in May 1959 by the nationalization of its plantation business. The banking business – the last Dutch business in Indonesia – followed in December 1960.

Alternatives to nationalization, such as the sale of the banking business in Indonesia or its transfer to a joint venture, were considered during the 1950s, but rejected as unrealistic. Sale of the plantation business as a whole was not feasible, because no private Indonesian parties had sufficient capital. NHM had to part with its assets for knock-down prices, and even those were never paid in some cases. Well before nationalization, the book value of the plantations was a mere 1 franc, so the 1959 nationalization did not have far-reaching accounting consequences. Naturally, nationalization also had implications for the Asian branch offices, whose main line of business was the financing of imports and exports to and from Indonesia. As early as the late 1940s, therefore, the company decided to expand its network in Asia, Africa and North and South America, subject to the condition that a reasonable degree of political stability prevailed in the countries concerned. The strategy proved successful: whereas in 1949 NHM had 38 overseas agencies, by 1964 it had 45, despite having lost its Indonesian offices in the interim.

The loss of the Indonesian offices also had consequences for the company's profit-and-loss position. Prior to nationalization, the majority of NHM's profits were generated in Indonesia and the other overseas branches. After nationalization, the bulk of the profits came from the Dutch business, partly because the latter became much more profitable following the opening of numerous new branches and the introduction of new products. NHM also looked for other locations where it could continue its plantation business. Ethiopia was considered but rejected. Eventually, NHM acquired interests in two existing companies: one in French Equatorial Guinea and one in Peru. Nevertheless, when the Indonesian plantation business was nationalized in 1959, the company was forced to accept that plantations were no longer in keeping with the product portfolio of a general bank. In the early 1960s, the operations in Africa and South America were accordingly wound up. Naturally, the final step in the process was the sale of the Suriname-based Mariënburg sugar company in early 1964. When it became apparent that nationalization of the business in Indonesia was imminent, the company recognized that it had to change. Talks were accordingly held with two overseas banks: first *Hollandsche Bank-Unie* (Holland Banking Union, or HBU) in 1954 and then *Nederlandse Overzee Bank* (Netherlands Overseas Bank, or NOB) in 1960. In that period, the priority for the NHM board was expansion of the overseas business. Negotiations with HBU and NOB yielded no material results, however.

By early 1964, both NHM and *Twentsche Bank* had reached the point where there was little choice but to seriously consider a merger. The possibility had been on the table for some years, but the plans had always foundered. Finally, however, the two companies' boards were able to work around the personal interest issues that had previously formed a barrier to progress. The merger of NHM and *Twentsche Bank* – in reality NHM's takeover of *Twentsche Bank* – was announced in June 1964, leading to the creation of *Algemene Bank Nederland* (General Bank of the Netherlands) in October 1964. Thus ended the independent existence of *Nederlandsche Handel-Maatschappij* and a presence in Indonesia stretching back almost 140 years.

Dutch colonial banking: South Africa

The story of Dutch banks in South Africa is quite different, and a little bit of previous history is needed to understand it.[9] Since 1652, the Cape had been governed by the VOC, but in 1806 the area was taken over by the British. Many of the white inhabitants of Dutch origin – called Boers or later on, Afrikaners – disliked the British colonial government, because it was not sensitive to their traditions or religious beliefs. During the Great Trek (1836–1838), they left the Cape in great numbers to settle in the interior, where they founded their own independent republics, Transvaal and Orange Free State. Threatened by the original black inhabitants and opposed by the British, the settlers developed strong nationalistic feelings. These incited the Boers to revolt against the British annexation of Transvaal, and in the first Boer War (1880–1881) they regained their independence. In the Netherlands, which up to that point had paid little attention to South Africa, the conflict stirred enormous sympathy for their kinsmen.

A scramble for colonial banking

Support actions were organized on a large scale, and Dutch teachers and civil servants went to South Africa to help build up the new state. The business community also became interested in what the country had to offer, all the more so when large gold deposits were discovered on the *Witwatersrand*. Foreign capital was needed, particularly to develop a railway system and to establish a national bank. The Transvaal government was prepared to give concessions for these purposes, but did not like the idea of becoming dependent on a single country, even the Netherlands. The railway company, although formally a Dutch enterprise, was partly financed by German capital. After ten years of wrangling, in 1891, a National Bank was set up by a consortium of Dutch, German and English financiers.

In addition to the new National Bank, with its special privileges, various private banks entered the South African Republic, as Transvaal was officially called. As early as 1877, during the British occupation, Standard Bank of South Africa opened a branch, and it continued to do business in the new republic. After the promising gold finds in 1886, other overseas banks followed, both from the Cape and one from Natal, another British colony. Swept along by the warm feelings for South Africa and attracted by the prospect of new commercial opportunities, a new, Amsterdam-based Dutch bank was established in 1888 to engage in credit activities in and with South Africa. This company, *Nederlandsche Bank voor Zuid-Afrika* (Netherlands Bank for South Africa, NBvZA), was a consortium of

South African sympathizers and Amsterdam financiers.[10] The latter put their stamp on the bank, in the form of very prudent banking policies. Although the bank in Transvaal attracted local deposits, it was mainly financed by its own capital provided from Amsterdam. In the highly speculative environment in Transvaal, deposits were not a stable basis for expansion; nor was the issue of banknotes. The new bank also refrained from involvement in gold mining and from financing the gold trade. As a result, it was able to withstand the various bank crises in the last decade of the nineteenth century and to pay regular dividends up to 1899. The same holds true for its mortgage banking subsidiary, which was financed by mortgage bonds issued in Holland. Nevertheless, the bank had to cope with severe problems. Connections with Amsterdam were slow (four weeks by boat and a week from Cape Town to Pretoria), staff were difficult to recruit and, after the early years, new capital was hard to attract. As a result, expansion had to be slow, with just three branches opened, in addition to the main agency in Pretoria.

Ten years after the creation of NBvZA, a second Dutch bank for South Africa was established: *Transvaalsche Handelsbank* (Transvaal Commercial Bank, THB).[11] It was founded as a trading firm by two Dutchmen who had come to Transvaal in the early days of the republic. In 1898 it was transformed into an Amsterdam-registered bank with two branches in Transvaal. The rough South African trading climate in which this bank had its roots made it more adventurous than its counterpart; so too was its affiliated mortgage bank, which did not declare any dividends in its first ten years of existence.

The outbreak of the Anglo-Boer War (1899–1902) ushered in a difficult period for the Dutch banks. Although the fighting caused neither of them any great direct damage, a government decree was issued, limiting the amount of interest that could be recovered on outstanding debts. After the British victory, the two Boer republics were annexed, so that all four regions in South Africa – Cape, Natal, Transvaal and Orange River Colony – were brought under British rule. The annexation was particularly threatening to NBvZA, because it had always maintained good relations with the old Transvaal government of President Kruger. There were fears that working under a British regime would be very difficult, if not impossible. However, after the peace treaty of 1902, the bank was able to resume its normal business. Initially, there was a strong economic recovery, from which both banks benefited. NBvZA soon opened branches in Cape Town and London, while THB established a presence in Hamburg, to facilitate their overseas trade financing business. Soon, however, a severe recession started, depressing banking activity until about 1910 and causing losses to the banks. Capital reconstruction was ultimately required to eliminate the losses. Things began to improve after 1910, when the four regions joined to form the Union of South Africa, providing better opportunities for banks.

Dutch colonial banks facing British colonial banks within a British colony

General developments in the banking sector did not favour the small Dutch institutions. Nearly all local banks had disappeared in the previous decade, and from

1910 there was further concentration amongst the bigger banks. In particular, the old Transvaal National Bank started an expansion drive, absorbing three other banks in the space of a few years (National Bank of the Orange River Colony in 1910, Bank of Africa in 1912 and Natal Bank in 1914). Standard Bank did not respond until 1920, when it took over African Banking Corporation. From then on, two big banks – National Bank and Standard Bank – dominated the field, the first being an indigenous institution, the second a British colonial bank. The small Dutch banks were no match for them. The following figures illustrate the relative strength of the various institutions around 1920: Standard and National had capital and reserves of £5.1 million and £4.3 million respectively. Both had more than 300 branches throughout the Union.[12] NBvZA had 12 branches and a capital and reserves of £290,000. THB had slightly less capital and only one office, in Johannesburg.

Clearly, the Dutch banks had little room for manoeuvre. However, they were not prepared to give up their independence, because they valued their Dutch identity highly. Their activities were concentrated in the Dutch (Afrikaans) speaking population and business community, and they were afraid of losing that market if they amalgamated with one of the other banks. They did not have the means to expand their branch networks, because for most of this period there was little scope for raising additional capital in the Netherlands – partly because the Dutch ceased to feel a special affinity with South Africa after the British annexation. The Dutch banks were also wary of offering better conditions to clients than their big competitors, for fear of provoking potentially disastrous retaliation.

Indeed, the Dutch banks welcomed the agreement on interest rates and other conditions first concluded amongst the banks in 1912, because it removed the risk of a tariff war, in which they were unlikely to prosper. NBvZA therefore joined the agreement,[13] although it sometimes tested the limits of what its partners were prepared to accept, and even got a concession on rates for certain types of deposits, because of its small branch network.[14] The bank's policy was to deliver a good service to its customers and to operate in a cautious and prudent manner. The continued importance of such a strategy became clear when National Bank got into difficulties as a result of its reckless expansion policy. Assistance from Barclays Bank in London was required to save National, which was taken over by the British bank in 1925. Barclays brought together National Bank and two banks in other territories to form Barclays DCO.[15]

Small as it was, NBvZA was a respected institution in the Union. Its managers were active in various banking associations and, in a personal capacity, acted as advisors to the authorities on financial policy matters. NBvZA's status is illustrated by the protracted process that led to the establishment of a central bank. As early as 1912, an NBvZA official pleaded for the creation of such an institution, but it was not until the early 1920s that action was taken. At hearings of a special government committee, NBvZA again spoke in favour of a central bank. Standard Bank, which always had recourse to its London head office, did not see the need for a central bank. The government decided to establish a Reserve Bank, and when this started operating in 1921, a former manager of NBvZA was appointed vice-governor. He was succeeded by another NBvZA manager, who in 1932 was chosen as governor.[16]

The 1920s and 1930s were turbulent years for the South African economy. After a short recovery a new depression set in, followed by renewed growth up to 1929. In 1931, South Africa did not follow Britain when it left the gold standard, which caused a substantial deterioration of its competitive position, adding to the difficulties of the Great Depression. Substantial capital flight, however, forced the government to abandon gold parity in December 1932. The consequent rise in gold prices favoured the gold mining industry in particular, but in its wake the economy as a whole started to improve, and South Africa did rather well in the remaining years before WWII. For THB, however, the situation remained precarious. Until 1920, it still had to cope with earlier losses on property and mining investments and for more than a decade was unable to pay dividends. It ultimately lost its independence, being taken over by NBvZA in 1925. The latter fared better and from 1910 up to 1939 it regularly paid dividends of 4–7 per cent, with the exception of 1932 when the depreciation of the South African pound caused a loss. The affiliated mortgage banks, however, did not survive the depression years and had to be liquidated.

Imperial banking, from colonial empire to Dominion and independence

Meanwhile, various socio-political developments occurred, which were to have important consequences for NBvZA in the long run. The bank was affected not so much by the gradual growth of the black opposition movement (African National Congress, 1912) against the policy of 'separate development' that was introduced in those years – after the Union agreement had already denied political rights to blacks – but by the rising tide of Afrikaner nationalism. Although the British had defeated the Boers militarily, within the Union the Boers or Afrikaners gradually became stronger and gained the upper hand politically. In 1924, an outspoken Afrikaner became prime minister for the first time. He succeeded in gaining a more independent position for South Africa within the British Empire, and internally he strengthened the Afrikaners' position by formalizing a preference for white labour and businesses. Nationalist sentiments reached a high in 1938 when the centenary of the Great Trek was celebrated with much enthusiasm. Participation in WWII was a subject of fierce disagreement between the British-minded and the extreme Afrikaners. Then, in the 1948 elections, the nationalist parties won power, ushering in half a century of nationalist government. As is well known, the National Party took the policy of separate development to the extreme ('apartheid'), despite growing opposition both internally and from the outside world.

In parallel to the struggle for political power, the Afrikaners started to organize themselves culturally – supported by the churches – and economically. The economy was still dominated by the country's English-speaking community and by British capital, and the banking industry reflected that overall picture. Because the Boers had relatively little capital, they started with small initiatives. First a little cooperative fund was established, followed in 1918 by a trust company and an insurance company. Understandably, Barclays' entry to the market in 1925 was greeted with suspicion by the Boer community, who regarded Barclays as a foreign bank. It was another ten years, however, before the first Afrikaner bank was founded: Volkskas.[17] The new institution started slowly, but received growing support from the Afrikaner population. The bank was followed by a finance company and an investment company.

Volkskas was not a direct threat to NBvZA, but it had the potential to become a strong competitive force in the Afrikaner segment of the banking market. Furthermore, some within NBvZA were in favour of the local management having more independence from the Amsterdam head office. Amsterdam was not opposed to the idea, and, before WWII, discussions about the possible incorporation of the South African business had already started. The rationale behind the proposal was to make the bank more flexible and more popular among the Afrikaners. During WWII, ties between Amsterdam and the bank in South Africa (and its London branch) were cut, obliging the South African business to operate autonomously. It did rather well, albeit under a government supervisor, because the head office was located in enemy territory. During the war years, Volkskas continued to grow and saw its market share increase. Those developments, together with the growing sense of Afrikaner identity, strengthened the desire for greater independence, with a separate South African company as a first step and a South African majority as the ultimate goal. In 1946, a new general manager was appointed in Amsterdam: someone who had worked as assistant general manager in Pretoria for nine years, including the war years. He was therefore sympathetic to South African sentiments and became the central figure in discussions between South Africa and Amsterdam. A particular issue was that South Africa needed more capital for its expansion, but Amsterdam had also plans to develop its own business. Pending further negotiations, a share issue took place in 1946 to raise money for both purposes.

In principle, Amsterdam was willing to grant more autonomy to South Africa and to form a local company to which the bank's South African activities would be transferred. However, efforts to realize such an autonomous arrangement in cooperation with another bank came to nothing. Volkskas was interested in a link-up, but its more extremist stance was not acceptable to the management in Amsterdam; it would only accept parties that were friendly to the Dutch. In the Netherlands, *Nederlandsche Handel-Maatschappij* was interested in participating in the bank or in a new venture, but the South Africans were not happy with that idea, because it would imply a new and even more powerful foreign party assuming control.[18] The participation of other South African institutions was also difficult to accept, since they would have their own agenda and might try to overrule Dutch wishes.

In the end, it was decided that a separate South African company with a Dutch majority should be established and governed by a board consisting of friendly directors. The next question was how large the African participation should be. The South African banking authorities demanded at least 50 per cent, but this was rejected by Amsterdam. The management there was not even prepared to commit to relinquishing its majority in the future, so this question was left open. Initially, 25 per cent of the capital would be made available to South African parties, on the understanding that they would be acceptable to the bank. The make-up of the board of directors was a thorny question, because many of the capable people in South Africa already had other interests. It was therefore agreed that the experienced and trusted general manager in South Africa would be chairman of the board, while the two Amsterdam managers would become members (with deputies in the Union). Of the seven board members, four would be Dutch nationals. On this basis, the new South African company was established on 2 January 1951 and registered as a bank on 15 January. It was named *Nederlandse Bank van Suid-Afrika beperk* (Netherlands Bank of South Africa Ltd.), the Dutch parent company retaining the old name of *Nederlandsche Bank voor Zuid-Afrika*. The fact that the institution in South Africa became Netherlands Bank *of* South Africa, rather than Netherlands Bank *for* South Africa, may have been a small change, but was a significant one in South African eyes. Of the share capital of £2 million, £500,000 was reserved for South Africa; the latter part was issued – and well received – in March. So the result was that the parent company in Amsterdam had a 75 per cent interest in the South African bank, with the rest being held domestically.[19]

It was a compromise that both sides could live with for the time being, although it had been a long and complicated process reaching it, involving many more technical and legal problems – including foreign exchange regulatory issues – than have been mentioned here. Cooperation between the two institutions went quite well, but developments in the two countries began to diverge, and it gradually became more difficult to accommodate both in a single concern. The bank in South Africa grew quickly, gaining market share by opening more branches and introducing innovative products.[20] It also expanded into neighbouring countries. It consequently needed more and more capital, which was not always easy for the parent company to provide. The latter was focused on expansion in the Netherlands, which it pursued by taking over several smaller banks and securities firms, while also taking interests abroad.

This process was accelerated in 1954 by a merger with *Amsterdamsche Goederen Bank* (Amsterdam Commodity Bank), an institution specializing in commodity financing and the clearing of commodity futures contracts. The name of the new bank, *Nederlandse Overzee Bank* (Netherlands Overseas Bank), could be interpreted as indicative of a shift in interest from South Africa to other regions. The last step in this diversification and expansion process was its amalgamation with the old firm of Mees & Hope in 1969. The new name, Bank Mees & Hope, had no echo of the old specialization in overseas banking. It was now a fully fledged bank in the Netherlands with an American shareholder and affiliates in a number of other countries.

In the course of this process, which was stimulated by the creation of the European Economic Community (EEC) in 1958, relations with South Africa began to weaken, also because new managers were not acquainted with the South African business. Moreover, the situation in that country became tenser as the policy of apartheid was continued with more vigour. The riots in Sharpeville in 1960 could be seen as a warning signal. All these elements ultimately led to a complete separation of the South African bank from the parent company. In 1957 there was still no question of the Dutch participation being reduced, and NOB participated in a share issue by its subsidiary, thus maintaining its 75 per cent stake. Within a few years, however, the situation had changed. It was then deemed advisable for the parent-subsidiary relationship to be superseded by a more equal relationship. There was a further share issue in South Africa, in which NOB did not participate. It even sold part of its existing shareholding, as a result of which its participation was reduced to 49 per cent – a minority position, in other words. The South African bank, on the other hand, acquired 12 per cent of the capital of the Dutch company, with a view to participating in developments in the EEC. In 1964, NOB sold more of its participation, thus reducing its holding to 25 per cent. When Bank Mees & Hope was formed in 1969, the new bank did not see holding a stake in a South African bank as consistent with its strategy, and the shares were accordingly disposed of. That move was followed in 1974 by the sale of the South African participation in the Dutch institution, thus severing the last of the longstanding ties between the Netherlands and South Africa.

It will be noted that the question of apartheid played no role in the process of the separation – certainly no public role. It was mainly the growing Afrikaner movement that continued to press for greater independence; the Dutch management was happy to accommodate the South Africans' wishes, because increasing separation fitted in with developments in the Netherlands. The strong inter-racial tensions in South Africa, the extreme nationalistic policy of the Union and the growing resistance from other countries to South African policy (leading ultimately to boycotts) all date from a later period. Those developments finally forced Standard and Barclays to divest their interests in South Africa towards the end of the 1980s, having already reduced their holdings to comply with government regulations. By comparison, the separation of the Dutch and the South African banks was quite a smooth and amicable process.

Dutch imperial banking in South America

Hollandsche Bank-Unie (Holland Bank Union, HBU) first established a presence in South America in the early twentieth century. The continent was perceived as offering boundless opportunities, being blessed with enormous natural riches, which had barely been exploited, due to chronic shortages of labour, knowledge, capital and capital goods. In that era, Europe was the primary source of the means of production. A steady flow of immigrants from Southern and Eastern Europe provided the manpower and expertise for the development of agriculture and industry, while Britain often provided the finance. People in the Netherlands also began to recognize the economic potential of South America. Staple produce, such as wheat, tobacco, maize and coffee, were imported in increasing quantities, for domestic consumption, for onward shipment to other countries and for processing to make other products. The goods were frequently transported across the Atlantic by Dutch shipping lines. Such activities quickly generated a demand for the advance financing and subsequent financing of commercial transactions between the Netherlands and South American countries, as well as for information and support for importers and exporters trading with the region.[21]

Hollandsche Bank voor Zuid-Amerika (Bancolanda) was founded in Amsterdam in March 1914 by *Rotterdamsche Bankvereeniging* (Rotterdam Bank). A number of trading houses were also involved. In South America, the bank originally traded under the name *Banco Holandés de la América del Sud* (Dutch Bank of South America), opening a branch in Buenos Aires, Argentina, in October 1914. Several branches soon followed in Brazil, in Rio de Janeiro (1916), Santos (1917) and São Paulo (1919). In November 1919, the bank's capital was increased to allow the expansion of activities to Hamburg and Santiago (Chile). In the course of 1920, however, the South American branches encountered problems. In response, the management thoroughly reorganized operations, closing the branches in Chile and Germany.

In 1924, Rotterdam Bank withdrew from Bancolanda because of an internal financial crisis. From 1925, the bank was headed up by N. E. Rost Onnes, under whose leadership the reforms and reorganizations previously set in motion were implemented, paving the way for the rapid growth seen in later years. Nevertheless, Bancolanda was perceived to have insufficient geographical coverage. To address that issue, it was agreed in June 1933 that the bank should take over *Hollandsche Bank voor de Middellandsche Zee* (Midzee), which had a branch in Istanbul. Following the takeover, the name of the bank was changed from *Hollandsche Bank voor Zuid-Amerika* to the *Hollandsche Bank-Unie* (Holland Banking Union). In March of the following year, *Hollandsche Bank voor West-Indië* (Dutch Bank for the Dutch West Indies, or Westbank) – which had sub-branches in Willemstad (Curaçao) and Caracas (Venezuela) – was also acquired. HBU's activities remained concentrated largely in South America, where the bank was engaged primarily in import and export financing, the provision of credit and securities services, the financing of international commodities trading and the settlement of foreign currency transactions and arbitration. In the Netherlands, the bank expanded by making acquisitions in Rotterdam (1939) and The Hague (1941).

Despite their serious effect on the lives of countless Dutch people, WWII and the German occupation of the Netherlands had no direct consequences for the activities of most Dutch banks. Overseas banks such as *Hollandsche Bank-Unie* formed an exception, however. Occupation of the Netherlands in May 1940 made the legal status of HBU's various overseas branches very unclear, because of the company's headquarters being in enemy territory. One particular consequence was that HBU's assets with banks in New York and London were frozen, and the branches around the globe were barred from making international transactions. To resolve these difficulties, the company's registered office was moved from Amsterdam to Curaçao in June 1940. It was eventually transferred back to Amsterdam in October 1945, a few months after liberation of the Netherlands.

The United States' entry into the war in December 1941 triggered a major expansion in inter-American trade – from which HBU's branches in the western hemisphere benefited greatly. The turnover of those branches was further boosted by the intensification of the commodities trading amongst the various South American countries, which became more reliant on each other for agricultural and industrial products because of the turmoil in Europe. After 1945, expansion of HBU's overseas branches gathered greater pace. The post-war economic boom and flourishing world trade generated more and more business in all the regions where HBU was active. HBU businesses in various countries were able to profit from the economic expansion, and numerous additional overseas branches were opened in the post-war years. In the period 1946 to 1950, new offices opened on Aruba in San Nicolas, city agencies were established in Willemstad on Curaçao and a presence was established in Maracaibo (Venezuela) and Tel Aviv (Israel).

During this phase of expansion, HBU repeatedly found itself in competition with another Dutch bank with a large overseas network: *Nederlandsche Handel-Maatschappij* (NHM). In 1949, at the request of the Dutch government, HBU investigated the possibility of opening a branch in Paramaribo, in collaboration with Surinaamsche Bank. Quite unexpectedly, NHM then made a successful bid for the shares of Surinaamsche Bank, thus scuppering HBU's plans. The eventual appearance of an HBU office in Paramaribo in 1957 has to be seen against the background of that manoeuvring. The minutes of the HBU board record that the motivation for having a branch in the city was to reinforce the bank's prestige relative to that of NHM; the board recognized from the outset that a Paramaribo office would generate a negligible income. In Uruguay, by contrast, HBU was able to get the better of NHM. Only one banking licence was available to a Dutch bank in that country, and HBU moved a little more quickly than NHM, establishing a Montevideo branch in 1952.

Although they had their tussles, there was also amicable contact between HBU and NHM. Post-war expansion demanded a great deal of HBU, both organizationally and in terms of capital requirements, prompting the bank's management to consider whether a merger might expedite progress. Cautious, informal merger talks between NHM and HBU began in 1951, but the time was not ripe for the two banks to join forces. Fresh discussions were held in 1954: HBU's strong South American presence was regarded as a good fit for NHM's Asian and African network. Although the 1954 merger talks ultimately came to nothing, negotiations ended amicably. In February 1960, Chase in New York expressed an interest in acquiring a majority stake in HBU, on account of its South American network. These overtures too led nowhere. In the early 1960s, further South American branches opened, in Ecuador and Brazil, and in 1963 HBU acquired 50 per cent of the shares in the Brazilian finance company *Cia. Aymoré de Creditos, Investimentos e Financiamentos*. The remaining 50 per cent was acquired in 1970. The company formed the basis for the strong position that HBU, and later ABN AMRO, enjoyed in Brazil's home loan and car loan markets.

It would be an exaggeration to say that *Hollandsche Bank-Unie* had two faces. Nevertheless, it is clear that the bank had both progressive and conservative characteristics – possibly reflecting the personality of its chief executive, Rost Onnes.

The bank was ahead of other Dutch banks in terms of PR and the marketing of its business and its products. The HBU used newspaper advertising well before WWII, for example. One product that was actively promoted was the bank book, introduced in 1935. HBU bank-book holders received significantly more interest on their deposits than the savings banks paid. Yet, where the credit market was concerned, the bank showed a different side to its character. Personal loans – introduced to the Netherlands in 1958 by *Twentsche Bank* – were not available from HBU until after Rost Onnes's death in 1964. The chief executive had always fiercely opposed the new form of consumer credit, which he regarded as involving unacceptable risk, even though it was known that personal loans generated a lot of spin-off business. Onnes's successors clearly did not share his reservations about innovative financial services.

Until the 1950s, HBU's overseas business generated the lion's share of the company's profits, with Argentina and Brazil in the lead. From the 1950s on, however, the Dutch business became an equally significant contributor. Foreign exchange dealing proved particularly lucrative in this period, and the volume of credit provided to the Dutch business community also increased. One of HBU Rotterdam's clients was shipbuilder Cornelis Verolme. Operating a bank with both a domestic business and an overseas business necessitated the formalization of many different procedures in an operations manual. Against the background outlined above, the extensive and detailed rules and directives laid down for the overseas branches by the head office were quite understandable, but the instincts of Rost Onnes, a lawyer by training, are likely to have been a factor too.

In 1961, Onnes stepped down as chief executive, but joined the Supervisory Board and remained a member until his death in 1964. Day-to-day management of the bank passed to Onnes's nephew Pieter Willem Rost Onnes (PW), and in 1966 PW's brother Albert Willem was also appointed to the Executive Board. After the death of chief executive and proprietor N. E. Rost Onnes in 1964, some of his HBU shares, representing about 30 per cent of the company's value, were acquired by investors. Between 1965 and 1967, discussions were held with three overseas banks about possible alliances or takeovers. Once HBU had disposed of its two branches in Israel, a takeover of HBU by *Algemene Bank Nederland* (ABN Bank) was announced in December 1967, ahead of implementation at the end of January 1968. The merger was advantageous to both banks. HBU lacked the capital to continue its overseas expansion, while ABN Bank stood to benefit from uniting its own overseas networks in the Arabic world and the Far East with HBU's networks in South America and around the Mediterranean.

The amalgamated bank had a more balanced and comprehensive geographical distribution than either bank had on its own. Another advantage was that the merger removed the need for HBU to add to its domestic network in order to support the overseas branches. HBU's existing city sub-branches in the Netherlands were either absorbed into the ABN Bank branch network or closed. After the takeover, HBU became a wholly owned subsidiary of ABN Bank, but continued to operate under its own name. Indeed, HBU went on opening new branches – some deliberately using the *HBU* name, such as the branch opened in Taipei, Taiwan, in 1980 (so as not to compromise ABN Bank's relations with the People's Republic of China). When ABN Bank merged with Amro Bank in September 1991, the new bank's management wanted to streamline its overseas activities under a single *ABN AMRO* label. Hence, HBU's overseas activities were gradually transferred to ABN AMRO during the period 1992 to 1995. The final branches to be relabelled were those in Argentina, Ecuador, Paraguay, Uruguay and Istanbul, leaving HBU with a single branch in Rotterdam. Later on, following the takeover of ABN AMRO by Royal Bank of Scotland, Fortis and *Banco Santander* in October 2007, ABN AMRO's South American branches were transferred to *Banco Santander* in 2008, thus joining Spanish influence overseas.

Conclusion

The history of overseas banking covers a period of approximately 150 years. It ended, on the one hand, in the disappearance of institutions focused on particular countries or regions and, on the other hand, in the emergence and growth of large multinational banking corporations. With all the individual differences, a strongly localized focus proved to be a significant disadvantage, which was aggravated by economical and political developments in the countries where the banks were active. After 1970, the rise of multinational groups was clearly not to be halted. The history of the Dutch institutions covered by this chapter is illustrative of such industry-wide developments.

From 1860, banks began to appear alongside *Nederlandsche Handel-Maatschappij* in the Dutch East Indies, to be followed in due course by banks in South Africa. The banks of the period were independent institutions, unlike the later overseas banks, which were allied to larger banking groups. NHM was always a broad-based organization that traded commodities and operated plantations before providing banking services, first in the Dutch East Indies and elsewhere in Asia and then in the Netherlands. The breadth of the NHM's activities enabled it to adapt to changing circumstances (albeit with some difficulty) and thus, ultimately, to secure a prominent position in the Dutch banking industry. By contrast, the other Dutch banks active in the Dutch East Indies eventually foundered, mainly as a consequence of political developments during and after WWII. The Dutch banks in South Africa had nowhere near the mass of the large British institutions. Furthermore, NBvZA's history was shaped by the strong nationalist sentiments of the era, which generated a desire for greater Afrikaans control.

After 1945, that desire and the wish of the Dutch management to expand the domestic business led to increasing distance between the South African and Dutch businesses, culminating in formal separation in 1974. In the Netherlands, further independent growth was initially achieved under the name Bank Mees & Hope, but that institution was ultimately obliged to seek a union with a larger entity, namely ABN Bank. By that stage, ABN Bank had also absorbed HBU – itself an amalgamation of once independent banks for South America, the Dutch West Indies and the Mediterranean region – which had run into the buffers in terms of independent growth. The outcome of those developments was that ABN Bank became a truly multinational institution, with centres of activity in Europe, the United States and South America. For some years, ABN Bank (and ABN AMRO as it became) enjoyed continued growth, but in the early years of the twenty-first century it encountered serious difficulties, leading to the disposal of large parts of its overseas business. So ended the global expansion of the Dutch banking industry, which had begun in 1850.

Appendix: a note on sources

The authors have refrained from directly quoting archival sources, because most are in Dutch. For his research into *Nederlandsche Handel-Maatschappij*, Ton de Graaf made extensive use of the company's archives, which are kept in the National Archive in The Hague (NA 2.20.01). The little that remains of the archives of *Nederlandsche Bank voor Zuid-Afrika* is kept in ABN AMRO Art & History Department in Almere (AAAHD). The remaining documents include a complete set of annual reports of the two Dutch banks, which formed an important information source for Piet Geljon's survey of those banks. The archives of the South African operation remain in South Africa but are now inaccessible. However, information was previously extracted from them by researchers. Of particular significance in that regard was the work of J. L. A. Pfundt, a former secretary to the bank, who produced an unpublished account entitled 'Reports and records of the *Nederlandsche Bank- en Credietvereeniging voor Zuid-Afrika* and the Netherlands Bank of South Africa 1888–1950.' A copy of his manuscript is held in AAAHD. In anticipation of Nedbank's hundredth anniversary, a research project on its history was set up by the Randse Afrikaanse Universiteit, which resulted in two masters' theses and one doctoral thesis by Joubert, Van der Merwe and Verhoef, listed in the footnotes. The archives of *Hollandsche Bank-Unie* and its predecessors are preserved in the archives of ABN Bank in AAAHD. The references include only the most important titles from the secondary literature in Dutch.

Notes

1 This text was originally intended for the session Imperial Banking at the 2012 World Economic History Conference in Stellenbosch. Due to circumstances it was not possible to present this paper at that conference. The presentation was completed in June 2013 in Warsaw at the EABH Conference *Foreign Financial Institutions & National Financial Systems. Studies in Banking and Financial History*.
2 Mira Wilkins, 'The free-standing company, 1870–1914: an important type of British foreign direct investment,' *Economic History Review*, 41, May 1988, pp. 259–82. Mira Wilkins and Harm Schröter (eds), *The Free-standing Company in the World Economy 1830–1996*, Oxford, Oxford University Press, 1998.
3 Albert Stephen James Baster, *The International Banks*, London, P. S. King & Son, 1935. Albert Stephen James Baster, *The Imperial Banks*, New York, 1929; reprint, New York, 1977.
4 This section is based in particular on Geoffrey Jones (ed.), *Banks as Multinationals*, London/New York, Routledge, 1990. Geoffrey Jones (ed.), *Multinational and*

International Banking, Aldershot, Edward Elgar Publishing, 1992. Geoffrey Jones, *British Multinational Banking, 1830–1990*, Oxford, Oxford University Press, 1993. Many particulars can also be found in the memorial volumes published by overseas banks and in Manfred Pohl and Sabine Freitag (eds), *Handbook on the History of European Banks*, Aldershot, Edward Elgar, 1994. See also Ton de Graaf, Joost Jonker and Jaap-Jan Mobron (eds), *European Banking Overseas, 19th–20th century*, Amsterdam, 2002. Philip Cottrell, 'Conservative abroad, liberal at home,' in Stefano Battilossi and Jams Reis (eds), *State and Financial Systems in Europe and the USA*, Farnham/Burlington, Ashgate, 2010.

5 Philip L. Cottrell, *The Ionian Bank. An Imperial Institution, 1839–1864*, Farnham/ Burlington and Athens, Ashgate, 2007.

6 Rolf E. Breuer, Jurgen Fitschen, Werner Plumpe and Hermann Wallich, *Deutsche Bank in East Asia/Deutsche Bank in Ostasien*, Munich-Zurich, Piper, 2004. Martin L. Müller, *Woven in. 125 Years of Deutsche Bank in Latin America*, Munich-Zurich, Piper, 2012.

7 This section is based on the history of *Nederlandsche Handel-Maatschappij*, published in 2012. Because the publication is in Dutch, no specific references to its text are included. The book includes a comprehensive English-language summary and conclusion; see Ton de Graaf, *Voor Handel en Maatschappij. Geschiedenis van de Nederlandsche Handel-Maatschappij, 1824–1964*, Amsterdam, Boom, 2012, pp. 441–69.

8 W. L. Korthals Altes, *Tussen cultures en kredieten. Een institutionele geschiedenis van de Nederlandsch-Indische Handelsbank en Nationale Handelsbank, 1863–1964*, Amsterdam, 2004.

9 To complement the following references in the footnotes: E. H. D. Arndt, *Banking and Currency Developments in South Africa* (1652–1927), Cape Town/Johannesburg, 1928. K. H. Berres, *Das Bankwesen der Union von Südafrika*, Cologne, 1959. I. Skinner and E. Osborn, 'Changes in Banking in South Africa in the 1980s,' in Stuart Jones (ed.), *Financial Enterprise in South Africa since 1950*, Basingstoke/London, MacMillan, 1992, pp. 62–79.

10 The original name was *Nederlandsche Bank en Credietvereeniging voor Zuid-Afrika*, which was changed in 1903. For simplicity, only the new name is used here. J. F. H. van der Merwe, *Die geskiedenis van die Nederlandsche Bank voor Zuid-Afrika, 1903–1945*, Randse Afrikaanse Universiteit, 1988. A.M. Joubert, *Die geskiedenis van die Nederlandsche Bank en Credietvereeniging, 1888–1902*, Randse Afrikaanse Universiteit, 1986.

11 Originally called *Tranvaalsche Bank & Handels-Vereeniging*, previously Baerveldt & Heyblom. The personal names and the word *handel* (trade) reflect its origin as a trading firm.

12 Stuart Jones, *The Great Imperial Banks in South Africa*, Pretoria, University of South Africa, 1996, pp. 182–92.

13 THB was not involved, because it attracted very few local deposits.

14 G. Verhoef, *Strategies for market monopolisation. The Register of Co-operation and the Imperial Banks in South Africa, ca 1920–1980*, paper at World Economic History Congress Stellenbosch 2012; and her chapter in this book (Chapter 5).

15 Stuart Jones, *The Great Imperial Banks*, op. cit., pp. 42–50. Julian Crossley and John Blandford, *The DCO Story. A History of Banking in Many Countries*, London, Barclays Bank International, 1975, pp. 1–17.

16 Gerhard de Kock, *A History of the South African Reserve Bank, 1920–1952*, Pretoria, J. L. van Schaik, 1954, pp. 4, 17.

17 Grietjie Verhoef, 'Afrikaner Nationalism in South African banking: The case of Volkskas and Trust Bank,' in Stuart Jones (ed.), *Financial Enterprise in South Africa since 1950*, Basingstoke/London, MacMillan, 1992, pp. 115–50.

18 See also Ton De Graaf, *Voor Handel en Maatschappij*, op. cit., p. 398.

19 Grietjie Verhoef, *Die geskiedens van Nedbank, 1945–1973*, Johannesburg, Ph.D. thesis, 1986, pp. 3–56. J. L. A. Pfundt, Reports and Records (AAAHD), pp. 358–80. H. W. J. Bosman, 'The separation of Nedbank, South Africa, from the parent institution in the Netherlands,' in Stuart Jones (ed.), *Banking and Business in South Africa*, Basingstoke/London, MacMillan, 1988, pp. 69–79. Grietjie Verhoef, 'Nedbank, 1945–89: The continental approach to banking in South Africa,' in Stuart Jones (ed.), *Financial Enterprise in South Africa since 1950*, Basingstoke, Hampshire, MacMillan, 1992, pp. 80–114.

20 Grietjie Verhoef, 'Aspects of Nedbank's international activities, 1945–1973,' in Stuart Jones (ed.), *Banking and Business in South Africa*, New York, St Martin's Press, 1988, pp. 81–103.

21 This section is based on Ton de Graaf and Jaap-Jan Mobron, *Van Rio tot Rotterdam. Negentig jaar geschiedenis Hollandsche Bank-Unie*, Amsterdam, Stichting ABN AMRO Historisch Archief, 2004. Since that publication is in Dutch, no specific references to its text are provided.

5 Strategies for market monopolization

The Register of Co-operation and the 'imperial banks' in South Africa in the 1920s–1980s

Grietjie Verhoef

The introduction of British colonial banking had a profound impact on the development of a competitive financial system in South Africa. The nature of the banking system that had emerged in the settler economy of the various British colonies in South Africa facilitated the international expansion of the 'imperial banks,' as was characterized by Stuart Jones[1] writing on the colonial banking system active there, but had a dual impact on the development of the local financial system. On the one had it secured stability in an unstable settler banking system but on the other hand it entrenched a monopolistic situation, which in the long run compromised competition in the South African banking system. This chapter explores the role of the banking cartel in shaping the financial system of South Africa. British colonies extended over almost two-thirds of European colonial presence in Africa, with the strongest presence in what later became 'South Africa.' Financial systems in British colonies reflected British dominance, well into the twentieth century. The British imperial banks had a direct impact both on the supply of funds and the demand for funds.

By facilitating savings, the banks accumulated funds for investment, but by allocating investment funding, the banks also affected the choice of areas of application of funds.[2] As development gained momentum, the number of transactions rose dramatically, involving financial intermediaries, private individuals and firms.[3] A 'market' for financial intermediation emerges. In a developing market a growing demand for funds offers an opportunity for market entrance and competition. How did this development manifest itself in the financial services sector in South Africa? What was the impact of the specific development path?[4]

Cartels: the debate

It is generally accepted that cartels had exercised a strong influence on market structures during most of the twentieth century. Collusive agreements of various forms were entered into in industries across the economic spectrum. The notion of 'horizontal agreements,' or cartels, reflects agreements between rivals in the same industry with the aim to eliminate some avenue of rivalry among signatories of the agreement.[5] Adam Smith had noted in the seventeenth century: 'People of the same trade seldom meet together, even for merriment and diversion, but the conversation ends in a conspiracy against the public, or in some contrivance to raise prices.' The outcome, Smith argued, was that 'In a free trade an effectual combination cannot be established but by the unanimous consent of every single trader, and it cannot last longer than every single trader continues of the same mind.'[6] For a long time, especially around WWI, Bram Bouwens and Joost Dankers observed the prevalence of cartels in Europe and a tolerance towards such collusive institutions by governments, because these were perceived to promote coordination of business and to safeguard order in the business environment.[7] For most of the twentieth century, cartel formation was frowned upon, but although it was perceived negatively in public, legislation was not passed to forbid the operation of cartels. In the reconstruction of the world economy after WWI, cartels were seen to be useful instruments that supported the coordination of the market, which contributed to economic order whereby it supported reconstruction and growth.[8]

Jeroen Kuipers and Norma Olaizola even state that cartels can induce positive externalities on firms outside the cartel, which could lead to those outside firms seeking a 'free ride' within the cartel arena. This development might make the cartel less stable.[9] Cartels were not, though, seen to be a threat to the functioning of the market, e.g. in the Netherlands during the 1920s and 1930s,[10] and the same applied for early twentieth-century banking in the British Empire. Both in 'South Africa' and Australia, agreements between banks existed and were tolerated. These agreements were seen to coordinate banking operations, keep costs down and ensure good services to clients. The bank agreements were seen to stabilize markets through coordinated production and profits.[11] As business systems change, the sustainability of cartels comes into question. The market-oriented economic policies of the post-1980 period placed the operations of cartels in a different perspective.[12] Governments began to implement 'anti-trust' or anti-cartel legislation more systematically, because the business system had changed to stronger emphasis on free market operations.

The operation of cartels needs careful analysis in the context of operation. The banking cartel in South Africa can be seen in the context of international tolerance of horizontal collaboration at a time when markets were not open, but experienced government intervention, trade protection policies were rampant and the cost of conducting business in imperial peripheries was high and prone to risk.

Colonial banking development: the background

How the banks in South Africa developed from small institutions in a colonial economy into competitive intermediaries can be explained by reflecting on the history of the development of the banking system since the initial settler society in the seventeenth century. The development of the banking system in South Africa was the direct outcome of capitalist economic development of primary production in the colonies. The investment in resources extraction in South Africa led to essential linkages to inter alia 'financial, transport and final demand linkages that were of most significance in the 19th century rather than those to manufacturing.'

Industrialization was therefore initially encouraged by the capital accumulated from resource wealth rather than from exports.[13] The 'dependence' of colonies on the 'imperial governance framework of liberalisation and specialisation on *capitalist* primary production were comparatively beneficial in the British settler economies.'[14]

The history of the banking sector in the settler society of South Africa shows how the local and, later, foreign financial intermediaries gradually promoted the savings-investment process by reducing transaction costs for savers, reducing the level of asymmetrical information between savers and the receiving firms and, finally, improving the liquidity of assets whereby risk-averse savers might experience a greater sense of safety.[15] South African history shows that in the early stages of economic growth those financial intermediaries were primarily engaged in mobilizing available savings rather than increasing savings. When did the economic development of the settler society in South Africa then start mobilizing domestic savings and develop new growth sectors in the local economy?

This development will give a clue to when new intermediaries appeared and the 'totally new organizations'[16] emerged in South Africa. What characterized the development of the banking sector in South Africa – were there any similarities or unique aspects compared to other British colonies? The chapter explores the history of banks in the British colonies, which eventually became the Union of South Africa in 1910. Much of this development path correlates with Lance Davis and Robert Gallman's explanation of financial intermediaries in settler societies. South African financial intermediary development both reflected the nature of British banking but also introduced cartelization, which went counter to the British 'free trade' policies. The chapter argues that the banking cartel in South Africa created non-competitive conduct in the industry, which served the market during times of high interest rates and speculative activity, but could not be sustained in liberalized markets.

Background in twentieth-century South Africa: colonial banking gathering momentum towards imperial banking

Banking developments in South Africa[17] followed the expansion of economic activity. The banking activities in the Dutch colony, the Cape of Good Hope, were opened up by the introduction of British colonial government in 1806. The Dutch colonizers did not allow competition in the market for financial services. The first bank in the Cape Colony, the Lombard Bank (*Bank van Leening*), was introduced by the Dutch East India Company in 1793; it was a government mortgage bank. In 1808, the British colonial government established the Discount bank, following liquidity constraints. These government-owned banks were the first banking institutions in southern Africa. The British colonial authority was opposed to the privatization of banking operations, since it was feared such a step would undermine colonial government revenue substantially. The banks yielded annual profits of between £6,000 and £7,000, and colonial revenue 'notwithstanding the objections that may attach to the Government being engaged in banking transactions, ought not in the present state of the Colony Finances, to be unnecessarily compromised.' By the law of the colony, the business of banking would remain exclusively in the hands of government.[18]

The British authority in the Cape Colony was reluctant to allow the establishment of private banks, even after the introduction of non-chartered joint-stock banks in England in 1826. Only in 1837 was permission granted for the establishment of the first privately owned bank, the Cape of Good Hope Bank.[19] This step was hailed as a 'triumph for private initiative.' Only later in the nineteenth century, after 1850, was the market allowed to determine access into the British-ruled parts of Africa, as in other parts of the British Empire. 'The Australian banking system during the latter half of the nineteenth century was relatively unregulated, and is considered to be a good example of a free banking system [...]. It had few legal barriers to entry, no branching restrictions and no credible restrictions on assets, liabilities or bank capital.'[20]

Shortly afterwards followed the introduction of the wool sheep to the Eastern Cape in the 1830s. Eighteen years after the first settlers arrived, the Eastern Province Bank was established in Port Elizabeth in 1838,[21] and by the middle of the century both the Eastern and Western Cape were dotted with small unitary banks – 27 unit banks with paid-up capital of £924,021.[22] These banks resembled the early Australian banks: they had unit bank structure, were owned and managed by merchants of the locality concerned, were based on the principle of unlimited shareholders' liability, issued their own banknotes and were virtually uncontrolled by government. These small banks were not the only enterprises undertaking banking business, as some well-established mercantile firms conducted their own 'private banking,' by issuing their own banknotes, e.g. the Barry & Nephews merchants of the Overberg area, or the Mosenthal Brothers of Graaff-Reinet.[23] What is important is the emergence of formal and informal networks of financial intermediation after the demise of government-controlled banking in the Cape, paving the way for extensive networks of savings and credit to support flourishing business. Not all such enterprises were eternally successful: during the mid-1860s, severe drought and adverse agricultural conditions and an international collapse of the wool price, coupled with extensive credit creation, led to the liquidation of many of these small local unit banks in the Cape.

The collapse of the small local banks did not result in economic or financial instability, since the so-called imperial banks had entered the market by 1861. As in 1835, when the Australian Bank was established in England to extend its capital in the colonies where interest rates were higher than in England, so various other banks followed almost 25 years later. The London & South African Bank (LSAB) was established and incorporated under Royal Charter London in 1861 in terms of the limited liability laws. It was established solely to conduct business in the Cape, with ambitious plans to extend a branch network in the colony. In 1862, Standard Bank of British South Africa (SB) was also established with the same purpose and under the same conditions. The small unit banks suited the needs of the communities, but their limited capital base and inability to extend operations geographically, together with the close ties to local fortunes, placed them at risk when disasters affected the agricultural economy. The small banks in the Cape Colony were often family affairs that had no interest in expanding business across the colony or into other British possessions. The banking industry in the Cape Colony resembled more the dealings of private mercantile firms than the business of banking establishments scattered across the colony. The demise of the small agricultural banks ushered in the era of the 'imperial banks.'[24] The 27 small unit banks had total capital in 1861 of £1,572,815. The largest bank among these had capital of £120,000; LSAB had capital of £4,000,000 and the SB £1,000,000.[25]

The 'imperial banks' were prudently managed. These banks could not be likened to the US 'wildcat' banks that disfigured the banking industry in the United States. The banking functions introduced by the 'imperial banks' were the classic banking functions of issuing banknotes, taking deposits and making short-term loans to merchants and farmers by discounting bills of exchange. Conservative adherence to the basic functions of conservative banking was determined by the need of banks to pay gold upon demand under the gold standard. This did not happen in practice, but it served to discipline banking operations in the Cape Colony. Some banking consolidation happened since the 1870s. In 1879 SB absorbed LSAB, which had been a rival since 1862. In 1873 the *Oriental Bank Corporation* was formed in India and commenced business in South Africa, but by 1879 it restructured its operations, giving birth to the Bank of Africa (BA) (with capital of £250,000) to continue its business in South Africa. Finally, in June 1890 a new bank, The African Banking Corporation (ABC), was established with paid-up capital of £350,000. Business commenced in 1891. The post-gold discovery speculative boom, which was followed by a severe depression, resulted in the takeover by ABC. This gave it a firm basis in the Cape Colony and left only one local bank, namely the Stellenbosch District Bank, to compete with the 'imperial banks.'

In the Natal Colony, Natal Bank was established in Pietermaritzburg in 1854, but its capital was small, and it also had to compete with the expansion of the imperial banks' operations into that colony. In the independent Boer republics, small banks were established. A state bank, National Bank of the Orange Free State, was established in the Orange Free State in 1877. In the South African Republic, *De National Bank* was established in 1888 (with joint German, Dutch and London capital). In 1888 a Dutch bank, *Nederlandsche Bank en Credietvereeniging (NBenCV)*, was established with the hope of being awarded the concession for the national bank in the South African Republic.[26] This effort failed, but *NBenCV* remained a small but innovative bank in South Africa; however, none of these interventions prevented the expansion of SB and LSAB branches into the republics.

The Boer republics were rural, and prior to the mineral discoveries these conditions did not offer much attraction to the imperial banks. After the discovery of gold, SB was the first imperial bank to open a branch in Johannesburg. By the time of the formation of the Union of South Africa, SB and BA dominated the banking scene. The absence of a sustained demand for change was reinforced by the success of the imperial banks. They survived, when all the local banks failed. Banking in the Cape Colony was dominated by Standard Bank and Bank of Africa.[27] The imperial banks' strategy was different from that of the local banks. From the beginning, the London-based banks set out to cover the whole colony with a network of branches, and, in determining policy, they took into account the interests of the whole economy and not that of single localities.[28]

This strategy required a larger capital base which in turn provided the imperial banks with greater security. It also provided them with the means to take over small local banks when the business cycle moved downwards. It was notably SB that capitalized on its extensive branch network by signing agency agreements with many banks unable to reach into remote areas of the country.[29] The imperial banks brought stability by offering capital when there was a shortage, extended branch networks and limits on volumes of discounts and restive covenants concerned with collateral and skills.[30] These benefits resulted from the direct links with the London directors and offices of the imperial banks that were available to the banking operations in the colonies.

The dominance of the imperial banks in South Africa was enhanced during the 1920s. SB absorbed its long-time rival ABC. National Bank ran into difficulties in 1926 and was taken over by Barclays Bank (Dominion, Colonial and Overseas – DCO). Barclays Bank (BB) merged the operations of National Bank with a small West Indies Bank and an Egyptian bank.[31] By 1930, the banking scenario in South Africa was dominated by two imperial banks, SA and BB. This dominant position of the imperial banks sent out a message of stability and confidence in the South African banking environment. The imperial banks were, as in other parts of the British Empire, more cautious with their credit policies than the local banks, rarely venturing their capital in long-term and speculative enterprises.

Competition and market control

The restructuring of the banking landscape which followed the demise of ABC and National Bank, and the entrance of BB, presented a position of domination to two banks that was unprecedented since the 1860s. Where the British colonial government was reluctant to allow freedom of competition in the colonial banking arena, no barriers to entry existed into the market. The Banks' Act of 1891 of the Cape Colony introduced capital, reporting and audit requirements and terminated note-issue practices of the past. Banks were required to purchase Cape government stock to the value of its notes in issue, not exceeding the banks' paid-up capital. Between 1862 and 1930, Standard Bank was the most successful bank – well capitalized and strictly managed. In the absence of a central bank, the London-based banks established 'market control' based on the traditional banking practices exercised in their business. Unconventional lending practices of especially the National Bank resulted in a strategy to manage competition. NB absorbed National Bank of the Orange Free State in 1910, BA in 1912 and Natal Bank in 1914. This concentration reduced competition in the Orange Free State, and interest rates fell, because despite a reduction in the number of competitors, competition between SB and the NB increased and pushed interest rates down.[32]

Curbing competition

The economic depression and the increase in bankruptcies, which peaked in 1906 and inaugurated three years of losses in commerce, mining and banking, was a powerful argument in favour of forming a banking cartel. It was already apparent in 1912 that competition for new business was unsettling the imperial banks. NB held the government accounts in the Transvaal and the Orange Free State, and the Natal Bank held the government accounts in Natal and the SB government accounts in the Cape, but when SB failed to obtain the Union government accounts, it induced a new sense of urgency with the SB to seek an agreement among the banks. Competition was not characteristic of the banking arena of British banks in the empire.

The general managers of SB, ABC and NB met on 4 September 1912 and agreed to devise a strategy to curb excessive competition. The rationale for such collusion was that it would allow banks to offer more secure services at a price of the reduction of competition and risk-taking. This course of action was justified by the general manager of NB, since the bank's resources had been fully employed and the bank could not afford a rate war.[33] NB had already allowed its cash ratio to drop to 21 per cent compared to the 30 per cent maintained by SB.[34] NB had pushed business in its anxiety to compete, which resulted in proper controls apparently being neglected. NB was not in a position to engage in any aggressive expansion policy. NBenCV also called for collaboration among the banks, which resulted in a meeting of the general managers of the South African banks on 9 and 10 December 1912 to discuss 'very divergent and in some cases undignified methods [...] employed by Branch managers in their efforts to acquire business.'[35]

A circular was prepared in which any form of 'touting' was 'sternly repressed.' Resolutions were passed to lay down office hours to the public, ledger fees to be charged, the rate of advances against fixed deposits ('1.5% over that rate at which the deposit runs'), fixed charges for stationery, fees for 'letters of guarantee' (10 shillings and 6 pence on a letter advance against fixed property, and on 'railway guarantees 0.5% for every six months'). Agreements were reached on matters such as rebates on bills, registration of shares, safe custody, letters of credit and commission on transfers, as well as the rates for advances. An agreement was reached between SB, African Bank and National Bank on a minimum charge for new advances. It was strongly advised that a lower rate should not be charged at the ports, but that a single minimum rate should be adhered to.[36] Follow-up meetings were held in March 1913 in Pretoria. The next meeting in March 1913 had to deal with 'friction' that arose as a result of the decision to charge for the registration of shares. The banks subsequently decided to replace the earlier decision with enforcement of fees 'wherever possible' – for fixed deposits, advances against fixed property, commission on transfers (except if existing arrangements excluded such charges), commission on the extension of overseas bills, guarantees to shipping companies, importation of silver, cheque forms and the exercise of 'powers of attorney to pass a bond,' and the clearing of country cheques minimum fees were agreed upon. For the second time, no agreement could be reached on exchange rates.[37]

The general managers were most concerned about 'the "serious inroads now being made into legitimate banking business by non-banking firms and institutions," which necessitated "some joint course of action."'[38] It was especially National Bank that had brought claims of serious inroads by outside competition. Netherlands Bank had concerns about the clearing of continental bills and banks clearance in Bloemfontein; SB had concerns about exchange rates, advances in ports and specific agreements that the bank had in place with certain clients. The strategy to contain competition among the banks was the successive agreements between general managers since 1912. These meetings were held every three months and developed a comprehensive set of agreed minimum rates charged for services rendered, advances extended, maximum interest rates to be offered on deposits and rates for discount and foreign exchange sales. The banks agreed on concessions to insurance companies and how much the agreed rates could be adjusted for government, municipal or provincial facilities. Initially these agreements were entered into by the London Banks' London offices, to be ratified by NB and NBenCV, but soon matters were discussed in the local conferences first. The banks insisted that their London offices ensure these agreements were 'applicable to the Continent of Europe and America, in order that business from the Continent of Europe and America should not be in a better position.' A very strong stand was taken against 'the extremely undesirability of extending the principle of allowing interest on Current Accounts.'[39] Instances were recorded where one of the participating banks had acted outside the agreement, but broadly speaking the agreements served to encourage compliance.

The London Agreement (1934)

These successive meetings of the general managers of the South African Banks between 1912 and 1930 finally resulted in the London Agreement, signed in London in 1934,[40] which went through several amendments until it was renamed the 'Register of Co-operation' (ROCO) between the South African banks after WWII. The London Agreement was signed by BB, SB and NBenCV. It comprised the most comprehensive cartel agreement in the South African banking sector at the time. The cartel included 'business with the Union of South Africa, Basutoland, Bechuanaland Protectorate, Nyasaland and Portuguese East Africa, herein-after collectively referred to as "South Africa."' The agreement also included transactions by the bank offices, agents and agencies in Great Britain, Europe and North America. If any unusual transactions were incurred, the phenomenon had to be brought within the scope by presenting it for discussion to ensure that a common policy was adopted.[41] Since a central bank was only established in South Africa in 1922,[42] bank operations were regulated by mutual agreement. The *Cape Bank Act* of 1891 was the only statute on banking prior to union, and in 1920 the *Currency and Banking Act* introduced provisions regarding reserves for the first time. The general managers of the banks opposed the establishment of the South African Reserve Bank (SARB) in 1922, because the scope of their interbank agreements functioned to that effect.

The size of these colonial banks gave them an effective 'monopoly' in the South African banking market, but they could not regulate the conduct of non-bank financial intermediaries, such as building societies and other disintermediation. The London Agreement was indeed utilized to entrench the market position of its signatories. After the establishment of *Volkskas* in 1934, the London Agreement signatories refused clearing facilities to the bank, which was seen as national-ist Afrikaner competition. Volkskas did not make significant inroads into the established business of the three banks of the London Agreement, but it had the potential to erode that basis gradually. The London Agreement introduced a regu-latory framework among the commercial banks, which dovetailed neatly with the conservative currency policies of the SARB. While the SARB was concerned foremost about the stability of the South African currency during the interwar period, having just abandoned the gold standard in the wake of the depression, the relative 'order' in the banking environment suited the central bank. An oligopoly in the bank sector created by the imperial banks was reinforced by non-market monetary policies of the central bank.[43]

The scope of the London Agreement was, in effect, a restrictive practice which discouraged the entry of new banks. After WWI and depression, a sharp contrac-tion in money in circulation occurred. Demand deposits of the commercial banks declined consistently between 1920 and 1932, which made an agreement contain-ing competition imperative.[44] The bank market was dominated by SB and BB. In 1926, SB and NB together held more than 90 per cent of all demand deposits of all commercial banks in South Africa. By 1933 this ration had dropped to 77 per cent, as a result of increased competition by new banks, such as Volkskas.[45] The recov-ery in the South African economy followed from the rise in the gold price after 1933 and continued until after WWII. Economic expansion promoted monetary expansion, and the demand for money created a demand for more flexible finan-cial instruments. New financial intermediaries emerged, and bank legislation was amended accordingly.

In 1942 a new Banks' Act, No. 38 of 1942, was promulgated. This act cat-egorized banking activities into commercial banks, people's banks, loan banks and deposit-taking institutions.[46] Since the Technical Committee preparing this legislation argued that commercial banks were the primary 'creators of money' as they, together with SARB, comprised the actual 'monetary banking sector,' stringent measures were introduced to regulate operations of commercial banks. These included the submission of quarterly reports to the Registrar of Banks and compliance with liquid asset, capital, reserve and cash reserve require-ments, which impaired banks' capital and reserves.[47] In a more regulated bank-ing environment, the London Agreement was the only mechanism the imperial banks could utilize to contain competition. Since the establishment of Volkskas in 1934 as a cooperative bank or people's bank, it had increased its share of total deposits from 4.36 per cent of all people's banks to 47.27 per cent in 1940. In 1942, the Treasury allowed Volkskas to register as a commercial bank when its paid-up capital reached R60,000,000. Between 1940 and 1947 Volkskas' total deposits as a proportion of the total deposits of all commercial banks rose from

0.93 per cent in 1940 to 3.25 per cent in 1947, and its cheque deposits increased from 0.72 per cent in 1940 to 2.16 per cent in 1947.

The most notable competition to other commercial banks was in the savings and fixed-term deposits: the former rose from 3.86 per cent in 1940 to 13.06 per cent of all the commercial banks in 1947 and the latter from 3.57 per cent in 1940 to 8.76 per cent in 1947.[48] In 1945, the NBvZA total deposits as a proportion of that of all commercial banks was only 2.93 per cent,[49] which illustrates the impressive performance of Volkskas. By 1945, Volkskas' advances as a portion of the total advances of all the commercial banks was 14 per cent, and this rose to 28.4 per cent in 1947 – clearly presenting a competitor to the existing clearing banks under the London Agreement.[50] Volkskas was not a signatory to the London Agreement and posed a future threat to the other South African banks. To be able to draw more than 13 per cent of total savings deposits and 8 per cent of fixed deposits was sufficient reason for the signatories to the London Agreement to take action to protect their own sources of funding. Between 1940 and 1947, Volkskas approached each of the signatories to the London Agreement several times for permission to sign clearing agreements, since Volkskas had far less branches than the imperial banks and needed to clear country cheques of clients drawn on the other banks. Persistent refusal was expressed until finally in 1947 the situation became untenable and Volkskas was permitted to enter the clearing agreement of the signatories of the London Agreement.[51]

Cartel control and the post-war boom

The market for financial services boomed in the post-war era. SARB administered interest rates to prevent the cost of credit from rising too steeply at a time of economic growth. WWII stimulated economic activity as South Africa supplied food, clothing and general war demand to the Allied powers. After the war, the government played an interventionist role in stimulating economic growth. In typical Keynesian fashion, government was committed to policies of full employment with a managed currency and reduced barriers to international trade. Economic growth was exceptionally strong, as was that of the entire post-war Western world. There was no post-war slump, and deflation after 1945 compared to the post-WWI era. Inflation was persistent, but only rose beyond 6 per cent in the period after 1960. National income in South Africa rose by 1,080 per cent between 1933 and 1960.

After 1960, sustained economic growth transcended political instability, but eventually undermined the political dispensation. Gross domestic product (GDP) growth exceeded 8 per cent during the 1960s, but double-digit inflation undermined the achievement. It dropped to an average of around 3 per cent during the 1970s and 1980s. The most striking growth in the post-war period was in the financial services sector. The financial sector increased its contribution to the GDP from 3.4 per cent in the early 1960s to 11.9 per cent by the end of the 1980s.[52] International pressures only began to have noticeable adverse effects on the economy towards the late 1980s, when monetary policies slowly adjusted to international trends towards market-related policies.

The strong growth in the South African economy stimulated the demand for credit, and the conservative imperial banks were not ideally positioned to respond to these demands. The dominance of the imperial banks was firm before the market changed: SB and BB together had 631 branches across South Africa out of a total of 699 branches of commercial banks by 1945. NBvZA's policy was not to expand into remote rural areas or the *platteland*, since its business was primarily wholesale and urban.[53] Volkskas was only beginning to develop a branch network, which was the banks' main reason for the persistent request to be permitted admission to the clearing house of the other commercial banks. SB and BB jointly held 84 per cent of total demand deposits of the banks in South Africa, and by 1953 this ratio had risen to 90.9 per cent, but it declined to 80.9 per cent by 1961.[54]

Towards more competition

Such strong growth and increased competition for funds among the banks affected the operations of Standard Bank and Barclays and then, as the decade progressed, also Volkskas and NBSA – NBvZA changed its name to 'Netherlands Bank of South Africa' (NBSA) in 1951, when a South African holding company was formed and incorporated in South Africa.[55] In the early 1950s, both the London-based banks were slow to recognize the threat posed by Volkskas, while the country's foreign trade was still predominantly tied to Great Britain. Since 1922 a concession existed for NBSA to charge higher interest rates on certain deposits, to balance out the fact of its limited branch network. By the 1950s the NBSA could no longer tolerate the persistent refusal by the imperial banks to act in a more competitive manner in order to open up a more steady flow of funds. In 1953, Netherlands Bank broke ranks from ROCO and began to quote lower rates for the transfer of funds to South Africa.[56] It also began to pay higher interest on deposits to counter competition from the building societies and increased the ceiling on savings deposits agreed to in ROCO. NBSA acted in typical Dutch entrepreneurial fashion – the bank created new categories of fixed deposits, for which no regulatory category had existed in ROCO, e.g. an eighteen-month fixed deposit. The NBSA then paid higher interest rates on those fixed deposits in order to attract more funds.

This conduct infuriated the imperial banks, which then either had to follow suit or lost out on the new flow of funds created by the NBSA ingenuity.[57] Volkskas, with its domestic branch network, provided the real threat: the proportion of its total bank assets rose from 3.17 per cent in 1947 to 10.3 per cent ten years later. The proportion of advances grew at a slightly slower rate, from 6.3 per cent to 11.4 per cent, and that of total deposits rose from 2.8 per cent to 9.9 per cent.[58] The newly established Trust Bank provided further competition in the later 1950s. For over 30 years, the two imperial banks were the epitome of gentlemanly capitalism in South Africa,[59] but sustained economic growth in the 1960s led up to the changes in both function and ownership of banks in the last decades of the century. Trust Bank offered small personal loans repayable in monthly payments and marketed personal loans energetically, appealing to a new middle class. In the 1960s, wealth generation was neither sufficiently vigorous nor yet sufficiently extensive to induce a major change in banking functions.

The competition of banks that were not signatories to ROCO forced a reconsideration of the agreement. It was entered into to set reasonable minimum rates of interest and commission that the signatories could observe and that would avert competition between banks to lure clients away from existing relationships. This could only function well when all banks complied, but the entry of Volkskas and, in 1956, Trust Bank undermined the operation of the restrictions under ROCO. Volkskas charged higher fees for services, and actually compromised its own position – BB, SB and NBSA did not mind about that, but the loss of market share in attracting deposits as a result of higher interest rates paid by Volkskas hurt the original ROCO members. NBSA was granted a concession to offer higher interest on savings deposits and fixed-term deposits than the ROCO maximum, because NBSA had a much small deposit base as a result of its limited urban branch network. The imperial banks did not feel overly threatened by the conduct of NBSA, but Volkskas constituted another matter. Volkskas was beginning to extend its branch network and showed success in growing its deposits.[60] NBSA anticipated that Volkskas would, in future, apply for admission to ROCO, but was not expecting it too soon, since Volkskas had not yet gained admission to the clearing house of the commercial banks. The imperial banks were actually delaying the admission of Volkskas, because they were looking for a mechanism to increase their own bank charges to the level charged by Volkskas to improve their own profitability.

The signatories of ROCO then lodged another strategy to delay Volkskas's application to ROCO. The signatories considered abandoning ROCO, but BB finally opposed this plan, arguing that the existence of commercial banks had to be accepted as an axiom, and a rate war would be more damaging to the imperial banks. An added risk was that the state might interfere in such a case. BB admitted that Volkskas had outperformed the other commercial banks by entering into sound business, delivering good service and thereby attracting clients from existing banks. The solution lay in extending ROCO by inviting Volkskas to join. BB proposed on 12 September 1946 that Volkskas be admitted to the clearing house on condition that the bank subscribed to ROCO. Volkskas became a signatory to ROCO from 20 October 1947.[61]

With Volkskas as a member of ROCO, the commercial banks enjoyed only short-lived peace of mind. Under conditions of rapid economic growth, the demand for funds and credit extension rose continuously. Banks sought alternative ways of offering services such as hire purchase facilities, factoring, leasing etc. to clients. The NBSA was especially innovative in establishing subsidiaries to perform specialist financing functions outside commercial banking. Since the early 1960s, traditional bank functions were transformed extensively. The clearing banks acquired their own merchant banks; each of the big commercial banks set up their own financing subsidiaries. Soon, banks adopted a new structure of financial services – they formed holding companies to control an entire 'empire' of financial services companies. This allowed commercial banks to conduct lending business outside the agreement of ROCO. Commercial banking functions constituted only a portion of the business of diversified financial services conglomerates.[62] At the same time, the building societies began to perform more functions resembling that of clearing banks. A revolution in bank functions was looming. Rising per-capita incomes put pressure on the financial system, because the demand for current accounts and relatively easy access to credit encouraged the diversification in banking functions.

NBSA was especially frustrated by the limitations ROCO had placed on competition. As a bank with a limited branch network, NBSA needed to 'buy' funds in the market. The concession to the bank within ROCO to charge higher interest rates on certain types of deposits was still not affording it sufficient flow of funds to respond to the opportunities the bank had identified in the market. The general manager of the NBSA, Bernard Holsboer, had extended repeated requests to the English banks to permit the bank to offer higher interest rates. He decided to create a new investment instrument, 'to contribute to a more competitive commercial bank sector in South Africa.'[63]

By 1964 NBSA developed a new product, negotiable certificates of deposit (NCDs), to attract funds. They were sold in the money market at competitive money-market rates and resulted in a substantial increase in the banks' liabilities to the public. NBSA sold the first NCDs in August 1964, but the competition for funds was so strong that other commercial banks had no choice but to follow the example of NBSA. Its highly innovative product was instrumental in increasing the commercial banks' liabilities to the public from R129 million in February 1967 to R149 million by the end of the year. Since NCDs were money-market instruments, increased liquidity resulted in a decline in NCD purchases. In this way, NBSA forced the imperial banks to be more competitive.[64]

The reform of 1965

In 1965, this change in the financial landscape resulted in an amendment to the 1942 Banks' Act. The new Banks' Act of 1965 therefore responded to cries of 'unfair competition' by the clearing banks. The latter had to comply with liquid asset requirements and hold deposits with SARB, while other non-commercial banks were undercutting their lending activities by quoting higher interest rates and lower charges. The 1965 Banks' Act increased the power of SARB to impose credit ceilings and increase the liquid asset requirements of the commercial banks. The new act also recognized the 'money creating' abilities of the new 'near banks' and categorized them all as 'deposit-taking institutions,' which were placed under the supervision of the Registrar of Financial Institutions.[65] These direct monetary policy mechanisms did not contain the high inflation or the competition between the banks. The commercial banks were especially dissatisfied about the stringent direct monetary control they were subjected to.

Renewed efforts were made to strengthen the ROCO agreement and observe compliance. Trust Bank only signed ROCO in 1964, and then only with respect to its commercial banking operations.

The Inter-bank Standing Committee of ROCO members met regularly to assess compliance with the ROCO agreement. During the 1960s, a great deal of attention was spent on fixing the hours of business of banks, and agreement was reached in August 1964 to introduce harmonized hours of business throughout the South African currency area. Hours of business were 9.00 am to 3.30 pm on Mondays, Tuesdays, Thursdays and Fridays, while on Wednesdays banks closed at 1.00 pm. On Saturdays, banks were open between 8.30 am and 11.00 am. The NBSA immediately informed the other ROCO members that it would not comply with the decision – NBSA observed Wednesdays as a full bank day.[66] It was beginning to become increasingly difficult to enforce compliance, given the highly competitive market. During 1964, BB, Volkskas and the NBSA put pressure on the SB to agree to an amendment of ROCO on the fees for the handling of script transactions.[67]

During the 1970s, the members of ROCO were feverishly meeting to adjust charges for services, to discuss strategies to circumvent the competition posed by savings institutions and building societies and to seek ways of closing off competition from Trust Bank.[68] In the age prior to computers and electronic clearing systems, detailed schedules were prepared on the per-item charges for the clearing of cheques, especially country cheques.[69] The banks were planning to introduce magnetic-band clearing facilities and needed to get the pricing correct, although the ROCO members argued that 'customers will have to accept the new pricing as they cannot go elsewhere [...]. In fact it could do serious damage to the banking system as such, and could possibly even invoke governmental interference as a fixed agreed charge through ROCO could be interpreted as a monopolistic approach by the banks.'[70] It was clear that the signatories of ROCO were experiencing the changes in the market for banking services, which undermined the sustainability of ROCO. Furthermore, the government was observing the developments closely.

The micro-management required to ensure compliance with ROCO was not sustainable. Contextual pressures mounted against the cartel. First, international pressures against South Africa resulted in changes in the Banks' Act in 1972 which required banks to invest in government stock and change the ownership structure to a local majority shareholding. Members of ROCO were constantly seeking ways of increasing bank charges in order to contain competition with non-commercial banks.

Market changes and the end of the cartel: imperial banking and growing South-Africanization

Banks operating in South Africa were required to invest a substantial proportion of their long-term liabilities in prescribed investments, which would be used to finance domestic economic development. In 1972, the government required foreign shareholding in banks operating in South Africa to be reduced to 50 per cent of total shareholding. Netherlands Bank had already disinvested in 1970, and

Standard Bank became a South African company in 1969 with a portion of its equity held locally. Barclays followed two years later.[71]

The British-controlled banks were still the two dominant players in the market for commercial banking services, but the competition of the local banks as well as Nedbank (as NBSA was renamed in 1971) changed the landscape of the banking sector fundamentally. Nedbank posted stronger growth than the two British banks for most of the 1970s and 1980s. By 1980, total deposits of Nedbank exceeded 10 per cent of the total deposits of all the commercial banks, while Volkskas and Trust Bank jointly held 32 per cent of total bank deposits.[72] None of these banks had extensive branch networks comparable to the former imperial banks, but they succeeded through effective competition in challenging their dominant position. The business market was changing. The cartel ROCO was no longer stable.

Rapid changes were observed in the operations of banks. In 1977, the government appointed the Commission of Inquiry into the Monetary System and Monetary Policy in South Africa.[73] The first report dealt with exchange rates and exchange rate practices (RP112/1978), followed in 1982 by a report on building societies, financial markets and monetary policy (RP93/1982) and, finally, a report on broad monetary policy. In a decade of global financial instability and considerations of monetary reform, South Africa's position was made more acute as a result of international hostilities that were mounting against the country. Under waves of high inflation during the 1970s, more and more countries of the world were adjusting their economic policies away from full employment towards policies aimed at price stability through the control of the money supply, realistic interest rates and the promotion of competition. The financial markets of most industrial countries became increasingly open and competitive. This led to growing internationalization of financial activities – and the banks in South Africa could hardly ignore these trends.

The [Gerhardus] De Kock Commission observed that the past direct monetary policies failed to contain the growth in the money supply and led to growing disintermediation in financial markets – the matching of borrowers and lenders outside the conventional channels of bank lending funded across the balance sheet from the deposit intake.[74] The direct monetary control mechanisms prevented banks from freely attracting funds and lending to the best borrower. Disintermediation actually increased the transaction velocity, and a given money supply circulated faster, thus undermining the stated direct monetary policy.[75] The recommendations of the De Kock Commission were that a market-oriented monetary policy needed to be implemented in order to remove artificial barriers to the operations of all financial institutions. This implied the scrapping of the strict categories of banking institutions since the early 1940s and the opening up of the market for financial services to all interested institutions. Building societies were subsequently permitted to perform functions previously reserved for commercial banks, and the latter were permitted to engage in long-term housing finance.

The distortion of the 'market' through direct regulatory mechanisms could no longer be sustained, since these invoked inefficiency in the market for financial services. In an open-market-oriented environment, the De Kock Commission observed, ROCO had to be dissolved. The end of the banking cartel was to be expected. Two developments pointed towards this demise. First, the imperial banks had been challenged in the market for financial services by innovative banks. NBSA led the way in product development while the bank was seeking ways of strengthening its deposit book as an institution with a limited branch network. Furthermore, Trust Bank challenged the commercial bank consensus by refusing to submit to ROCO with respect to all its operations. The imperial banks failed to compete effectively in the rapidly growing post-war market of the 1950s and 1960s. They persisted with traditional banking functions and services, while the strong growth of the 1960s demanded innovative financial services. Towards the end of the 1970s it was abundantly clear that the cartel was no longer stable. Strong incentives existed for competitors to challenge its existence, and signatories to the cartel were also no longer insulated from competition. The cartel no longer created 'positive externalities' for banks outside the cartel which offered incentives for them to 'free ride' on the cartel. Second, the imperial banks effectively withdrew from the South African banking market when majority shareholding passed to local shareholders. This happened during the mid-1980s, effectively removing any need for them to attempt market domination. Strong cash-rich insurance companies were able to acquire their shareholding.

Conclusion

Although Kathleen Monteith argued that such collusive agreements amongst banks in the West Indies did not exclude competition completely amongst the commercial banks,[76] ROCO in South Africa curbed competition and restricted access in favour of the imperial banks. The bank cartel performed a stabilizing role in the bank sector in South Africa, especially during the interwar period and, for a while, after WWII. When the nature of the business market changed, the cartel was unable to adapt. The suffocating effect of ROCO became apparent when strong growth in the domestic economy demanded innovative thinking to respond to those demands. In the typical European mode, the cartel ensured discipline and consistency in financial services provision, but when the market opened up, the imperial bank model could not be sustained. English banking was never highly competitive. Collusion suited the conservative model and kept rising costs at bay. The presence of three non-imperial banks forced the cartel open. Effective competition by local banks and the global move towards market policies rang the toll on imperial banking in South Africa.

Notes

1 Stuart Jones, *The Great Imperial Banks in South Africa. A Study of the Business of Standard Bank and Barclays Bank, 1861–1961*, Pretoria, UNISA Press, 1996.
2 Lance Davis and Robert Gallman, *Evolving Financial Markets and International Capital Flows. Britain, the Americas and Australia, 1865–1914*, Cambridge, Cambridge University Press, 2001, p. 42.

3 Stanley Engerman, Philip Hoffman, Jean-Laurent Rosenthal and Kenneth Sokoloff, *Financial Intermediaries in Economic Development*, Cambridge University Press, Cambridge, 2003, p. 1.

4 We consulted archives from National Archives of South Africa (NASA): Treasury (TES) Selected correspondence Treasury-Volkskas, 1940–1947. Netherlands Bank Archives (NBA) Minutes of Board Meetings, 1922–1970. NBA, Minutes of General Management, 1922–1975. RP/70/1984, *Die monetêrestelsel en monetêrebeleid in Suid-Afrika*, Pretoria, Government Printer, 1984. RP 50/1964, *Report of the Technical Committee of the Banking and Building Society Legislation*, Pretoria, Government Printer, 1964. South African Reserve Bank (SARB) (1940–1957), *Quarterly Bulletin of Statistics*, Pretoria, SARB. Standard Bank Archives (SBA), various correspondence, memoranda and agreements between South African banks, 1879–1975. SBA, General Manager's Office (GMO), selected correspondence with London office, 1930–1943.

5 Mark Jephcott, *Horizontal Agreements and EU Competition Law*, New York, Oxford University Press, 2005, p. 82.

6 Quoted by Alan Moran, 'Competition and the cartel crusade,' *Institute of Public Affairs Review: A Quarterly Review of Politics and Public Affairs*, 58(4), January 2008, pp. 57–9.

7 Bram Bouwens and Joost Dankers, 'The invisible handshake: Cartelization in the Netherlands, 1930–2000,' *Business History Review*, 84, 2011, pp. 751–71.

8 See Harm Schröter, 'Cartelization and decartelization in Europe, 1870–1995: Rise and decline of an economic institution,' *Journal of European Economic History*, 25(1), 1996, pp. 129–53. Jeffrey Fears, 'Cartels,' in Geoffrey Jones and Jonathan Zeitlin (eds), *The Oxford Handbook of Business History*, Oxford, Oxford University Press, 2008, pp. 268–82.

9 Jeroen Kuipers and Norma Olaizola, 'A dynamic approach to cartel formation,' *International Journal Game Theory*, 37, 2008, pp. 397–408.

10 Bram Bouwens and Joost Dankers, op. cit., 2010.

11 SBA, Minutes of the Proceedings of a Conference of the General Managers of the South African Banks, 2 December 1912, 14 March 1913.

12 See Richard Drummond Whitley, 'Societies, firms and markets: The social structuring of business systems,' in Richard Whitley (ed.), *European Business Systems: Firms, Markets in their National Context*, London, Sage, 1992.

13 Christopher Lloyd and Jacob Metzer, 'Settler colonization and societies in history: Patterns and concepts,' unpublished paper delivered to CISH 20th International Conference of Historical Sciences, session 'Settler Economies in World History,' Sydney, 3–9 July 2005. Text published in Christopher Lloyd and Richard Sutch (eds), *Settler Economies in World History*, London, Brill, 'Global Economic History Series,' 2013, chapter 1, p. 25.

14 Ibid., p. 26.

15 Lance Davis and Robert Gallman, op. cit., 2001, p. 42.

16 Stanley Engerman et al., op. cit., 2003, p. 2.

17 'South Africa' only comes into existence in 1910, when four British colonies united into a constitutional union – the Union of South Africa. Nevertheless, reference is generally made to 'South Africa' prior to 1910, which points to the entire development of the Cape Colony, the Natal Colony, the independent Boer Republics of the Orange Free State and the South African republic.

18 Ernst Heinrich Daniël Arndt, *Banking and Currency Development in South Africa, 1652–1927*, Juta, Cape Town, 1928, p. 223

19 Ibid., pp. 176–234. V. E. Solomon, 'Money and banking,' in Francis L. Coleman (ed.), *Economic History of South Africa*, Pretoria, HAUM, 1983, pp. 130–1, 137. D. Hobart Houghton, *The South African Economy*, Cape Town, Oxford University Press, fourth edition, 1976, pp. 190–1.

20 Charles Hickson and John Turner, *The Trading of Unlimited Liability Bank Shares: The Bagehot Hypothesis* (Working paper/ESRC Centre for Business Research, University of Cambridge) [Paperback], p. 147.

21 A. C. M. Webb, *The Roots of the Tree. A Study in Early South African Banking: The Predecessors of First National Bank, 1838–1926*, Johannesburg, First National Bank of Southern Africa, 1992, p. 6. Ernst Arndt, op. cit., 1928, p. 238.

22 Ernst Arndt, op. cit., p. 254

23 V. E. Solomon, op. cit., 1983, p. 138

24 Stuart Jones, *The Great Imperial Banks*, op. cit.

25 Ernst Arndt, op. cit., 1928, p. 257. Stuart Jones, op. cit., 1996, pp. 6, 11, 24.

26 A. M. Joubert, *Die Geskiedenis van die Nederlandsche Bank en Credietvereeniging, 1888–1902*, Johannesburg, Randse Afrikaanse Universiteit, 1986, pp. 93–136. Grietjie Verhoef, 'The establishment of the Netherlands Bank and Credit Association in South Africa, 1888. Establishment and perspective on the future,' *Historia*, 34(2), 1989.

27 Christian Gustav Waldemar Schumann, *Structural Changes and Business Cycles in South Africa, 1806–1936*, London, P. G. King & Son, 1938, pp. 77–9. Stuart Jones, 'The amalgamation movement in South African banking, 1863–1920,' *The South African Journal of Economics*, 67(1), 1999, pp. 111–56, here p. 111.

28 Stuart Jones, op. cit., 1999, p. 113. Ernst Arndt, op. cit., 1928, p. 295.

29 SBA: Memorandum of Agreement between the Standard Bank of South Africa and the National Bank of the Orange Free State, 16 April 1887; Agency Agreement between the Standard Bank of South Africa and the Natal Bank, 3 May 1896; The Standard Bank of South Africa Limited Agency Agreements with the African Banking Corporation, 28 October 1897.

30 Merret, 1992, pp. 306–8.

31 Stuart Jones, op. cit., 1996, pp., 42–52. Solomon, op. cit., 1983, pp. 144–6.

32 Stuart S. Jones, op. cit., 1996, p. 168.

33 SBA, General Manager's Office (GMO), Private-official, Letter GM-secretary, 30 April 1912.

34 Ibid., 23 August 1912.

35 SBA: Minutes of the proceedings at a conference of the general managers of the South African banks held at Cape Town on 9 and 10 December 1912.

36 Ibid.

37 SBA: Minutes of proceedings at a conference of the general managers of the South African banks held in Pretoria on 14 March 1913.

38 Ibid.

39 SBA, Minutes of proceedings at a conference of the general managers of the South African banks, 26 and 17 June 1913.

40 SBA, London Agreement, 31 December 1934.

41 Ibid., p. 1.

42 Michiel Hendrik De Kock, *Central Banking*, fourth edition, London, Crosby Lockwood Staples, 1976. Stuart Jones and A. L. Muller, *The South African Economy, 1910–1990*, London, MacMillan, 1992, p. 104.

43 RP 70/1984: Finale Verslag van die Kommissie van Ondersoekna die Monetêre Stelsel en Monetêre Beleid in Suid-Afrika, Pretoria, Government Printer, pp. 57–8.

44 Theunis Willem De Jongh, *Analysis of Banking Statistics in the Union of South Africa, 1910–1945*, Pretoria, SA Reserve Bank, 1947, p. 140.

45 Ibid., p. 140. Stuart Jones and A. L. Muller, 1992, op. cit., p. 101.

46 RP 70/1894, p. 42.

47 'Commercial banks' were defined as 'persons who carry on a business of which a substantial part consists of the acceptance of deposits of money withdrawable by cheque.' See Grietjie Verhoef, *Die Geskiedenis van Nedbank, 1945–1973*, Johannesburg, Randse Afrikaanse Universiteit, 1986, pp. 109–11. H. A. F. Barker, *Principles and Practice of Banking in South Africa*, third edition, Cape Town, Juta, 1952, pp. 210–11, 218–19, 317–33. Colin L. McCarthy, 'On the definition of money and its development,' *Finance and Trade Review*, 12(1), 1976, pp. 124–35.

48 SARB Quarterly Statistics, 1940–1947; Volkskas Annual Reports, 1934–1950.

49 Grietjie Verhoef, op. cit., 1986, p. 422.
50 Grietjie Verhoef, op. cit., 1992. Grietjie Verhoef, 'Afrikaner Nationalism in South African Banking: the cases of Volkskas and Trust Bank,' in Stuart Jones (ed.), *Financial Enterprise in South Africa since 1950*, London, MacMillan, 1992, p. 122.
51 SAB, Selected Correspondence GMO-Volkskas, 1940–1947. Volkskas Archives, Correspondence General Manager-Standard Bank, Barclays Bank and NBvZA, 1940–1947. See also G. J. Klopper, *Die vestigingsjare van Volkskas*, unpublished MA dissertation, Randse Afrikaanse Universiteit, Johannesburg, 1991, pp. 120–45.
52 Stuart Jones and A. L. Muller, op. cit., 1992, pp. 128–30, 229–33.
53 Grietjie Verhoef, op. cit., 1986, pp. 425–50
54 Stuart Jones, op. cit., 1996, p. 233.
55 Grietjie Verhoef, 'The Nederlandsche Bank voor Zuid-Afrika N.V. becomes a South African Bank, 1945–1973,' *Bankhistorisches Archiv, Zeitschrift Für Bankgeschichte*, 13(2), 1988, pp. 113–20.
56 Grietjie Verhoef, *Die Geskiedenis van Nedbank, 1945–1973*, Johannesburg, Randse Afrikaanse Universiteit, 1986, pp. 441–2. Stuart Jones and A. L. Muller, op. cit., 1992, pp. 62–3.
57 See Grietjie Verhoef, op. cit., 1986, pp. 442–54.
58 Grietjie Verhoef, op. cit., 1992, pp. 131–2.
59 Peter Cain and Anthony Hopkins, 'Gentlemanly capitalism and British expansion overseas: New imperialism, 1850–1945,' *South African Journal of Economic History*, 7(1), 1992, pp. 182–215.
60 BBA, Barclays Bank Report-Banks' Clearing House, 1 March 1941–31 December 1947.
61 NASA, TES, Letter Registrar of Banks-Volkskas, 4 July 1945. Volkskas admission to clearing house, 12 September 1946.
62 Grietjie Verhoef, 'The dynamics of banking in South Africa, 1980–1993,' *The South African Journal of Economic History*, special issue: *The South African Economy in the 1980s*, (2), 1995, pp. 84–109.
63 NBA: DD/5: Letter Holsboer-NOB 7 September 1963.
64 NBA: BesprekingAlgemeenBestuur, 6 August 1964; HK/S: Minutes NBSA Board, 2 February 1968; 22 October 1968; 1 December 1970.
65 See RP70/1984, pp. 152–5.
66 SAB: Inter-Bank Standing Committee Minutes, 6 August 1964.
67 Ibid., Minutes 13 August 1964; 21 August 1964.
68 Ibid., Minutes 21 August 1972; 22 September 1972; 4 October 1972.
69 Ibid., Minutes 21 August 1972; 28 November 1972.
70 Ibid., Minutes 8 January 1973.
71 Grietjie Verhoef, 'Concentration and competition: The changing landscape of the banking sector in South Africa, 1970–2007,' *The South African Journal of Economic History*, 24(2), 2009, pp. 157–97; here, p. 188.
72 Grietjie Verhoef, 'Nedbank, 1945–1989: The continental approach to banking in South Africa,' in Stuart Jones (ed.), *Financial Enterprise in South Africa since 1950*, Basingstoke, MacMillan, 1992, pp. 96, 148–9.
73 This commission was under the chairmanship of Dr Gerhardus De Kock, Governor of the SARB. The commission was often referred to as 'the De Kock Commission.'
74 RP70/1984, pp. 42–5.
75 See Diederik Goedhuys, 'South African monetary policy in the 1980s: Years of reform and foreign financial aggression,' *South African Journal of Economic History*, 9(2), 1994, pp. 152–3.
76 Kathleen A. Monteith, 'Competition between Barclays Bank (DCO) and the Canadian banks in the West Indies, 1926–1945,' *Financial History Review*, vol. 7, Cambridge University Press, 2000, pp. 67–87.

6 From colonial and imperial banking to independent banking

A dialectical perspective of the evolution of Angola

Nuno Valério and Palmira Tjipilica

It is possible to divide the evolution of the banking system of Angola into three periods. These are the colonial period, during which banking activity in Angola was exercised by Portuguese (mainly private) banks; the period immediately after independence, during which banking activity in Angola was exercised only by banks controlled by the Angolan government; and the period since the 1990s, which saw the gradual development of a combination of a government-controlled central bank and several private commercial and investment banks, with both Angolan and foreign branches and affiliates. Colonial banking had prospered, opened more and more to competition. However, the move to independence opened doors to a system 'nationalist' views were balanced. On the one hand, this was a gain for anti-imperialism. On the other hand, this assisted in the necessary preservation of internationalized tools and levers to connect with transnational business, thus avoiding isolationism and the destruction of existing commercial connections. The new State needed this to foster its economy and revenues.

Angola as a target for Portuguese colonial banking

Banking in Angola started in the 1860s with the creation of the BNU-*Banco Nacional Ultramarino* (National Overseas Bank). This was a joint initiative of the Portuguese government and the entrepreneur Francisco Chamiço (linked to a Lisbon banking house headed by his brother Fortunato Chamiço, which later became *Banco José Henriques Totta* and *Banco Totta-Aliança*, mentioned again in this chapter), inspired by the example of French colonial banks, and mainly aimed at providing the capital resources needed to ease the transition from an economy based on slave trade to an economy based on plantation production for the African provinces of the Portuguese colonial empire.[1] It received the exclusive legal right to issue banknotes in the Portuguese colonial empire for a 20-year period, and enjoyed a monopoly of banking activity in the empire for a ten-year period. It was allowed to act as a commercial bank, but not as an issuing bank, in Portugal proper.

Colonial banking in Angola: the case of Nacional Ultramarino

Although originally designed to act as a banking organization for the whole of the empire, BNU gave priority to its activity in Angola. The bank started its activity by opening its headquarters in Lisbon on 2 January 1865. Its first branch was opened on 21 August of the same year in Luanda, and the first banknote issue in Angola followed almost immediately afterwards. Another branch was opened in the colony of Cape Verde, also in 1865. But the development of the network in other colonies had to wait for a few more years: the first branches were opened in Portuguese India and São Tomé and Príncipe in 1868, in Mozambique in 1877, in Macao in 1902, in Portuguese Guinea in 1903 and in Portuguese Timor in 1912. The first banknote issues only occurred in Mozambique in 1877, in São Tomé and Príncipe in 1891, in Cape Verde in 1897, in Macao in 1905, in Portuguese India in 1906, in Portuguese Guinea in 1909 and in Portuguese Timor in 1915. Angola also received the first branches to be opened outside the capital of the colony, in 1868, in Benguela and Moçâmedes (present-day Namibe). In the other Portuguese colonies, the opening of branches outside the capital of the colony only occurred in Mozambique in 1883, in Cape Verde in 1894, in Portuguese India in 1916, in Portuguese Guinea in 1917 and in São Tomé and Príncipe in 1919; no branches outside the capital of the colony were ever opened either in Macao or in Portuguese Timor.

BNU remained the only banknote issuer and the only banking organization active in the empire until the 1920s (except for some South African banks and privileged companies in Mozambique that started their activity during the 1890s), despite the fact that it did not fulfil the hope that it would prove to be an important instrument in fostering the economic development of the empire. This was partly the consequence, on one hand, of the fact that BNU's activity as a commercial bank in Portugal proper (and in Brazil, beginning on the eve of WWI) always exceeded its involvement in the overseas territories, which were supposed to be its main area of operation. On the other hand, in a certain sense, the empire that was to exist between the late 1910s and the early 1970s was still in the making until WWI. As such, it could not be an attractive field for banking, or for investment in general.

It was the end of the phase of the establishment of colonial rule and the beginning of the phase of investment and modernization that brought the creation of further branches of BNU in Angola: in 1915 in Novo Redondo (present-day Sumbe); in 1918 in Lobito and Malange; in 1919 in Cabinda; and in 1921, in Bié (later called Silva Porto, present-day Kwito) and Lubango (later called Sá da Bandeira). However, this new phase also brought ill-considered moves that caused a deep economic crisis in Angola.

The crisis started during WWI as a local case of wartime scarcity and inflation triggered by the reduction of foreign supplies and foreign outlets for local production and by the increase in public expenditure needed to pay for military operations.[2] After the end of the war, the crisis was exacerbated by rash expenditure on public investments designed to promote the territory's economic recovery and development. Price increases and exchange-rate depreciation were brought to an end in 1924 (with the value of the currency around 25 times lower than on the eve of the war), but the problems of external payments persisted.

In 1925, an attempt was made to bring in *Banco Angola e Metrópole*, a banking initiative of the entrepreneur Artur Alves Reis, to complement BNU's contribution to financing the economic development of Angola, but this move failed miserably. Not only did *Banco Angola e Metrópole* fail to produce the promised investments in Angola, but it became the linchpin of a financial swindle involving about 100,000 *contos* (£909,091 at the existing exchange rate) in duplicate 500-*escudo* banknotes, obtained from the printers in London (Waterlow & Sons), and used to finance a number of business deals, including the bank itself. The discovery of the swindle in December 1925 brought an end to the dealings of Artur Alves Reis and his associates, all of whom were convicted and received heavy prison sentences, and undermined the credibility of the existing democratic republican regime. This paved the way for the military coup that replaced it with a military dictatorship in 1926, and later with a right-wing authoritarian regime in 1933.

In 1926 the military dictatorship opted for devaluation, establishing a currency board regime and replacing BNU as the issuing and commercial bank in Angola with a particular bank for the colony. Thus, the Angolan escudo was replaced as the currency of Angola by the angolar (with 1 *angolar* = 1.25 Angolan *escudos*), and the *Junta da Moeda de Angola* (Currency Board of Angola) and *Banco de Angola* (Bank of Angola) were created, respectively, as the currency board administration and the new issuing and commercial bank of the colony. Plans were put forward to create a development bank to complement the activity of the Bank of Angola, which was restricted to currency issues and commercial business, but they never came to fruition.

At first, Bank of Angola was a joint venture of BNU and the government of the colony. It had its headquarters in Lisbon, received the assets and liabilities of BNU in Angola (and a branch in Léopoldville, in the neighbouring Belgian Congo) and was authorized to act as a commercial bank in Portugal proper. During the 1930s, the colony's shares in the stock of the Bank of Angola had to be ceded to the Portuguese government in compensation for the assumption of the colony's debts; the BNU's shares in the stock of the Bank of Angola were acquired by *Caixa Geral de Depósitos*, the bank of the Portuguese government, as it intervened to bail out BNU, which had been badly affected by the consequences of the Great Depression in the Portuguese empire. Thus, the Portuguese government became in practice the sole owner of Bank of Angola. However, it was not formally nationalized, and its stock was eventually privatized during the 1950s.

The measures taken in 1926 did not solve the problem of the external payments of Angola. The Currency Board's existence as a separate entity was short lived. It was disbanded in 1929, and its role as administrator of the colony's Exchange Fund was taken over by Bank of Angola. The final solution to this protracted crisis of the external payments of Angola only came about in 1931, with significant restrictions being imposed on these payments, namely in the form of import duties and the control of capital movements.

By then, the colony was already suffering the effects of the Great Depression. Although it was in a better condition than BNU, Bank of Angola had no means of countering these effects. It sought to expand the branch network inherited from BNU, but the depressed mood of the economy during the 1930s thwarted those efforts: new branches were opened in Nova Lisboa (former and present-day Huambo) in 1929 and in Santo António do Zaire (former Sonho, present-day Soyo) in 1930, but the latter had to be closed down in 1935. Attempts to supplement the activity of Bank of Angola with the foundation of a government-managed *Fundo de Fomento de Angola* (Angola Development Fund) in 1939 were also thwarted by WWII.

After the war, a development department, specializing in the provision of credit for agricultural, fishing and industrial purposes, common mortgages and loans for colonization, was at last created at Bank of Angola. It was replaced in 1959 by the Luanda branch of *Banco de Fomento Nacional* (National Development Bank), designed to operate as an investment bank for the whole Portuguese metropolitan and overseas territory. Bank of Angola became one of the shareholders of National Development Bank, as the latter had taken over the assets and liabilities of the development department of the former.

During the 1950s, 1960s and early 1970s, Bank of Angola developed a much larger branch network. Branches were opened in 1954 in Carmona (former and present-day Uíge), Gabela and Luso (former and present-day Luena); in 1961 in Salazar (former and present-day N'dalatando); in 1963 in Henrique de Carvalho (former and present-day Saurimo); in 1964 in Mariano Machado (former and present-day Balombo), Robert Williams (former and present-day Caála) and São Salvador do Congo (former and present-day M'banza Kongo); in 1965 in Cubal; in 1966 in Matala and a second branch in Luanda; in 1967 in Serpa Pinto (former and present-day Menongue); in 1968 in Porto Amboim; in 1969 in Kiculungo and in 1972 in Pereira de Eça (present-day Ondjiva).[3]

Towards a competitive banking system

In 1953, a new law was enacted governing the exercise of banking activity in the Portuguese Overseas Provinces. Under this regime (revised in 1963), several new banks started their activity in Angola: In 1956, *Banco Comercial de Angola*, an Angolan subsidiary of one of the largest Portuguese banks, Banco *Português do Atlântico*; in 1965, *Banco de Crédito Comercial e Industrial*, an Angolan subsidiary of another large Portuguese bank, *Banco Borges & Irmão*; in 1966, *Banco Totta-Standard*, a joint venture of *Banco Totta-Aliança*, another of the largest Portuguese banks (which in 1970 merged with *Banco Lisboa & Açores* to become *Banco Totta & Açores*), and the Standard Bank of South Africa; in 1967, *Banco Pinto & Sotto Mayor*, an Angolan extension of another large Portuguese bank of the same name; in 1969, *Instituto de Crédito de Angola*, a government initiative; in 1973, *Banco Inter-Unido*, a joint venture of *Banco Espírito Santo & Comercial de Lisboa*, another of the largest Portuguese banks, and First National City Bank of the United States of America.

These six banks developed bank networks that were comparable to that of *Banco de Angola* and succeeded in gaining important market shares. Thus, at the beginning of the 1970s, *Banco Comercial de Angola* was already the largest commercial bank in Angola with a market share of roughly one-quarter of total deposits; *Banco de Crédito Comercial e Industrial* had a market share of roughly one-fifth of total deposits, approximately the same as that of *Banco de Angola*; and *Banco Totta-Standard* and *Banco Pinto & Sotto Mayor* each had market shares of roughly half that size. The sophistication of the banking system in Angola was further enhanced by the introduction of credit cards from the BankAmeriCard network by *Banco Pinto & Sotto Mayor* in 1973.

This development of the banking system in Angola must be explained by the exceptionally favorable short-term and structural characteristics of the Angolan economy. The territory's economic growth was highly significant between the post-WWII years and the early 1970s: an index of economic activity based on the evolution of the geometrical average of exports, imports, tax revenue and public expenditure was multiplied by a factor of around ten[4]; gross domestic product (GDP) was multiplied by a factor of around 2.5; and GDP per inhabitant rose by almost 80 per cent. On the eve of independence, Angola enjoyed an intermediate level of development, with a GDP per inhabitant of roughly half the world's average, one and a half times the African average.[5]

Against colonial banking: independence and the centrally planned economy

At first, independence was the antithesis of the colonial period – in the banking domain just as much as everywhere else. From another perspective, independence itself might be seen as a dialectical synthesis, with the pre-colonial era of the independence of small local societies being the thesis, and the colonial era of the union of Angola under foreign rule being the antithesis. Of course, the synthesis combined the independence of the pre-colonial era and the union of the colonial era, rejecting the parochialism of the pre-colonial era and the foreign rule of the colonial era. The fact that independence had finally been gained after a bitter 13-year war of independence with Portugal made it unacceptable that the banking system still remained dominated by affiliates of Portuguese banks. Moreover, as the new government opted for a centrally planned economy for ideological reasons,[6] private banking organizations were also unacceptable. Such an option was reinforced by the fact that the new government had to face a protracted civil war for roughly one-quarter of a century.

In August 1975, the so-called takeover of the banks placed the whole banking system under the control of the government; in November 1976, the banking system was reorganized by Law no. 69/76 of 5 November, which established *Banco Nacional de Angola* (National Bank of Angola) as an issuing and credit bank, and by Law no. 70/76 of 10 November, which created *Banco Popular de Angola* (People's Bank of Angola) as a deposit bank. Both banks were completely controlled by the government. The activities of all other banking organizations were handed to these two banks, and these same organizations were definitively closed according to Law no. 4/78 of 25 February.[7]

The new structure of the Angolan banking system may be seen as a simplified version of a Soviet-type banking system of the epoch: a complex of specialized banks – e.g. an issuing bank, a savings bank, a bank for foreign trade, banks for particular sectors of the economy – all fully owned and controlled by the government, as instruments of the central planning of the economy.

From independent banking to globalized banking: back to the market economy

Total control of the banking system of Angola by the government lasted for nearly two decades. In 1979, Angola became a member of the International Monetary Fund, but this move did not have immediate consequences for its economic system. The first steps to dismantle the centrally planned economic system were only taken in the early 1990s, as a consequence of the collapse of the Soviet sphere of influence and a short break in the Angolan civil war.

In 1991, Law no. 5/91 of 20 April (Law of Financial Institutions) reorganized the banking system. Two Angolan banks were created as joint-stock firms completely owned by the state – *Banco de Poupança e Crédito* (BPC), resulting from the transformation of *Banco Popular de Angola*, and *Banco de Comércio e Indústria* (BCI), formally devoted to the development of industrial and tertiary activities. Another government credit organization, *Caixa de Crédito Agro-Pecuária e Pescas* (CAP), was created to support the expansion of the productive capacity of agriculture and fishing. This might seem just a step towards achieving increased sophistication of a Soviet-type banking system, but, at the same time, branches of foreign banks were once again authorized in Angola. The first of these branches to be created belonged to three Portuguese banks that had been present in Angola before independence: *Banco Totta & Açores* (BTA), *Banco de Fomento e Exterior* (BFE), which resulted from a transformation of the former *Banco de Fomento Nacional*, and *Banco Português do Atlântico* (BPA), the former owner of *Banco Comercial de Angola*.

In the long run, the trend was towards the triumph of private and foreign banking over government-owned banks. In 1996, the National Bank of Angola ceased to act as a commercial bank and became a typical central bank in keeping with Law no. 5/91. Its retail network was handed to BCI and CAP. The next year, this transformation was confirmed by the new Organic Law of the National Bank of Angola, Law no. 6/97 of 11 July. BCI and CAP had different fates thereafter: while BCI was privatized and developed as a commercial bank, CAP was closed down in 2000.

Also in 1996, Sonangol, the Angolan oil corporation, created *Banco Africano de Investimentos* (BAI). Besides its activity in Angola, this bank plays an important role abroad: it has a branch in Johannesburg, South Africa; an affiliate in Portugal, *Banco BAI Europa*, with branches in Lisbon and Porto; and an affiliate in Cape Verde, *Banco BAI Cabo Verde*. Moreover, it owns several joint ventures, namely BSA – *Banco Sul Atlântico IFI* in Cape Verde, *BPN Brasil Banco Múltiplo* in Brazil, and BISTP – *Banco Internacional de São Tomé e Príncipe* – in São Tomé and Príncipe. In 2011, it created a specialized affiliate for microfinance, *BMF-Banco BAI Microfinanças*, in Angola.

In 2002, the branch of *Banco Totta & Açores* was transformed into an Angolan bank, *Banco Totta Angola* (BTA). This bank is today a joint venture of the Portuguese Caixa Geral de Depósitos, Spanish *Banco Santander*, which acquired the Portuguese *Banco Totta & Açores* in 2000, and Sonangol. In the same year, the branch of *Banco de Fomento e Exterior* was also transformed into an Angolan bank, *Banco de Fomento de Angola* (BFA). The branch of *Banco Português do Atlântico* was similarly transformed into an Angolan bank, *Banco Millennium Angola* (BMA), in 2006.

The twenty-first century witnessed a significant increase in the number of banking organizations acting in Angola. Ten Angolan banks were created: in 2001, *Banco Sol* (BSOL); in 2003, *Banco Regional do Keve* (BRK), with its headquarters in Sumbe; in 2005, *Banco Internacional de Crédito* (BIC) (which in 2008 created a Portuguese affiliate, *Banco BIC Português*, and in 2011 acquired a Portuguese bank, BPN-*Banco Português de Negócios*, reprivatized after a bailout by the government in the wake of the 2008 financial crisis); in 2006, *Banco de Negócios Internacionais* (BNI), and *Banco Privado Atlântico* (BPA); in 2007, *Banco Angolano de Negócios e Comércio* (BANC), and *Banco de Desenvolvimento de Angola* (BDA), a govenment-owned investment bank, resulting from the transformation of the *Fundo de Desenvolvimento Económico e Social* (FDES), a development fund financed by oil and diamond royalties; in 2010, *Banco Quantum Capital* (BQC) (later transformed into *Banco Kwanza Investimento*), and *Banco Valor* (BVB); and in 2011, *Banco Comercial do Huambo* (BCH), with its headquarters in Huambo.[8]

Meanwhile, Angolan affiliates were created: in 1999 by the Amalgamated Banks of South Africa Limited (ABSA) under the name of *Banco Comercial Angolano*; in 2000 by the French bank Paribas[9]; in 2001, by the Portuguese *Banco Espírito Santo* under the name of *Banco Espírito Santo Angola* (BESA); in 2004, by NovoBanco (NVB) (a microfinance institution, which already existed in Mozambique since 2000); in 2006, by the South African Standard Bank under the name of Standard Bank de Angola (SBA); but it should be remembered that Standard Bank had already been present in Angola before independence, in the form of a joint venture with a Portuguese bank. Further affiliates were created in 2007, by the Russian *Banco VTB-África* (VTB)[10]; in 2008, by the Portuguese *FiniBanco* under the name of *FiniBanco Angola* (FNB) (which was acquired by the Portuguese *Montepio* in 2010); and in 2009, by *Banco do Brasil*.

To sum up, the last two decades have marked a new epoch in Angolan banking – one which has combined private initiative, as during the colonial period, with Angolan initiative, as during the period that immediately followed independence; while at the same time rejecting full dependence on foreign initiative, as during the colonial period, and full dependence on public initiative, as during the period that immediately followed independence. Such an evolution must, of course, be related to the fact that, after GDP per inhabitant had fallen in the late twentieth century to roughly half of its pre-independence level as a result of the civil war, Angola is now experiencing a very dynamic catching-up process and has become one of the world's fastest growing national economies in the early twenty-first century.

Notes

1 On the history of the Portuguese banking system in general, see Nuno Valério, Ana Bela Nunes, Carlos Bastien, Rita Martins de Sousa and Sandra Domingos Costa, *History of the Portuguese Banking System*, Lisbon, Banco de Portugal, 2006–2010 (two volumes). On the history of Portuguese colonial banking in general, see Ana Bela Nunes, Carlos Bastien, Nuno Valério, Rita Martins de Sousa and Sandra Domingos Costa, 'Banking in the Portuguese colonial empire (1864–1975),' *Économies et Sociétés*, series 'Histoire économique quantitative,' AF, 44(9), 2011, pp. 1483–554.

2 Note that Angola was, for a while, a theatre of war, with operations being conducted by troops from German South-West Africa (present-day Namibia) against the territory, until South-West Africa was occupied by South African forces in 1915.

3 During the same period, Bank of Angola also developed a significant branch network in Portugal proper (up to 20 branches).

4 For more information about this index, see Nuno Valério and Palmira Tjipilica, 'Economic activity in the Portuguese colonial empire: A factor analysis approach,' *Économies et Sociétés*, series 'Histoire économique quantitative,' AF, 39(9), 2008, pp. 1765–808.

5 Figures from Angus Maddison, *The World Economy. A Millennial Perspective*, Paris, OECD, 2001.

6 Note that MPLA – *Movimento Popular de Libertação de Angola* (People's Movement for the Liberation of Angola), which has been the dominant force in the Angolan government since independence, claimed at the time a Marxist-Leninist ideology, and was geo-strategically supported by the Soviet Union.

7 Of course, the remaining activities of the Bank of Angola in Portugal proper were not affected by the measures taken by the government of Angola. The Bank of Angola was nationalized by the Portuguese government in 1974. In 1978, it merged with two other small banks to form the *União de Bancos Portugueses* (Union of Portuguese Banks), later acquired between 1993 and 1996 and absorbed in 1996 by *Banco Mello* (Mello Bank), which in turn was acquired in 2000 and absorbed in 2004 by *Banco Comercial Português* (Portuguese Commercial Bank), later renamed Millennium BCP.

8 Unless otherwise stated, all Angolan banks have their headquarters in Luanda.

9 In the same year, Paribas was acquired by the National Bank of Paris (*Banque nationale de Paris*) to form today's BNP Paribas.

10 VTB (*Vneshtorgbank*) was originally the Russian bank for foreign trade, still within the framework of a Soviet-type system (although already in its disintegration phase). It was created in 1990 by the Russian government, designed to act as a Russian competitor to the Soviet bank with the same specialization, which had had the same name, but had become the *Vnesheconombank* in 1988 (and which has survived to the present day with the new name, as a Russian bank). We are grateful to Professor Sofya Salamatina for providing us with the necessary indications for disentangling this rather confusing evolution.

Part III
French colonial banking

7 Colonial banking in French North Africa

Banque de l'Algérie et de la Tunisie (1851–1963)

Samir Saul

French imperial banks have not been the subject of a general historical overview similar to that of their British counterparts.[1] Like Indochina, North Africa was a focal point of France's overseas possessions, and both regions became home to major imperial banks. Unlike *Banque de l'Indochine*,[2] *Banque d'État du Maroc*[3] and *Banque de l'Algérie*[4] have received sparse scholarly attention recently, and only a few monographs grappled with the history of North African banking.[5] Studies extant of the *Banque de l'Algérie* are of older descriptive vintage, mainly dissertations in law or economics.[6] Standing apart is the informative commemorative volume written by a former CEO for the centenary of the French conquest of Algeria.[7] Part of the reason lies in the difficulty of accessing the internal archives of *Banque d'État du Maroc* and, in the case of *Banque de l'Algérie*, of drawing historically meaningful substance from the sizable but largely day-to-day management records deposited at the *Centre des archives d'outre-mer* (CAOM) of the *Archives nationales* at Aix-en-Provence. The dearth of material of significance for historical investigation stands in stark contrast with the sheer volume of the records left behind by the bank. Minutes of the board of directors are terser than the norm for this sort of literature. Astonishing also is paucity of exchanges or debates over strategy or policy in the correspondence and other documents. As for annual reports to the general assembly of shareholders, they are more loquacious about the Algerian economy than about the bank.

Banque de l'Algérie (from 1904 onward, *Banque de l'Algérie et de la Tunisie*, or BAT) seemed to be supreme and omnipresent in Algeria. A measure of its importance can be gauged by comparing the total commerce between France and Algeria (then Tunisia) and discounts of commercial paper by the bank. The latter were sometimes higher than the yearly sum of France's imports from and exports to the two North African countries (Table 7.1).

Although its banknotes were not legal tender, it was treasurer to the state; it had branches in all nodal points of the Algerian economy; it discounted bills. BAT even engaged – disastrously – in agricultural banking and later branched into industrial banking. It was also, perhaps more than anything, an imperial bank active in France's closest and one of its most economically valuable overseas domains. Manifestly a diversified financial establishment, it defies categorization and is particularly baffling to characterize. What banking purpose it served and

Table 7.1 Statistical data (millions of francs)

| Yearly average or year | France–North Africa commerce | | | | | | Discounts by Banque d'Algérie et de la Tunisie |
| | Algeria | | | Tunisia | | | |
	Imports	Exports	Imports + exports	Imports	Exports	Imports + exports	
1827–1836	1.2	6.3	7.5	—	—	—	—
1837–1846	2	42	44	—	—	—	—
1847–1856	21.9	72.9	94.8	—	—	—	—
1857–1866	51.7	126.2	177.9	—	—	—	69
1867	67.6	114.7	182.3	—	—	—	97.5
1868	71.1	116.6	187.7	—	—	—	112.3
1869	63.7	129.5	193.2	—	—	—	125.5
1870	47.3	109.5	156.8	—	—	—	153.1
1871	78.8	118.2	197	—	—	—	150.9
1872	138.1	140.6	278.7	—	—	—	203.3
1873	148.6	140.3	288.9	—	—	—	218
1874	113	135.6	248.6	—	—	—	230
1875	108.6	146.1	254.7	—	—	—	185.7
1876	122.6	148.5	271.1	—	—	—	175.4
1877	122.1	138.1	260.2	—	—	—	193.9
1878	120.2	128.9	249.1	—	—	—	203.7
1879	122.3	139.3	261.6	—	—	—	265.4
1880	126.9	161.8	288.7	—	—	—	351.1
1881	92.1	169.9	262	—	—	—	485
1882	96	165.4	261.4	—	—	—	515.7
1883	95.5	154.5	250	—	—	—	475.9
1884	102	146.7	248.7	—	—	—	484.8
1885	123.6	167.7	291.3	—	—	—	526.4
1886	124.5	189.2	313.7	—	—	—	525.3
1887	133.9	153.2	287.1	—	—	—	465.9
1888	158.1	133.6	291.7	—	—	—	415
1889	200.6	178.7	379.3	—	—	—	430
1890	208.5	194.9	403.4	—	—	—	420.5
1891	186.7	207.1	393.8	—	—	—	418.6
1892	195.3	189.6	384.9	—	—	—	425.6
1893	142.4	184.8	327.2	—	—	—	396.6
1894	207.7	199.3	407	—	—	—	442.4
1895	245.7	203.2	448.9	—	—	—	434.5
1896	196.8	217.8	414.6	—	—	—	436.9
1897	237.9	216.2	454.1	—	—	—	415.9
1898	224.5	225.5	450	—	—	—	352.8
1899	271.5	260.4	531.9	—	—	—	421.2
1900	165.9	259.4	425.3	—	—	—	501.8
1901	197.8	259	456.8	—	—	—	458.1
1902	253.7	269.2	522.9	—	—	—	469
1903	262.8	286.7	549.5	—	—	—	560.7
1904	233.8	314.9	548.7	52.8	57.5	110.3	713.1
1905	216.3	326.8	543.1	40.7	63.7	104.4	781.4
1906	243.7	355.4	599.1	55.8	69.4	125.2	966.5

(continued)

Table 7.1 (Continued)

Yearly average or year	France–North Africa commerce						Discounts by Banque d'Algérie et de la Tunisie
	Algeria			Tunisia			
	Imports	*Exports*	*Imports + exports*	*Imports*	*Exports*	*Imports + exports*	
1907	290.6	392.7	683.3	70.4	84	154.4	1,187.7
1908	273.1	399	672.1	62.6	89.4	152	1,222.2
1909	272	397.1	669.1	56.7	100.4	157.1	1,229.8
1910	446.6	438.9	885.5	72.7	87.2	159.9	1,275.3
1911	425.6	489.9	915.5	79.3	90.2	169.5	1,460.6
1912	427.3	568.5	995.8	85.2	109.5	194.7	1,705.1
1913	330.8	552.6	883.4	81.5	100.1	181.6	2,086.9
1914	313	444.6	757.6	41.5	77.8	119.3	1,533.1
1915	546.9	367.7	914.6	77.8	78.8	156.6	649
1916	538.6	520.5	1,059.1	87.3	89.3	176.6	952
1917	682.5	523.7	1,206.2	186.8	85.7	272.5	1,386.4
1918	623.6	604.3	1,227.9	185.7	107.6	293.3	1,405.8
1919	1,223.7	958.6	2,182.3	437.4	166.5	603.9	1,492.8
1920	1,053.5	2,290.1	3,343.6	269.4	369	638.4	2,877
1921	1,111.6	1,415.1	2,526.7	256	265.3	521.3	4,220.3
1922	984.5	1,716.3	2,700.8	224.1	265.6	489.7	3,358.3
1923	1,283.7	2,127.8	3,411.5	309.3	446	755.3	4,243.3
1924	1,652.9	2,613.4	4,266.3	294.6	568.2	862.8	7,461.7
1925	1,726.8	2,980.7	4,707.5	393.6	614.5	1,008.1	8,343
1926	2,702.1	3,369.3	6,071.4	642.9	938.4	1,581.3	9,107.6
1927	2,601.2	3,426.3	6,027.5	398	804.4	1,202.4	8,799.4
1928	2,831.7	3,964.7	6,796.4	589	908.9	1,497.9	8,475.3
1929	2,989.6	4,500.8	7,490.4	704.1	1,006.5	1,710.6	12,491.9
1930	3,299.5	4,563.5	7,863	664.7	915.5	1,580.2	17,273.6
1931	3,428.2	3,976	7,404.2	584.9	800.5	1,385.4	16,592.6
1932	3,290.7	3,270.7	6,561.4	724.7	754.5	1,479.2	15,547.6
1933	3,864.6	3,309.6	7,174.2	449.9	665.8	1,115.7	17,003.9
1934	2,813.3	3,082.9	5,896.2	415.5	616.6	1,032.1	17,268.1
1935	2,329.8	2,577.9	4,907.7	464.5	567.1	1,031.6	13,804.6
1936	2,842.6	2,692.5	5,535.1	534.5	610.3	1,144.8	13,425.1
1937	3,807.3	3,289.7	7,097	741.4	798.6	1,540	14,962.19
1938	4,864	3,779.5	8,643.5	878.5	980.5	1,859	19,584
1939	4,759.7	3,702.1	8,461.8	923.9	1,011.7	1,935.6	23,031.1
1940	4,879.3	2,816.8	7,696.1	1,050.1	782.3	1,832.4	24,566.6
1941	6,611.8	3,045.5	9,657.3	1,644.3	611.9	2,256.2	30,713.9
1942	5,706.5	3,354.4	9,060.9	1,644.2	1,170.3	2,814.5	8,659.6
1943	35.5	—	35.5	22.1	—	22.1	9,275.3
1944	38.7	15.6	54.3	134.3	7.4	141.7	15,450.7
1945	1,933.2	2,681.5	4,614.7	1,601	717.3	2,318.3	19,032.1
1946	24,627	13,358	37,985	2,145	4,416	6,561	52,033.85
1947	36,897	31,645	68,542	4,332	10,652	14,984	72,355
1948	80,496	67,308	147,804	7,351	20,472	27,823	11,448
1949	80,822	107,770	188,592	15,160	29,127	44,287	15,138

(continued)

Table 7.1 (Continued)

Yearly average or year	France–North Africa commerce						Discounts by Banque d'Algérie et de la Tunisie
	Algeria			Tunisia			
	Imports	Exports	Imports + exports	Imports	Exports	Imports + exports	
1950	92,357	121,818	214,175	21,055	36,680	57,735	17,000
1951	97,874	163,502	261,376	19,096	44,880	63,976	26,850
1952	114,387	178,658	293,045	20,163	45,235	65,398	26,300
1953	108,012	159,364	267,376	25,957	42,619	68,576	25,677.6
1954	115,791	172,615	288,406	28,701	42,031	70,732	24,217.9
1955	130,533	200,046	330,579	23,388	46,069	69,457	19,187.5
1956	133,282	215,852	349,134	24,680	43,869	68,549	18,676.1
1957	161,016	298,762	459,778	35,928	42,387	78,315	19,680.7
1958	190,390	412,376	602,766	45,093	45,696	90,789	17,263
1959	167,648	471,109	638,757	37,526	56,932	94,458	—
1960	1,841	5,356	7,197	345	615	960	283.1
1961	1,750	4,353	6,103	329	554	883	—
1962	3,246	2,777	6,023	344	540	884	—

Sources: Official statistics of French customs (under various titles); CAOM, 80S/1,2,3,4.

how it went about accomplishing its aims remain perplexing questions even after consultation of primary sources. Was it mainly an issue bank and a guardian of the money supply? Was it above all a facilitator of commercial transactions by way of its discounting function? Did it act primarily as banker to the state, advancing cash, holding and managing its current accounts? To what extent did it play the role of a bankers' bank, rediscounting bills from other institutions and providing a lender of last resort? BAT was simultaneously a quasi-central bank, or a precursor thereof, evolving in a monopolistic framework and a private commercial operator on the market. The object of this chapter is to disentangle and consider the various functions with a view to providing an overall portrait of a bank active in a colonial economy for over a century.

Why was *Banque de l'Algérie et de la Tunisie* founded?

The conquest of Algeria in 1830 led to 17 years of warfare as indigenous tribal confederations battled the invading army. At the same time, French economic interests strove to gain a foothold in areas coming under French rule. Aiding commerce and providing a currency that might replace Spanish *piasters* were leading concerns, the latter having also as an object the visible demonstration of France's political authority. Supporting commercial activity by the discount of bills, making available means of exchange and consolidating political control went hand in hand.

Projects to create local banks duly emerged. In February 1836, the idea of creating a local issue bank was under study, but it failed to materialize. Later in 1836,

Tricou, a Bordeaux merchant, and Goupy, another Bordeaux merchant, each came up with plans for issue banks. But authorities in Algiers and Paris were wary of granting the privilege to print bearer banknotes. Projects for commercial, colonial, mortgage and other types of banks followed, but none came through. In 1841, the Chamber of Commerce of Algiers put forward another project for an institution to discount bills and issue notes, *Banque algérienne*. Attention then turned to the idea of inviting *Banque de France* to operate in Algeria and, in November 1844, the French government formally appealed to it. *Banque de France* undertook a feasibility study, but several members of its board of *Régents* were not keen to take risks in the unstable environment of Algeria. Finally, a compromise was reached; the *comptoir* of *Banque de France* in Algiers would not be a wholly owned branch but would be a partly owned affiliate in which *Banque de France* held 2 million out the 10 million francs equity. Despite the adoption by the French legislative chambers in 1845 and growing impatience in commercial circles in Algeria, there were further delays, partly due to the onset of political unrest in France and, eventually, to the revolution of February 1848. In July 1848, *Banque de France* let lapse its right to create the *comptoir*, much to the dismay of French merchants in Algeria.[8]

An economic crisis in France reinforced the need to revive activity by making credit available and prompted the creation of a nation-wide network of discount houses (*comptoirs nationaux d'escompte*) by the revolutionary authorities on 7 March 1848. They were intended as a temporary three-year substitute for bankers, who had stopped lending. Their capital was shared one-third by the central government, one-third by departments and communes and one-third by investors. Conditions were even bleaker in Algeria, and a campaign to set up a *Comptoir national d'escompte d'Alger* (CNEA) got underway in April 1848. The French government obliged and took steps in that direction, while limiting the functions of the Algiers *comptoir* to discounting bills and excluding issuance of notes. In 1849, the Minister of Finance approved the statutes, and the *Banque de France* agreed to rediscount the Comptoir's bills. The equity was established at 1.5 million francs, provided one-third by the state, one-third by the city of Algiers and one-third by private shareholders. In fact, paid-up capital amounted to no more than 188,900 francs, and CNEA was not allowed to rediscount its bills in France. Although it could collect deposits, it clearly lacked the means to fulfil expectations in the colony. CNEA started business on 1 October 1849; its shortcomings quickly became apparent.[9]

Two pieces of legislation highlighted the need for an overhaul of the original design of the establishment. On 11 January 1851, a law modifying France's customs system opened the French mainland to Algerian products. What was previously external trade between France and a foreign land now became internal commerce, destined to grow appreciably and to require banking support beyond what CNEA could offer. The idea that Algeria needed an issue bank or, at least, a genuine bank of greater scope than CNEA came back to the fore. It was given impetus by the law of 11 July 1851 on colonial banks which set up issue banks in Martinique, Guadeloupe and La Réunion, in whose capital was invested part of the indemnity paid to planters following the abolition of slavery in 1848 and its replacement by wage labour. The purpose of the banks was to lend short term in order to finance agricultural activity. Like investment banking promoted by the Saint-Simonians, issue banking in overseas territories was in the limelight, even if Algeria's context differed from that of the slave colonies. Nor was it similar to that of France. In the name of security, *Banque de France* restricted its discounting to bills bearing no less than three signatures. But, with every intermediary, interest edged upwards. Since Algerian rates were high and the stimulation of commercial activity required that they be lowered, it was agreed that the new bank would be satisfied with two signatures. At the same time, it was assigned the task of fighting usury, which was rife in many quarters, and of lowering the exchange rate between France and Algeria. Security was not sacrificed. Safeguards were put in place to insure that its banknotes[10] would enjoy the public's confidence. The amount in circulation, plus current accounts, could not be greater than three times the amount of cash on hand; its portfolio was to contain only short-term liquid assets; the amount of liabilities exceeding cash could not be greater than three times paid-up capital; one-half of yearly net profit had to be allocated to reserves and the latter were to be maintained at a level equal to one-half paid-up capital. Like CNEA, the new bank enjoyed state support, which came in the form of a line of credit of 1 million francs at 3 per cent.[11]

Replacing CNEA, *Banque de l'Algérie* was created by the law of 4 August 1851, drafted under the aegis of Finance Minister Achille Fould. Its manager-chairman (*directeur-président*) was Édouard Lichtlin, a merchant who, as president of the Chamber of Commerce of Algiers from 1844 to 1850, played a major role in the establishment of a multipurpose bank in Algeria. *Banque de l'Algérie* was an issue, discount and deposit bank endowed with a 20-year privilege, renewable after parliamentary review for another 20 years. It had a capital of 3 million francs represented by 6,000 shares, of which 2,000 were earmarked for the state as a guarantee of its 1 million franc loan. In October 1851, when a tranche of 2,000 shares was offered to the public, the issue was oversubscribed by 60 shares. Other banks did not acquire shares, and ownership of the new bank gives the impression of relative diffusion. With four-fifths of the shares located in mainland France (Table 7.2), *Banque de l'Algérie* was not a homegrown firm, a status not unusual for companies operating overseas.

Table 7.2 Shareholders of *Banque de l'Algérie* (October 1851)[1]

Shareholders	Number	Number of shareholders	Average shares owned	Percentage of shares per holder
Residing in Paris	68	1,260	18.5	61.2
Residing in Marseille	49	400	8.2	19.4
Residing in Algeria	79	400	5.1	19.4

Note
1 *Ibidem*, p. 117. Forty extra shares were created for directors of *Banque de l'Algérie* as their *statutory* surety.

The humdrum beginnings of *Banque de l'Algérie* (1851–1880)

Several years and stages were required to favour the embeddedness of *Banque de l'Algérie* simultaneously in Algeria and on the Paris marketplace.

The building of activities during the Second Empire

The beginnings of *Banque de l'Algérie* were surprisingly modest, considering repeated vocal demands for the services of precisely such a financial institution. Its banknotes were accepted by European merchants, settlers and state officials but not by the Arab population, which was already suspicious of French coins. 'Circulation of our notes,' wrote the board, 'is developing extremely slowly and only metallic currency will for a long time be admitted on Arab markets, where banknotes are practically excluded.'[12] *Banque de l'Algérie*'s notes found takers in Algiers, but few beyond and practically none in the interior of Algeria. It opened branches in Oran (1853), Constantine (1856) and Bône (1868), but to no immediate avail. 'Circulation of the Bank's notes still leaves much to be desired. It is 1 million francs less than issued capital and the reserve find combined,' reiterated the board.[13] Paradoxically, the diminishing supply of coins due to hoarding threatened to force the bank to limit the circulation of its banknotes or risk breaching the rule of proportionality inscribed in its statutes. At great cost, it even had to import metallic currency from France because hoarding had deprived commerce of means of exchange.

The line of credit extended by the state amounted, in fact, to no more than 525,000 francs, or one-half paid-up capital. In 1853–1854, the state advanced another 300,000 francs, which were repaid in 1856. But business remained slack, and bank commitment prudent and lackluster. More means were thought necessary to spark banking activity. A second tranche of 2,000 shares was offered to the public in 1856, and a third in 1857. Nominal capital of 3 million francs was now fully paid up. Attention turned to resources tied up in the reserves and lying idle instead of being put to productive use. In 1857, permission was sought from – and denied by – the government to limit reserves to one-quarter of paid-up capital, instead of one-half, and to reduce the allocation of the year's net profit from 50 per cent to 20 per cent. Caution was the watchword in official circles. The bank persisted and, on 30 March 1861, was allowed to lower the limit to one-third of paid-up capital and the allocation to one-third of yearly net profit. It was also granted the right to raise its capital from 3 million to 10 million francs. Nevertheless, paid-up capital attained only 4 million francs in 1861 and 5 million in 1863; the full amount was not raised until 1872.

In the meantime, the impatience of the merchant community turned into discontent. There was regret that *Banque de l'Algérie* neglected agriculture and a project by a member of the Algiers regional council (*Conseil général*) for another bank to fill the void.[14] The Chamber of Commerce of Algiers, an erstwhile promoter of *Banque de l'Algérie*, lost faith and began calling on *Banque de France* to open branches in Algeria and absorb *Banque de l'Algérie*. The latter's perceived timidity in extending credit and its high interest rates came under severe criticism from Algiers businessmen.[15] *Banque de France* discounted bills for 4.5 billion francs, or 22.5 times its capital of 200 million francs, whereas the *Banque de l'Algérie*'s figure was 30 million, or 10 times its capital of 3 million.[16] But was not an issue bank obliged to view its capital primarily as a guarantee for the bank-notes it put in circulation and adjust its lending to its business milieu? A rejoinder came from a banker who reminded his readers that Algeria's economic conditions, being less developed than France's, explained the dearth of credit and high rates, and were a more decisive factor than the size of the lending institution.[17] Discount rate at *Banque de l'Algérie* was pegged at 7 per cent; it came down to 6 per cent in 1861 but rose to 7 per cent in 1864.[18] A too important differential with the rate of the *Banque de France* had to be avoided, lest lower rates in Algeria produce an onrush of bills from France; the reverse was also detrimental because it could dry up local business for the bank. Strengthening its cash reserve was another motivation for raising rates. The three other banks in Algeria set their rates between 8 and 12 per cent, and private bankers (usurers) imposed a stiff 18 to 24 per cent, sometimes even charging 100 per cent.[19] *Banque de l'Algérie*'s average rate hovered around 6 per cent, occasionally edging higher or slipping below that level.

Throughout the 1860s and 1870s, competitors showed interest in Algeria. In 1860, *Crédit foncier de France*, the leading mortgage lender in France, received authorization to enter the Algerian market. A powerful investment bank, *Société générale algérienne*, was created in 1865 by Louis Frémy, the governor of Crédit foncier de France, and Paulin Talabot, general manager of the *Chemins de fer Paris-Lyon-Méditerranée*. Based on the model of the Pereire brothers' *Crédit mobilier*, it had a capital base of 100 million francs and Napoleon III as one of the shareholders. The timing was not right, because dire events struck Algeria in 1866–1868 (an earthquake, drought, bad crops, cholera), which spread misery throughout the land and dealt a blow to a struggling economy.[20]

In June 1863, Fould dispatched a Finance Ministry official to Algeria to appraise the situation. D'Artigue produced a report advising against extension of *Banque de France* in Algeria and favouring the maintenance of *Banque de l'Algérie*. Fould opted for the latter's reinforcement. His letter to the bank, dated 23 October 1863, outlined two important measures in that regard. First, *Banque de France* was to aid *Banque de l'Algérie* by rediscounting its paper up to 4 million francs. The rate was to be the one applied in France, lower than Algeria's. *Banque de l'Algérie* received treatment equivalent to that of banks in France. It benefited from the equivalent of a low-cost line of credit supplying it with funds for easing capital shortage and lending in Algeria. Thus, *Banque de France* was drawn into Algeria indirectly rather than through the opening of branches.[21]

Second, Fould ordered that funds of the public revenue office (*Trésor public*) in Algeria would be deposited in a current account at *Banque de l'Algérie* free of interest, and entrusted the bank with administrative payments on behalf of the state in regions where public services were not yet in place. Henceforth and for the rest of the history of the bank, the Treasury account and banknote circulation – in effect, a loan from the public to the bank – became its two sources of working funds. Deposits by the general public were minimal, in part because they earned no interest. Moreover, during the rest of the *Banque de l'Algérie*'s history, the Treasury account was destined to play an important role in the elimination of transaction costs between Algeria and France. Payment due in France was made to the Treasury account at the bank in Algeria, and its correspondent in France – *Comptoir d'escompte de Paris* (CEP) – or the Treasury paid the creditor in French francs. The reverse operation applied in similar fashion. Entries in registers obviated the need for transfers of cash. Over time, the Treasury current account at *Banque de l'Algérie* received two types of deposits: public funds for official use and payments made by importers in Algeria to exporters in France in representation of sums disbursed to them by the bank's correspondent in France.

Despite its monopoly of issue, *Banque de l'Algérie* was a private firm. With the state as its leading partner, it became more than an ordinary issuer of banknotes and took on the character of a quasi-official state bank, although it was never formally endowed with such a status.[22] A change in its statutes in 1868 empowered it to lend to other banks, underlining its special rank at the summit of the banking hierarchy. One further element of uncertainty remained to be lifted. The expiration of its issue privilege in 1871 weakened confidence in its banknotes, restricting ipso facto their circulation. On 15 January 1868, an imperial decree extended its privilege to 1 November 1881.

An interesting instance of relations between *Banque de l'Algérie* and *Banque de France* occurred in 1869. Algeria imported a wide range of goods from Rouen and, faced with exporters' demand for payment in Rouen rather than by drafts on Algeria, *Banque de l'Algérie* sought to open a current account at the Rouen branch of *Banque de France*. CEP, the *Banque de l'Algérie*'s representative, would pay *Banque de France* in Paris. For the latter, the operation amounted to a transfer yielding a commission. Baron Jean-Henri Hottinguer, a member of the *Conseil général* (board) of *Banque de France*, objected that the operation was a de facto domiciliation – *Banque de France* acting as the local representative of *Banque de l'Algérie* – and a service that the bank would be bound to provide others. The board concurred and the issue was sent to the *Comité des livres et portefeuilles* for further study.[23] Baron Alphonse Mallet[24] put the matter before the *Comité*. Article 63 of the internal rules and regulations of the *Banque de France* allowed the bank to pay for transactions of holders of current accounts, as long as there was acceptance of the drafts payable at the bank. But *Banque de l'Algérie* was, in effect, asking for the right to draw directly on *Banque de France*. Opening a current account at a branch where the holder is not represented locally (domiciled) was a precedent. Therein lay the problem. Some members of the *Comité* believed *Banque de l'Algérie* had to present drafts payable at the Rouen branch, while others were willing to make an exception.[25]

The case went back and forth between the *Conseil* and the *Comité*. Finally, a solution close to the proposal of *Banque de l'Algérie* was found. Rather than relying on drafts, *Banque de l'Algérie* would issue notes payable at the Rouen branch of the *Banque de France*. CEP would supply funds at the *Banque de France* in

Paris on account of *Banque de l'Algérie* in Rouen, all subject to a commission of 30 centimes per thousand francs. Thus, no privilege would be bestowed because prior deposit made it unnecessary to have a local representative. *Banque de l'Algérie* would have a partial current account, excluding borrowing rights. It was granted the portion not requiring domiciliation, that segment for which exemption was possible.[26] On this current account it would later purchase currency in France.

Banque de l'Algérie *and the Third Republic (1870–1880)*

No sooner were relations with *Banque de France* and with the state placed on a firmer footing than a change in the direction of political winds again put *Banque de l'Algérie* under pressure. In September 1870, the downfall of the Second Empire following France's military defeat at the hand of Prussia/Germany removed a pillar of support for the bank and left it exposed to suspicions of imperial allegiance on the part of the new republican regime. The bank lost the political backing it had come to rely on. Old antipathies towards its policies and the spectre of its replacement by the *Banque de France* came back to the fore, putting the bank at serious risk. Adolphe Villiers, the manager-chairman, exerted himself to assuage the new authorities. Their need for cash provided an opportunity. In October 1870, the bank agreed to make an advance of 10 million francs for 3 months at 6 per cent per annum, and in March 1871 another of 5 million on identical terms. It also relented in February 1874 to a request to pay 1 per cent interest on balances exceeding 4 million francs on the Treasury's current account – a revealing concession, since the *Banque de France* paid no interest on the state's account, and a costly one as deposits soared over the years.[27] Terms were renegotiated in January 1879 to make 1 per cent applicable on no more than 5 million francs.[28]

When *Banque de l'Algérie* broached the question of renewal of its issue privilege, the minister of finance Émile Dutilleul wrote to *Banque de France* on 6 December 1877 proposing merger between the two banks. It was fortunate for the Algiers bank that its Paris counterpart balked at the idea,[29] but it still had to tread softly, partly because the possibility of some form of linkage with *Banque de France* in Algeria was not completely laid to rest, partly because the opening of branches in Algiers and Oran by *Crédit lyonnais* in 1878 signaled more intense competition. Renewing its issue privilege took on added significance. The idea of merger was revived, and again the *Banque de France* turned it down. Jacques Lucet, a senator from Algeria, argued that the rules of *Banque de France* were too strict for an economy like that of Algeria, where some leniency was called for. It was reintroduced tangentially in the debate with a proposal to the effect that its banknotes be legal tender in Algeria in return for the same status being granted to *Banque de l'Algérie* banknotes in France. But *Banque de France*, aware that its notes fetched a premium in Algeria, could not accept reciprocity. Conferring the attribute of legal tender on its notes in Algeria was understandable; the same could not be said about *Banque de l'Algérie* banknotes in France. *Banque de France* expressed its willingness to establish business relations with *Banque de l'Algérie*. On 5 April 1880, the latter's privilege was renewed to 1 November 1897, a date which coincided with the expiry of the privilege of the Paris institution and perpetuated an informal association between the two banks.[30]

The overall growth of activities

Evolution of the bank's activity (Table 7.3) reveals a steady, if unspectacular, growth of the volume of discounts (number of bills discounted and amounts involved) from 1851 to 1867–1868. A greater-than-usual upward movement is registered as of 1864–1865, and its acceleration in the two years following the economic hardships of 1867 reflects recovery of the economy. There is a sharp drop in the number of bills discounted (but only a slight diminution of amounts) in 1870–1871 as war in France and an uprising in Algeria spelled a downturn for the economy. Within a year, the bank made up for the plunge and regular growth resumed.

There were significant jumps recorded in the number of bills discounted between 1875–1876 and 1876–1877 and between 1878–1879 and 1879–1880, despite the outbreak of an economic crisis in the eastern part of Algeria, around Constantine, and the country-wide recession it induced. On the other hand, amounts discounted fell between 1873–1874 and 1877–1878, probably due to smaller orders from importers in crisis-stricken Europe. Both the number of bills discounted and the amounts involved leapt forward between 1878–1879 and 1880–1881, and rose in tandem in 1881–1882. Banknotes in circulation were subject to a different tempo. There was a regular increase from 1851 to 1870, then a sudden doubling of the money supply from 1869–1870 to 1870–1871, setting a new floor from which to continue with moderate increases in subsequent years. Net profit rose at a consistent pace front every year. It nearly tripled between 1870–1871 and 1871–1872, the result of surges in discounts and banknotes put in circulation. As these two sources of income leveled off or fell slightly, so did profit. Making up on average less than one-tenth of discounts, rediscounts remained marginal business, an indication that *Banque de l'Algérie* was a privileged issue bank and a private commercial bank, but not primarily a bankers' bank.

Banque d'Algérie losing its bearings (1880–1900)

The renewal of privilege was accompanied with the right to double capital to 20 million francs and to issue banknotes for 20 million francs.[31] With little delay, on 28 October 1880, its equity was increased to the full amount permitted and paid up. This floatation raised the proportion of shareholders from Algeria in the *Banque de l'Algérie*'s capital. They subscribed to 7,084 shares out of the 20,000 issued, leaving 12,916 to investors from France.[32] It also more than tripled the proportion of large shareholders vis-à-vis smaller owners. Investors holding more than 150 shares – all above 300 shares – represented 12.9 per cent of the total before the doubling of equity. After the doubling, those above 300 shares were now 22.6 per cent of the total, while another 19 per cent held between 150 and 299 shares.[33] High dividends – 71 francs in 1879–1880 to 100 francs in 1882–1883 – had

Table 7.3 The activity of Banque de l'Algérie et de la Tunisie

	Number of bills discounted	Amount discounted (francs)	Amount rediscounted (francs)	Banknotes in circulation (francs)	Net profit (francs)	Paid-up capital (francs)
1851/2	11,906	8,755,964	9,322	729,939	32,929	1,050,000
1852/3	17,369	13,728,669	13,049	1,580,987	47,413	Id
1853/4	21,788	18,218,882	11,912	2,290,445	56,072	1,089,000
1854/5	25,025	20,491,439	12,976	2,621,000	68,997	Id
1855/6	31,718	21,840,707	17,320	2,743,150	90,510	1,966,500
1856/7	47,598	32,682,419	27,170	3,002,000	134,291	3,000,000
1857/8	57,736	39,595,268	—	3,475,000	—	Id
1858/9	66,233	43,342,538	33,044	3,735,000	175,466	Id
1859/60	79,000	53,942,530	43,522	4,085,700	208,957	Id
1860/1	88,169	61,983,728	52,971	4,179,800	193,647	4,000,000
1861/2	99,188	68,365,076	58,171	4,668,300	272,607	Id
1862/3	107,145	72,798,117	60,967	5,468,450	316,346	5,000,000
1863/4	102,569	77,884,541	59,250	5,036,950	320,816	Id
1864/5	104,552	78,324,612	—	6,047,300	—	Id
1865/6	121,586	96,329,727	97,674	7,162,800	323,634	Id
1866/7	118,872	97,503,296	95,483	7,496,600	320,456	Id
1867/8	120,867	112,340,899	106,892	10,210,300	330,592	Id
1868/9	146,385	125,525,783	111,585	13,344,250	330,558	Id
1869/70	178,757	153,151,647	—	15,812,875	—	Id
1870/1	111,098	150,931,116	197,183	34,732,450	360,580	Id
1871/2	202,588	203,288,351	230,050	42,744,120	914,211	10,000,000
1872/3	251,514	217,977,045	225,744	46,374,310	872,133	Id
1873/4	288,647	230,139,549	158,973	38,653,375	805,415	Id
1874/5	245,691	185,668,182	149,065	32,691,705	800,613	Id
1875/6	256,694	175,361,549	135,964	37,172,155	—	Id
1876/7	304,030	193,871,776	160,000	37,629,910	748,521	Id

1877/8	317,612	203,745,218	156,728	38,128,730	706,369	Id
1878/9	337,659	265,431,243	180,000	47,955,445	800,820	Id
1879/80	423,535	351,062,884	246,520	59,529,990	844,934	Id
1880/1	505,663	485,014,725	402,081	62,746,750	1,112,135	20,000,000 Id
1881/2	540,868	515,730,936	482,005	60,448,225	2,157,172	Id
1882/3	490,174	475,909,147	470,211	63,710,105	2,120,965	Id
1883/4	505,769	484,780,778	502,231	67,307,845	1,869,444	Id
1884/5	538,851	526,393,457	535,421	67,647,145	1,983,632	Id
1885/6	512,971	525,332,168	563,983	64,488,430	1,882,535	Id
1886/7	430,819	465,882,044	486,481	69,946,895	1,738,356	Id
1887/8	378,707	415,036,841	451,534	74,831,315	1,675,564	Id
1888/9	386,375	430,324,194	464,274	72,963,765	1,669,168	Id
1889/90	352,912	420,451,324	400,292	87,784,370	1,676,720	Id
1890/1	311,385	418,643,652	426,750	86,693,940	1,498,378	Id
1891/2	340,795	425,572,041	439,909	77,170,750	1,282,087	Id
1892/3	322,489	396,638,488	444,421	71,636,495	1,056,240	Id
1893/4	353,112	442,370,625	474,171	82,935,410	750,873	Id
1894/5	343,249	434,499,122	440,271	89,290,595	674,661	Id
1895/6	355,298	436,925,619	465,661	82,629,105	323,338	Id
1896/7	324,027	415,904,716	366,463	85,853,540	631,219	Id
1897/8	273,005	352,818,271	312,187	91,351,450	322,382	Id
1898/9	336,831	421,196,139	285,970	96,804,100	318,644	Id
1899/1900	410,837	501,784,374	329,725	95,902,490	430,589	Id
1900/01	400,944	458,064,714	278,481	101,923,000	639,994	Id
1901/02	486,233	468,966,934	288,191	104,365,930	642,605	Id
1902/03	545,927	560,673,043	366,558	120,696,690	636,583	Id
1903/04	622,447	713,075,494	455,165	118,492,060	841,979	Id
1904/05	700,042	781,464,747	401,746	116,913,660	850,670	Id
1905/06	866,217	966,515,859	574,216	126,271,480	847,001	Id
1906/07	957,068	1,187,715,031	899,937	142,427,950	1,180,777	Id

(continued)

Table 7.3 (Continued)

	Number of bills discounted	Amount discounted (francs)	Amount rediscounted (francs)	Banknotes in circulation (francs)	Net profit (francs)	Paid-up capital (francs)
1907/08	1,031,419	1,222,222,817	922,451	144,518,830	1,441,603	25,000,000
1908/09	1,067,268	1,229,764,183	867,544	145,781,510	2,649,022	Id
1909/10	1,054,152	1,275,275,864	1,135,118	183,229,910	2,720,781	Id
1910/11	1,148,467	1,460,580,701	1,449,130	204,814,560	3,256,867	Id
1911/12	1,187,792	1,705,128,620	1,591,566	216,326,620	4,747,365	Id
1912/13	1,309,822	2,086,946,232	1,801,436	228,466,150	6,606,705	Id
1913/14	1,062,393	1,533,068,394	455,310	354,207,225	7,808,605	Id
1914/15	122,275	649,044,944	1,151,249	416,583,835	4,406,613	Id
1915/16	204,815	952,103,796	1,098,266	469,817,995	4,732,610	Id
1916/17	269,213	1,386,476,224	1,976,392	593,992,560	6,226,891	Id
1917/18	228,464	1,405,793,600	2,697,983	884,106,360	6,339,724	Id
1918/19	231,312	1,492,839,284	1,384,948	1,148,671,620	7,663,894	Id
1919/20	354,063	2,877,041,092	3,494,035	1,212,706,315	9,281,430	Id
1920/1	398,478	4,220,256,998	2,900,265	1,024,976,855	12,257,958	Id
1921/2	414,919	3,358,270,202	1,817,786	802,314,095	14,010,290	Id
1922/3	598,301	4,243,309,725	4,043,588	1,034,341,915	14,452,392	Id
1923/4	747,761	7,461,702,580	5,018,242	1,173,191,200	15,756,261	Id
1924/5	984,442	8,343,020,725	8,429,815	1,157,065,470	16,602,028	Id
1925/6	1,046,790	9,107,590,008	6,601,072	1,483,178,660	17,923,387	Id
1926/7	1,039,492	8,799,375,452	7,334,242	1,375,799,925	20,293,216	Id
1927/8	1,150,741	8,475,250,493	6,985,271	1,807,499,680	22,950,864	Id
1928/9	1,640,033	12,491,921,017	8,060,000	2,203,755,725	25,104,461	Id
1929/30	2,019,529	17,273,571,577	8,278,819	2,146,520,320	24,607,198	Id
1930/1	2,036,517	16,592,597,213	7,513,986	2,043,940,860	23,036,129	Id
1931/2	2,140,536	15,547,550,515	5,501,000	2,009,714,000	16,660,507	Id
1932/3	1,765,012	17,003,926,690	5,640,430	2,079,274,320	16,582,592	Id
1933/4	1,539,302	17,268,056,377	6,739,769	2,100,675,760	16,722,555	Id

Year							
1934/5	1,347,304	13,804,555,380	6,168,817	1,954,139,105	16,941,019		Id
1935/6	1,244,724	13,425,089,264	7,379,474	2,110,878,365	17,139,625		Id
1936/7	1,206,134	14,962,088,569	9,167,426	2,382,682,030	17,220,461		Id
1937/8	1,348,052	19,583,956,425	10,860,660	3,185,939,380	18,535,100		Id
1938/9	1,300,020	23,031,149,713	11,066,211	4,124,916,940	19,042,098		Id
1939/40	515,066	24,566,617,718	15,105,698	5,740,658,920	20,688,440		Id
1940/1	286,982	30,713,942,105	33,445,565	8,010,714,340	20,761,217		Id
1941/2	178,903	8,659,552,805	—	14,746,145,060	37,929,541		Id
1942/3	74,091	9,275,255,799	—	26,435,499,615	36,644,254		Id
1943/4	96,416	15,450,658,098	—	—	—		Id
1945	—	19,032,089,015	—	32,303,845,870	36,676,313		Id
1946	—	52,033,806,435	—	39,803,949,310	19,627,233		Id
1947	—	72,355,000,000	—	47,354,100,825	230,841,211		Id
1948	—	11,448,000,000	—	59,433,150,415	193,081,749		Id
1949	—	15,138,000,000	30,485,170,000	69,624,213,630	547,897,604		Id
1950	—	17,000,000,000	32,312,166,000	80,289,363,670	570,039,141		Id
1951	—	26,850,000,000	47,490,694,000	90,753,958,450	474,869,506		Id
1952	—	26,300,000,000	60,745,985,000	102,372,564,020	1,401,393,513		Id
1953	—	25,677,594,000	52,628,880,000	107,538,444,990	1,637,182,486		Id
1954	—	24,217,942,000	51,600,000,000	121,533,698,000	1,587,018,152		Id
1955	—	19,187,513,000	34,669,067,000	143,124,471,000	1,394,595,067		Id
1956	—	18,676,142,000	38,288,004,000	191,342,872,000	1,555,534,281		Id
1957	—	19,680,700,000	18,406,539,000	207,349,553,000	1,625,353,916		Id
1958	—	17,262,973,000	17,966,042,000	206,539,360,500	2,266,254,319		Id
1959	—	—	—	206,081,619,000	2,500,078,540		Id
1960	—	NF 283,056,000	NF 1,080,977,000	NF 2,274,680,480	NF 2,172,591	2,000,000,000	Id
1961	—	—	—	NF 2,417,888,330	NF 2,383,755	NF 20,000,000	Id

Source: CAOM, 80S/1,2,3 (there are gaps in the internal records). Rediscounts from 1947 to 1960 are from annual reports.
Net profit is amount given in minutes of the board, lower than that presented to shareholders

boosted the price of *Banque de l'Algérie* stock. With shares quoted at 1,502 francs and new shares issued at 935 francs, directors and shareholders would pocket a substantial profit of 567 francs, if only share price could be maintained thanks to hefty dividends generated by way of an increase in business.[34] Moreover, volume of banknotes issued could now expand and total circulation gain greater velocity thanks to the new fractional currency.

A new stage of growth and diversification

The bank was now set for extension of its activities. Thirsting for easier credit and unfamiliar with the rules of issue banking, settlers wanted nothing more than a loosening of the tight policies of the bank and a redirection of the flow of lending towards the agricultural sector. Demand was brisk, and *Banque de l'Algérie* did everything to attract it, including the opening of local discount banking offices (*Comptoirs d'escompte*) in towns close to rural districts of the interior and the use of roving salesmen to canvass prospective borrowers. Other financial institutions entered the field. Under the aegis of the Crédit foncier de France, *Crédit foncier & agricole d'Algérie* was created in 1880.[35] Settlers were switching from wheat to grapes, a process that would cover northern Algeria with vineyards and make wine the leading Algerian export. On the one hand, wheat had become less profitable; on the other, phylloxera was wreaking havoc with the wine production of southern France. Timing was right to penetrate the French market with Algerian produce. Many crisis-stricken mainland winegrowers crossed the Mediterranean penniless and gave impetus to the transition by pursuing their trade with borrowed money in Algeria. *Banque de l'Algérie* acted as the financial agent of the process. It had been asked by the government to grant credit to *colons* during procedures for the renewal of its issue privilege. Tacit acceptance by the bank was a precondition for authorization to double its capital.

And so, *Banque de l'Algérie* embarked on lending on a large scale for the planting of vines.[36] But since a return was possible only at the end of three years, growers could not reimburse their loans quickly enough to restore to the bank its lending capacity. Instead it took the easy road of increasing the money supply. In 1883, when it sought a 10 million franc loan from *Banque de France*, it was turned down because of suspicion it did have the statutory minimum cash in hand to cover its banknotes in circulation.[37] *Banque de l'Algérie* used its newly increased capital. Net profit doubled between 1880–1881 and 1881–1882; the dividend was maintained; the share price was driven upward. A way to prosperity had been found, and everything was done to apply an apparently winning formula. Throwing caution to the wind, *Banque de l'Algérie* lent liberally. But its position was precarious.

It had strayed from the path of issue-cum-commercial banking and become an agricultural bank offering loans having crops as collateral as well as a de facto mortgage bank. Discounted bills went into its portfolio in greater quantity and amounts than ever, but they were more agricultural than commercial paper. Much of it was not secured by expected crops – in effect, agricultural collateral – but solely by the hope the land would be developed.[38] Its statutes forbade lending beyond 100 days. As a rule, an issue bank has to hold liquid assets like cash (foreign currency), bullion or commercial bills as a guarantee for its banknotes; but, violating orthodoxy, *Banque de l'Algérie* took to renewing short-term advances and filled its portfolio with mortgage contracts, becoming immobilized with longer-term assets, difficult to realize in case of need. The volume of banknotes in circulation was higher than what the statutes authorized in relation to the immediate cashable value of the portfolio.

Banque de l'Algérie *and the phylloxera and rural crisis*

In the summer of 1885, the forces of nature acted in the opposite direction. While vineyards were back in operation in France, those in Algeria produced poor crops and had to contend with phylloxera. The following year, drought, locusts and hail were visited upon Algerian farmland. Crop yields were dismal, and crisis spread quickly to the entire agricultural sector. Previously boosted to artificial heights by open-handed credit, land values plummeted; lending ground to a halt; borrowers forewent repaying altogether. Alarm bells sounded. The attention of authorities was drawn to the bank. According to its statutes, the general manager is appointed by the president of the Republic, on recommendation of the minister of finance. In October 1886, chairman Ernest Chevallier, a man closely identified with freewheeling growth and quick profits, was replaced by Félix Nelson-Chiérico, a government paymaster (*trésorier-payeur général*) and a former prefect. The choice of a civil servant with no banking background signaled a change of direction.

The new course outlined in the program of 24 November 1887 did nothing to make hard times more bearable. Euphoric years were a dim memory and the lending spree a thing of the past. The bank now demanded immediate repayment from borrowers, tightened credit, foreclosed, expropriated and dispossessed as vigorously as it had lent. Clearing out bad debts was the order of the day. Planters whose estates and livelihood depended on credit were cut adrift just as they found themselves in dire straits. Adding to the misery, mildew made its appearance in vineyards in 1890. There ensued bitter denunciations of the harshness of management's new policy, along with all of the bank's doings from day one, excoriated as nothing more than swindles and deceitful moneymaking schemes.[39] A brochure expressing satisfaction with the bank was published, but the author preferred anonymity.[40] Land acquired at inflated prices quickly depreciated; it was often barren and worth little. Auctions by the bank found few buyers despite rock-bottom opening prices. Algeria's issue bank turned into the country's largest landowner, saddled with overvalued property. Instead of secured banknotes, cash in hand or discounted bills, real estate became its core asset. It tended its domain while waiting for the appropriate moment to unload it at a profit. The bank's situation remained perilous.

Returning on course (1900–1914)

Setting its account on a better footing was the prime task of the bank throughout the 1890s. The immobilizations, a lack of available cash, a bloated portfolio containing questionable assets and circulation of banknotes far surpassing the statutory limit of three times cash or metallic currency in hand were the main problems. Book value of real estate had been 22.6 million francs; it was written down to 8 million.[41] Between 1887 and 1892, the portfolio was disencumbered of worthless paper. Outstanding bills valued at 32.1 million were withdrawn by way of redemption or levy on reserves; a remaining portion of unpaid bills estimated at 7.3 million was transferred to a new 'Liquidation' account.[42] The bank tried to improve its accounts by calling upon new resources. In 1889, the *Banque de France* relented to an advance of 40 million at 3 per cent, instead of 4 per cent.[43] *Banque de l'Algérie* complained that interest due on the growing credit balance of the Treasury's account amounted to one-half of its yearly profits. It worked out less stringent arrangements with the Ministry of Finance in 1893 and 1895. Dividend paid out was down to 50 francs in 1892–1893 and it kept sliding; by 1896–1897, it stood at no more than 15 francs.

The bank was at pains to shore up its accounts, demonstrate that it possessed appropriate assets to back up its banknotes and improve its reputation as the moment of renewal of its privilege approached. In 1897, it wrote branch managers to deny a rumour to the effect that it would no longer renew bills presented for discount. Rather than a draconian general rule, it urged managers to examine transactions one by one and to show prudence, tact and consideration in order to reassure customers.[44] The rumour was not baseless, as the sentiment of board members proved a few months later. When Amédée Rihouet, the manager-chairman, proposed to use the extraordinary reserve to reduce the portfolio by half, other board members objected, preferring to attain the same end by not renewing maturing bills of large debtors and demanding reimbursement.[45]

Government and parliamentarians subjected *Banque de l'Algérie* to intensive scrutiny and criticism. The specter of *Banque de France* being called in to Algeria reappeared to haunt *Banque de l'Algérie*, much to the chagrin of businessmen in Algiers, now largely supportive of their local bank. The latter had to part with its real estate by selling it at market value to a new and separate company, *Société domaniale*, which promptly went into bankruptcy. In 1897, its privilege was extended two years only, then a third until 31 October 1900. Marc Lafon, an *inspecteur des Finances* (that is a high civil servant of the Ministry of Finance), was appointed manager-chairman on 18 May 1898. The bank argued that it had cleared away a substantial portion of its illiquid assets, that its portfolio was now almost entirely of commercial origin, that it had lowered the costly Treasury account by two-thirds, that its reserves were nearly at par with capital and that its real-estate holdings had been written down by means of special reserves and sales.[46] In return for the one year extension, the manager had to commit to complete disappearance of real estate from the balance sheet, and to achieving by 31 October 1900 equilibrium between immobilizations and liquidations, on the one hand, and reserves, on the other.[47]

A law passed on 5 July 1900 finally renewed the privilege for a longer period, to 31 December 1920 – a date coinciding, tellingly, with that of the *Banque de France*'s privilege. The extension was subject to review in 1911, and there were conditions. While banknote circulation was freed from the obligation to hold cash in hand as a guarantee, it could not exceed 150 million francs (regime of the 'legal ceiling'). Head office had to be moved from Algiers to Paris in order to shield lending policy from local influences and temptations to loosen rules. Some deputies leaned towards the idea of lightening the burden that interest charged on the Treasury account represented for the bank by having *Banque de France* open a low-interest current account on its behalf; but nothing came of it. Instead, the bank had to pay the state an annual fee starting at 200,000 francs – rising to 250,000 from 1906 to 1912 and to 300,000 from 1913 to 1920 – and to lend it 3 million francs without interest for the duration of the concession. Both sums were to be deposited in a special Treasury account and eventually serve to provide agricultural credit, outside the purview of the bank.[48] As it did with real estate, the bank would withdraw from the countryside altogether. It could no longer discount bills relating to agriculture, whether for cultivation or for land development. But *colons* in Algeria were not in tune with central government in Paris. They continued to request working capital for seasonal planting needs and to protest the bank's refusal to discount bills based on rural property, calling in the governor general to plead on their behalf. The board responded by pointing to the law of 5 July 1900, by giving examples of the leniency shown to debtors in arrears and by stressing that safeguarding its banknotes was its primary responsibility.[49]

After hitting bottom between 1893 and 1895, the Algerian economy began to emerge from the doldrums in 1897 when demand for Algerian wines picked up in France. Prosperity was the hallmark of the years leading up to WWI, and the bank was one of the beneficiaries. Newcomers appeared on the North African scene; in 1913, *Société générale* and *Société marseillaise de crédit* opened branches in Algeria. Under the terms of the law of 5 July 1900, the bank was allowed to operate in France's African possessions; subsequently, the decree of 8 January 1904 granted it the power to discount bills to circulate Algerian banknotes bearing the stamp '*Tunisie*' in the neighbouring protectorate of Tunisia. On 11 April 1907, it was permitted to increase its capital to 25 million francs and its circulation to 200 million. Review of its privilege in 1911 concluded with a positive assessment and a law passed on 29 December 1911. Circulation limit was raised to 250 million. Payment of the fixed annual fee to the state was waived in favour of a fee proportional to banknote circulation above the volume of metallic currency held by the bank; minimum payment would be 750,000 francs. At the same time, the bank now had to advance to government 5 million for use in Algeria and to provide banking services free of charge to local administration. It was also allowed to open branches in Morocco, as part of France's penetration in the sultanate.

From 1900 onwards, discounts, circulation and performance were on the rise, a trend that continued until the war (Table 7.3). The value of discounts in 1913–1914 was more than three times the level of 1899–1900; rediscounting continued to be marginal. The bank assumed for free the service of the government of Algeria's loan issued on 19 July 1902. The progression of its activities was rapid and results appreciable, despite the cost inherent in launching operations in Tunisia. On 14 August 1912, a decree raised circulation ceiling to 300 million francs. The portfolio of discounted bills swelled, but profit flowing therefrom went almost completely to covering expenses, especially interest on the soaring Treasury current account. Consequently, to secure additional revenue, the bank raised the discount rate.[50] From 4.5 per cent in 1909, it rose to 5 per cent on 6 November 1912, to 5.5 per cent on 16 November 1912 and to 6 per cent on 28 December 1912. Reaction from the business community was not long in coming, sustained by the fact that the *Banque de France* rate for bills from Algeria was 4.5 per cent or 5 per cent. *Banque de l'Algérie* set the level of the discount rate in Algeria. It handled half of Algeria's discounts, the other half belonging to branches of French commercial banks. The author of a pamphlet noted that, as a counterpart of privilege, the bank held the Treasury account in Algeria. It had at its disposal 100 million francs on which it paid an average interest of 2 per cent and 200 million subject to payment of 2.375 per cent. It then turned around and lent at 6 per cent, pocketing an easy mark-up at the expense of local business. Logically, the author called for a repeal of the privilege of the bank and the opening of a branch of *Banque de France* in Algiers.[51]

War and its aftermath (1914–1939)

The outbreak of WWI led French authorities to take financial measures in France and in Algeria. A general moratorium left many outstanding debts unpaid. To prevent abandonment of banknotes in favour of metallic currency or bullion, the banknotes of *Banque de France* and those of *Banque de l'Algérie* became inconvertible legal tender in their respective territories on 5 August 1914. The ceiling for circulation in Algeria was raised to 400 million francs in order to provide means of exchange. Decrees in 1914, 1915, 1918, 1919, 1920 and 1925 raised the amount to 1,700 million. From 1914 to 1918, the bank advanced a total of 406,280,989 francs cash to the state[52] and received 3 month Treasury bills at 1 per cent, to be raised to 3 per cent after the end of hostilities.[53] It bought National Defence bills as assets. The authorities in Algeria, Tunisia and Morocco borrowed from the bank. Whereas banknote circulation increased during the war, discounting and profits, not unexpectedly, fell and then picked up as of 1916–1917 (Table 7.2). It is interesting to note that, while the amounts discounted after the war returned to pre-war nominal levels, their real value was down because of rise of prices and depreciation of the franc. The fact that the number of bills discounted remained low was an indication that business remained slack.

Algeria prospered during the war from the export to France of foodstuffs and other necessities at high prices, and *Banque de l'Algérie* was a stakeholder in the economy. Discussion of the bank's privilege following the war occurred in the light of its rising profitability. The law of 29 December 1918 extended its privilege to 31 December 1945. The annual fee remained along the lines set in 1911, the minimum being 750,000 francs.[54] The bank's advance free of interest to the state rose from 5 million to 18 million; if annual dividend was above 150 francs after tax, it would pay the state the equivalent of one-half of the excess amount; it had to service checks and transfers free of charge for the Treasury in Algeria. More original was the obligation to create and extend credit to a sister bank called *Banque industrielle de l'Afrique du Nord*, which was intended to foster the growth of industry, given that the fall of exports from France during the war had prompted entrepreneurs in Algeria to begin local production.[55] Having to lend long term, it would have to borrow long term, a calculus far removed from issue and discount banking.

During the debate, Marius Moutet, a socialist deputy (and a future minister of Colonies in the 1930s and 1940s), spoke on 12 September 1918 against renewal on the grounds that *Banque de l'Algérie* was not a state bank from which the state could borrow,[56] or a bankers' bank acting as a lender of last resort, but a private company. As an issue bank, it had to hold short-term assets, but as a private bank, it was expected to provide longer-term credit. The lesser number of bills discounted in relation to the stability of the total amount appeared to be a bias of the bank in favour of rich clients. Moutet was an advocate of putting up the privilege for auction, in effect launching a new bank.[57] The French government was opposed to turning *Banque de l'Algérie* into a state bank. Nor did it favour the old idea of substituting *Banque de France* for *Banque de l'Algérie*, precisely because the former was primarily an issue bank managing the money supply and a rediscount bank; Algeria was in need of more, to wit an issue bank that would also provide capital for ordinary economic activity. So the privilege of *Banque de l'Algérie* was extended, but in exchange for more concessions from the bank.[58]

It rendered services to the state, and vice versa. In 1921 and 1923, without charge, the bank represented Algeria in the negotiation of loans and accepted to be the intermediary for servicing the resulting debts. For its part, the government issued a decree on 5 December 1925 raising the 'legal ceiling' of the bank's circulation from 1,300 million francs to 1,700 million, then another on 6 August 1926 setting the maximum at 2,100 million. One concession the bank declined was a return to agricultural credit, despite appeals from local parties; memories of the near debacle of the 1880s and 1890s were still fresh.[59] In 1929, the question of the limit on the volume of banknotes issued by *Banque de l'Algérie* gave rise to instructive exchanges between the bank and French officials. The context was the stabilization of the French franc after years of inflation and monetary turbulence caused by WWI. In keeping with the law of 25 June 1928, *Banque de France* was subjected to stricter rules; it had to guarantee its banknote circulation by a much higher proportion of gold and cash. In effect, this meant a curtailment of issue, a lowering of profits and a scaling down of credit put at the disposal of the economy through discounting and rediscounting of bills, advances, loans, etc.

Would the same principle apply to *Banque de l'Algérie*, the only issue bank subject to a 'legal ceiling,' a system lacking flexibility and adjustable only through changes in the law? It was reluctant to be bound by a return to the 'cash in hand' rule, which would result in a lowering of the volume of banknotes in circulation, a rise in the discount rate and disengagement by the bank from the Algerian economy. As for the choice between maintaining the 'legal ceiling' or raising it, the bank professed to be indifferent.

> Shareholders are no more interested in seeing the issue limit elevated than they are in having it remain at the present level. If it rises, circulation increases and the rate of discount stays moderate. If its does not, the bank will have to take restrictive measures, the most efficient of which is a sharp ascent in the rate of discount, leading to an increase in profits, much to the advantage of shareholders.[60]

The *Mouvement général des fonds* of the French Ministry of Finance (the Treasury Department) proposed a project according to which *Banque de l'Algérie* would have on hand in bullion, gold currency,[61] *Banque de France* banknotes and current accounts at *Banque de France* the equivalent of at least 35 per cent of the total of its banknotes and creditor current accounts. If banknote circulation was less than 3 billion francs, the percentage of legal cover was scaled down according to echelon, the lowest being 20 per cent for a circulation of less than 2,200 million francs. As much as *Banque de l'Algérie* wished to be free of the limitations of a ceiling, it did not favour a return to the system of predetermined proportions of cash to keep idly on hand. Its board 'could not view without apprehension the application to Algeria's issue bank, whose role as a discount bank was of primary importance to the colony, of rigorous rules justified exclusively by monetary principles valid for banks whose discount role was negligible next to their monetary function.'[62] In Algeria, the consequence would be a rise in the rate of discount. The board countered with two proposals: the first accepted a proportion of 30 per cent of circulation, escalating to 35 per cent for a circulation exceeding 2,100 million francs; the second established a scale ranging from 20 per cent to 35 per cent with levels of circulation starting at 2,300 million and capping at 3,500 million. It also urged revision of the obligation to pay interest on the Treasury's current account for sums whose matching funds were up to 35 per cent immobilized and unproductive.

One month later, the *Mouvement général des fonds* resubmitted the idea of 35 per cent cover, coupled with the rule of one-third proportion in bullion and gold currency, but without a sliding scale applying to different amounts in circulation. A new scale of interest for positive balances on the Treasury's current account was submitted: from no interest for up to 25 million francs to 3.5 percent for over 250 million. Considering that the bank already held the required liquid assets to comply with the 35 per cent requirement, the board accepted, thus ending the 'legal ceiling' system instituted by the law of 5 July 1900.[63] The bank later obtained the possibility of temporarily lowering the proportion to 30 per cent under certain conditions.[64] In return for the lifting of the 'legal ceiling,' a convention signed on 4 July 1929 increased the interest-free advance to the state to 30 million francs and the annual fee from 750,000 francs to 10 million.

But the bill tabled in the French Chamber of Deputies on 5 July 1929 could not be adopted before summer break, and the 'legal ceiling' system remained in place: on 1 August 1929, it was raised to 2,400 million francs. Another convention signed on 3 July 1930 provided for an interest-free advance of 50 million to Algeria and 6 million to 10 million to Tunisia. But the ceiling system was not replaced. On 15 February 1932, the interest-free advance went up to 80 million francs, and, on 9 April 1932, the maximum banknote circulation was set at 3,000 million. The latter was raised to 4,000 million francs on 17 June 1938, a change stemming less from an increase in business transactions than from the repercussions of three devaluations of the French franc.[65]

Throughout the 1920s, the *Banque de l'Algérie*'s activity expanded regularly as evidenced by the rise in the number of bills discounted, the amount of discounts, circulation and net profit (Table 7.3). As it sought to reinforce its capacity to issue banknotes, authorities took into account the bank's performance and, as quid pro quo for their acquiescence in renewing its privilege, sought advantages in favour of France and Algeria. The world economic crisis reached Algeria in 1931, starting a downward trend in the discount business that accelerated with the onset of war. Pickup in amounts discounted from 1937–1938 to 1940–1941 was testimony the depreciation of the franc, not to improving commercial climate. The negative impact of slow business was offset by constancy in the issuance of banknotes. Thanks to this relatively inexpensive source of credit, profits, although sagging, avoided a tumble.

Strategic fanning out: Tunisia, Morocco, industrial banking

In addition to the ten branches it had opened in Algeria, *Banque de l'Algérie* looked beyond its main market. Means of payment were in short supply in neighbouring Tunisia. The decree of 8 January 1904 authorizing it to issue banknotes and practice discounting of bills in Tunisia provided for several measures it was obliged to carry out in return. It had to pay a fixed fee for the banknotes it put in circulation; the amount was set at 66,666 francs until 31 December 1905, 83,333 francs until 31 December 1912 and 100,000 until 31 December 1920. It also had to conduct ordinary banking services for the Treasury at no charge, and to lend the Regency 1 million francs free of interest throughout the duration of the privilege for use in developing agriculture.[66] The portfolio increased from 4 million francs in 1907 to 229 million in 1908; banknote circulation went from 18 million in 1910 to 49 million in 1915.[67] The decree of 30 December 1918 renewed the privilege for 25 years, from 1 January 1921 to 31 December 1945.

In Morocco, the hopes of *Banque de l'Algérie* were short-lived. The Algerian franc entered the sultanate in 1907 as a means of facilitating French military expenses. *Banque de l'Algérie*'s foray began formally with the law of 29 December 1911 that allowed it to open branches. It had to tread softly because of the creation in 1906 of the *Banque d'État du Maroc*, an international institution resulting from the Tangiers crisis of 1905 and the subsequent Algesiras conference.[68] In 1912, *Banque de l'Algérie* opened a subsidiary, *Banque algéro-tunisienne*, to promote use of the Algerian franc. When the international crisis of the summer of 1914 induced a run by depositors, that latter, flush with metallic currency, was able to come to the aid of other banks. By the decree of 5 August, like the banknotes of *Banque de France*, those of *Banque de l'Algérie* were made legal tender in the French zone of Morocco and were imported on a large scale.

After the war, French authorities tried unsuccessfully to bring about a rapprochement between *Banque de l'Algérie* and *Banque d'État du Maroc*. The former would become a shareholder in the latter by way of acquisition of the German portion of equity. The two banks would exchange directors and open reciprocal current accounts. Should the 8 March 1920 arrangement be successful, the *Banque de l'Algérie*'s subsidiary would be closed. But *Banque de l'Algérie* acquired the German share on 2 June 1921 and intended to absorb *Banque d'État du Maroc*. However, *Banque d'État du Maroc* was backed by the powerful *banque d'affaires* (investment bank), *Banque de Paris et des Pays-Bas*. Among other tensions, the presence side by side of two competing currencies was not conducive to amicable relations between the partners. In 1925, Algerian banknotes were withdrawn from Morocco, and BAT was bought out then liquidated by its rival: *Banque de l'Algérie* had thus failed to establish a foothold in Morocco.[69]

In addition to expanding geographically, *Banque de l'Algérie* diversified by attempting to enter the industrial sector. This was a novel activity for an issue and commercial bank. Shortages and the fall of imports from France during the war engendered unsatisfied demand in Algeria and created opportunities for local industrial production in Algeria. Some manufacturing got underway with the ebbing of outside competition, a form of natural unlegislated protectionism, and interest grew around the idea of sustaining this budding industrialization. *Banque de l'Algérie* pondered the feasibility of taking part. The inquiry it carried out in 1916–17 returned a positive assessment of Algeria's industrial potential, and the law of 29 December 1918 renewing the bank's privilege provided for the creation of *Banque industrielle de l'Afrique du Nord* (BIAN). It was constituted on 11 August 1919. It had a capital of 12.5 million francs, 10 million of which were to be subscribed by shareholders of *Banque de l'Algérie* with the balance made available to the public. An advance of 10 million francs free of interest from *Banque de l'Algérie* supplemented the new bank's working capital.

However, no sooner had the war ended than French imports returned on the Algerian market, driving out lower-quality local products and dashing hopes for further industrialization. Food processing and construction materials were the only sectors having a fair chance of holding their own. Uniquely favourable wartime conditions were a thing of the past, and BIAN had few available outlets for long-term industrial investment. In fact, after initial acquisitions of shares in companies, it began to sell out. Its portfolio of shares in companies fell from 3,046,000 francs in 1920 to 679,000 in 1927. Instead it used its funds in classical short-term discounting of commercial bills of modest unitary value. That item on the balance sheet went from 35 million (with 5,580 bills) in 1920 to 542 million (65,073 bills) in 1927. Even debtor current accounts fell off. BIAN never succeeded in acting as a genuine *banque d'affaires*; it quickly became less a banker for industry than a traditional commercial bank, competing to some extent with other discount houses.[70]

The Second World War and the nationalization of central banks

War in Spain, tension in the Mediterranean, the Czech crisis of September 1938, the outbreak of war in September 1939 and the defeat of France in the May–June 1940 provoked runs on banks in North Africa, withdrawal of deposits and, before the war, massive transfers of funds in search of security in France. Like other financial institutions, *Banque de l'Algérie* had to weather the storm. It endeavoured to keep capital in North Africa even while maintaining its rate of discount at a maximum of 5 per cent, a level lower than that of *Banque de France*.[71] With the signing of the armistice, money returned to bank accounts and accumulated in substantial amounts – a sure sign, not of wealth, but of stagnant business conditions drying up demand for credit.

Banque de l'Algérie advanced 1,000 million francs to the French government on 11 May 1939 and another 1,000 million on 30 December 1940, both operations at 0.75 per cent. It lent 8,000 million francs at 0.75 per cent on 31 December 1942, then 4,000 million on 12 July 1943 and 4,000 million on 4 July 1944, both loans at 0.50 per cent. By 1944, the outstanding amount lent to authorities stood at 16,000 million francs.[72] The war debt was gradually paid off and the slate cleared on 7 January 1952. Maximum banknote circulation was raised to 7,000 million francs on 31 December 1940, then to 10,000 million on 13 September 1941. During the war, hoarding was commonplace and widespread. As economic activity slowed, discounting of bills fell precipitously. Lending to the state shored up profits (Table 7.3). The bank concentrated on managing assets diverted from occupied France to North Africa, as well as accumulated payments on previous North African exports to France.[73]

The nationalization of *Banque de France* on 2 December 1945 pointed to a similar outcome for *Banque de l'Algérie*. Pending a decision, its privilege, ending on 31 December 1945, was extended 3 months, to 31 March 1946. On 17 May 1946, the French state became the owner of the bank, and former shareholders received compensation in the form of registered (*nominatives*) but negotiable bonds. Although the privilege had lapsed on 1 April 1946, the bank continued to operate. The public's indifference to the legal void was a measure of the extent to which its banknotes had become a part of daily life.

The situation in Tunisia required attention. The transfer rendered obsolete the bank's convention with the Regency. Its future there was in doubt, the more so given that operations in the Tunisian market had been a source of losses from 1943 to 1947.[74] Nationalism emerged as an economic factor after the war. The idea of setting up a purely Tunisian issue bank was mooted in the Arabic press and in the Tunisian section of the Grand Council, possibly through nationalization of *Banque de Tunisie*, *Banca italiana di credito* and *Banque franco-tunisienne*.[75] Separation of the issue and discount functions with the aim of establishing two distinct departments was under study.[76] There was resistance to renewal of the privilege of the bank in the Tunisian section of the Grand Council, where some advocated postponement of the decision.[77] Renewal was ratified on condition that the 25-year renewal be broken into an initial period of ten years, followed by five-year extensions. Facing an uncertain future, the bank expressed reservations about the idea of staggered renewal, and French authorities concurred.[78]

A decree issued on 5 August 1948 finally renewed the privilege retroactively for 25 years from 1 April 1946 to 31 December 1970. The advance free of charge to Tunisia went from 34 million francs to 500 million francs. France ceded for free half the ownership – 35 per cent to Algeria, 15 per cent to Tunisia – in the bank now renamed *Banque de l'Algérie et de la Tunisie*. Maximum authorized circulation was 60,000 million francs. On 31 December 1948, it stood at 59,433,150,415 francs (46,975,222,305 in Algeria; 12,457,928,110 in Tunisia).[79] At the request of the *Résident général*, the ceiling for Tunisia was raised to 20,000 million.[80] In 1950, the management of the business was split between two offices: one in Algiers for operations in Algeria, the other in Tunis for activities in Tunisia.[81]

Final reorientation and liquidation

The new owners of *Banque de l'Algérie et de la Tunisie* now appointed the governor and the board of directors, six of whose members were named by France, six by Algeria and three by Tunisia. Most directors were to be higher officials in the French Ministry of Finance, such as Jacques Brunet, Emmanuel Monick, François Bloch-Lainé, André Postel-Vinay, Roger Goetze and Pierre-Paul Schweitzer.[82]

The nationalization had a tangible effect on the policy and orientation of *Banque de l'Algérie et de la Tunisie*. Throughout the earlier part of its history, alongside its function as an issuer of banknotes, it was basically a commercial bank, discounting bills like any other private institution. Rediscounting, a function associated with a bankers' bank, amounted at most to one-tenth of its business as a discounter. *Banque de l'Algérie et de la Tunisie* was not a genuine central bank; and, after its nationalization, rediscounting increased significantly, so much so that, at least from 1949 on, it became more substantial than discounting (Table 7.3). The pattern set since the foundation of the bank in 1851 was reversed: 'This evolution conveys well the policy of the bank which never ceased during the last fifteen years to assert its role as a bank of issue, while continuing to provide credit necessary to guarantee the most favourable conditions for the economy.'[83] In 1948, the bank discounted commercial paper at 5 per cent; its rediscount rate was 3.25 per cent or 3.75 per cent.[84]

Strong emphasis was put on providing ample quantities of banknotes to lubricate economic activity. The legal maximum for circulation rose rapidly from 60,000 million francs in 1948 to 300,000 million in 1958.[85] The Tunisian circulation oscillated between one-quarter and one-third of Algeria's from 1945 to 1953.[86] The bank continued to advance sums in a steady stream to the state. For instance, in 1952–1953, these ranged from 1,000 million francs to 12,000 million francs for periods of one day to a few weeks.[87] State auditors pointed out the risky nature of the bank's accounts. The portfolio comprised paper based largely on immobilized assets and equipment whose market value would plummet in case of crisis. More than *Banque de France*, the *Banque de l'Algérie et de la Tunisie*'s fate was linked to the general economic environment.[88] Uncertainty justified an increase of share capital from 25 million francs to 2,000 million by incorporation of a part of the reserves in 1959.

In some respects, *Banque de l'Algérie et de la Tunisie* was a unique financial establishment. Revenue from discounts and rediscounts was insufficient to cover with any guarantee of stability the expenses inherent in banknote circulation and operation of an issue bank. Other banks, like *Banque de l'Indochine, Banque de l'Afrique occidentale* and *Banque de Madagascar* drew revenues from their stock-holding in various companies. All four colonial banks held accounts in France whose credit balances represented the equivalent of the amounts transferred from France to its overseas territories. *Banque de l'Algérie et de la Tunisie* built up liquid resources in Paris thanks to the cashing of bills it discounted in Algeria and to Treasury transfers waiting to be made in the direction of Algeria. It developed these interest-producing assets as a safeguard against sudden fluctuations in its commercial discount business in Algeria and Tunisia. The Paris account (Table 7.4), denominated in French francs, dispensed the bank from holding large amounts of gold as security for the banknotes it issued.[89] Assets in gold and metallic currency were approximately equivalent in value to other, more liquid,

Table 7.4 Banque de l'Algérie et de la Tunisie accounts in Paris and Algiers

31 December	Credit balance in Paris (assets)	Treasury current account in Algiers (liabilities)
	Millions of francs	
1945	853	4,463
1946	1,138	5,227
1947	660	1,351
1948	1,052	3,658
1949	1,053	3,559
1950	1,199	83
1951	1,566	95
1952	2,622	27,896
1953	2,128	31,201
1954	2,192	33,005
1955	2,437	13
1956	2,527	20
1957	3,100	90
1958	2,899	5
1959	2,438	2,468
1960	25	122
1961	81	11
1962	44	1

The figure was 1,171m on 30 November 1961

Sources: Archives of Crédit lyonnais, DEEF 72958/3. CAOM, 80CO/813 CAOM, 80CL/19, letter to the Minister of Finance, 27 December 1961.

resources deposited in Paris.[90] Amounts in the Paris account were relatively stable. In the Algiers account of the Treasury, sharp swings and drawdowns after 1950 reflected public spending by the authorities, especially after the struggle against the nationalist uprising intensified from 1955 on.

The Algerian and Tunisian economies were apparently prosperous and expanding in the first half of 1955, and the monetary situation looked stable. The nationalist revolt did not yet impact on the economic outlook. There were no withdrawals of deposits from banks and no exodus of capital. Investment from France was still arriving.[91] Events in August 1955 created a feeling of insecurity that spread and had repercussions in France where exporters restricted credit to their customers in Algeria; business slowed down. By early 1956, the situation had worsened; private investment fell, demand for credit was sluggish and capital flowed out of Algeria.[92] Conditions improved in 1957 thanks to a bumper crop and the business activity that the presence of French troops generated. And oil was discovered in the Sahara the previous year. 'The harnessing of the vast Saharan resources will be the starting point of a profound transformation of the economy and the foundation of any lasting solution of the Algerian problem, while at the same time contributing significantly to balancing France's accounts.'[93]

In 1954, in the context of negotiations between Tunisian nationalists and French authorities, demands for an autonomous central bank prompted a review by Ministry of Finance officials in Paris of the advantages *Banque de l'Algérie et de la Tunisie* brought to Algeria and Tunisia: lower cost of credit, availability of means of payment, financial support to the economy, loans to the state, elimination of expenses for exchange. The French Treasury benefited as well by the use of its current account to allocate to Tunisia funds available in Algeria. The bank's business was profitable in Algeria and a loss-maker in Tunisia, but the latter gained from association with Algeria via a common bank. In the view of French officials, a separate Tunisian bank would lose money; it would have to raise the cost of credit and to stop remittance of the fee the bank paid to the Tunisian state. It represented a luxury Tunisia could not afford. But the advantage of a separate issue bank for the Tunisians was its greater responsiveness to national economic needs and policies.[94] The country's independence in 1956 made continuance of operations by the bank on Tunisian territory less likely. In a convention signed on 25 July 1958, it agreed to surrender its privilege of issue and to withdraw from Tunisia, subject to payment of an indemnity and compensations, and make room for the *Banque centrale de Tunisie* that was created on 9 September 1958 and obtained transfer of the privilege of issue on 31 October 1958.[95]

In Algeria, independence in 1962 sealed the fate of the *Banque de l'Algérie et de la Tunisie*. A protocol confirmed temporarily to 31 December 1962 its privilege of issuing banknotes. Upon creation of *Banque centrale de l'Algérie* on 14 December 1962, a convention was signed with *Banque de l'Algérie et de la Tunisie* on 31 December 1962 for transfer the same day of issue rights and all other business. The gold reserve was remitted at the *Banque de France* in Paris where it had been stored. In January 1963, a government-to-government agreement provided that an indemnity of 80 million new francs would be paid to

Banque de l'Algérie et de la Tunisie for its buildings and other material assets – it claimed 168.4 million francs.[96] The handover proceeded amicably, a transition facilitated by the fact that the general manager of the *Banque centrale de l'Algérie* had been an executive of the predecessor bank.[97] *Banque de l'Algérie et de la Tunisie* was liquidated and dissolved on 31 December 1963.

Conclusion

Swept away by decolonization, some imperial banks had an afterlife in the form of reconversion into homeland financial institutions or absorption by other banks. *Banque de l'Algérie et de la Tunisie* experienced no such metamorphosis; decolonization signaled its end. Unlike *Crédit foncier d'Algérie et de Tunisie, Banque de l'Indochine*,[98] Imperial Bank of Persia[99] or Hongkong and Shanghai Banking Corporation,[100] and others, it did not try to restart business elsewhere. Nor did it even seek to become a holder of equity of firms in the banking or non-banking sectors. It disappeared without leaving a trace. No doubt nationalization in 1946 had removed the private shareholders who might have attempted to revive or reinvent the BAT in some fashion.

Banque de l'Algérie et de la Tunisie was involved in various types of banking, and reconciliation between them required a delicate balancing act. From the start, the foundation was a response to two distinct necessities in Algeria. On the one hand, creation of a monetary system to provide adequate amounts of a common means of payment implied that Algeria needed an issue bank. On the other, ordinary economic activities such as importing and exporting goods had to be assisted by easily available credit. The two functions could not co-exist harmoniously. The object of the first was to attend to the money supply, to watch over its security and to keep its expansion within the limits of the assets designed to guarantee its value. As for the second function, it meant providing credit to the satisfaction of merchants usually eager to have as much of it as can be secured for as little cost as possible. This pull factor was compounded in Algeria by the fact that demand for credit came as much, if not more, from the agricultural as from the commercial sector. Ideally an issue bank should live on the revenue it generates from the circulation of its banknotes and the rediscounting of the bills of other actors in the economy. *Banque de l'Algérie et de la Tunisie* could not. Issuance of the needed amount of banknotes meant costly immobilization of large quantities of gold, bullion and metallic currency serving as security. And, as there was insufficient rediscounting to do, not enough revenue could be drawn from that source to cover the expense of banknote circulation. So *Banque de l'Algérie et de la Tunisie* worked in other areas, essentially in the discounting of commercial bills, at one time in agricultural lending – where it nearly came to grief – and, indirectly, in industrial banking. It was classical in one respect, that of a state bursar working in conjunction with the Treasury.

In essence, it was a near-public institution, in a category apart from other banks, and, at the same time, an ordinary commercial bank operating in the market like its competitors. It had one foot in each sector. It was a composite entity, combining features of distinct models of banking, but not perfectly. While it was an issue bank regulating the money supply, and while it extended recurrent short-term loans to the state, it was not an authentic central bank overseeing the commercial banking system. While it acted as a rediscount bank, it was not a lender of last resort to the banking sector and therefore not a bankers' bank. Even the nationalization of 1946 did not alter these facts.

Central banking has composite origins. Even archetypal issue banks, such as Bank of England or *Banque de France*, grew out of mixed institutions practicing commercial banking for a long time, alongside their monetary, 'last-resort' and 'official treasurer' functions. Only in 1970, for example, did *Banque de France* cease direct discounting. Although *Banque de l'Algérie et de la Tunisie* provided a specific combination of banking activities, it was not exceptional or atypical. Its amorphous nature can be attributed to its colonial-imperial environment. The rudimentary state of the North African market economy meant that a currency and a banking system were to be established simultaneously. There were too few other discounters for *Banque de l'Algérie et de la Tunisie* to concentrate on rediscounting their paper, as would a bankers' bank. It was not surprising that *Banque de France* tried to steer clear of North Africa. So it depended on discounting. Even that activity was restricted by the importance of agriculture in a colonial economy like North Africa's. Bills based on agricultural activity proved unsuitable because they were not liquid enough to be held by an issue bank. Commerce was the residual sector left to work in, along with operations on the Treasury current account. Moreover, the bank's environment subjected it to demand for credit pure and simple, occasionally at the behest of state authorities, in complete disregard for its role as an issue bank. In sum, the *Banque de l'Algérie et de la Tunisie* could not specialize or choose between models of bank behaviour. It combined issue banking with commercial banking, an awkward but unavoidable partnership. If its history is in any way representative of imperial banking, it underlines the difficulty for issue banks in colonial economies to concentrate on their monetary-regulatory function and evolve into central banks.

Notes

1 Albert Stephen and James Baster, *The Imperial Banks*, New York, Arno Press, 1977 [1929].
2 Marc Meuleau, *Des pionniers en Extrême-Orient. Histoire de la Banque de l'Indochine (1875–1975)*, Paris, Fayard, 1990. Yasuo Gonjo, *Banque coloniale ou banque d'affaires. La Banque de l'Indochine sous la IIIᵉ République*, Paris, Comité pour l'histoire économique et financière de la France, 1993.
3 Samir Saul, 'La Banque d'État du Maroc et la monnaie sous le Protectorat,' in Jacques Marseille (ed.), *La France et l'Outre-Mer. Un siècle de relations monétaires et financières*, Paris, Comité pour l'histoire économique et financière de la France, 1998, pp. 389–427.
4 Mohamed Lazhar-Gharbi, *Crédit et discrédit de la Banque d'Algérie (seconde moitié du XIXᵉ siècle)*, Paris, L'Harmattan, 2005.
5 Hubert Bonin, *Un outre-mer bancaire méditerranéen. Histoire du Crédit foncier d'Algérie & de Tunisie (1880–1997)*, Paris, Publications de la Société française d'histoire d'outre-mer, 2004 and 2010. Hubert Bonin, 'La Compagnie algérienne levier de la colonisation et prospère grâce à elle (1865–1939),' *Revue française d'histoire d'outre-mer*, 328/329, 2000, pp. 209–30. Hubert Bonin, 'Une histoire

bancaire transméditerranéenne: la Compagnie algérienne, d'un ultime apogée au repli (1945–1970),' in Daniel Lefeuvre et al. (eds), *La Guerre d'Algérie au miroir des décolonisations françaises* (En l'honneur de Charles-Robert Ageron), Paris, Publications de la Société française d'histoire d'outre-mer, 2000, pp. 151–76.

6 Guy Duménil, *La Banque de l'Algérie. Étude sur son rôle économique et financier*, Paris, E. de Boccard, 1927. Maurice Jaïs, *La Banque de l'Algérie et le crédit agricole*, Paris, Arthur Rousseau, 1902. Joseph-Jean-Vivien Saint-Germès, *La Banque de l'Algérie et le crédit pendant et après la guerre*, Algiers, Imprimerie La Typo-Litho, 1925. Pierre Bonifay, *Banque de l'Algérie. Influence de la guerre. Renouvellement du privilège*, Paris, Jouve, 1926. André Lejeune, *Le rôle du crédit dans le développement économique de l'Algérie depuis la fin de la guerre*, Paris, E. Duchemin, 1930.

7 Paul Ernest-Picard, *La monnaie et le crédit en Algérie depuis 1830*, Algiers, Jules Carbonel; Paris, Plon, 1930.

8 Paul Ernest-Picard, op. cit., pp. 72–82.

9 Ibid., pp. 87–101.

10 Denominations were large: 50, 100, 500 and 1,000 francs. The Algerian franc and the French franc were convertible at par.

11 Paul Ernest-Picard, op. cit., pp. 102–13.

12 Centre des archives d'outre-mer (CAOM), 80S/1, Comptes rendus annuels des assemblées générales, 27 November 1860.

13 Ibid., 30 November 1861.

14 A. Jaubert, *De l'institution d'une Banque mobilière-agricole de l'Algérie. Projet de statuts*, Algiers, Imprimerie mécanique de Dubos frères, 1859.

15 Eugène Ganzin, *De la situation du crédit commercial, industriel et agricole en Algérie et de son organisation par la Banque de France*, Algiers, Imprimerie de Dubos frères, 1858. Émile Robert, *De la transformation nécessaire de la Banque de l'Algérie en succursale de la Banque de France*, Paris, Imprimerie de H. Carion, 1860.

16 Émile Robert, *De la transformation nécessaire*, op. cit., p. 5.

17 J.-A. Rey, *La banque en Algérie*, Algiers, Dubos frères, 1858.

18 CAOM, 80S/1. It was lowered to 5 per cent in 1878, then to 4 per cent in 1879, but went up to 5 per cent in 1883.

19 Paul Ernest-Picard, op. cit., p. 142. M. Lazhar-Gharbi, op. cit., p. 93.

20 Having speculated and suffered losses, SGA was replaced by *Compagnie algérienne* in 1877.

21 *Banque de l'Algérie* requested a 4 million franc line of credit from *Banque de France* on 15 October 1863. It was granted the right to rediscount drafts up to that amount at the going rate on 22 October 1863. Archives de la Banque de France, Délibérations du Conseil général.

22 CAOM. 80S/122, Procès-verbaux du conseil d'administration, 1863. M.-L. Gharbi, op. cit., pp. 24–8.

23 Archives de la Banque de France, Délibérations du Conseil général, 22 April 1869.

24 Incidentally, the founder of the Mallet dynasty was a cloth merchant in Rouen in the sixteenth century.

25 Archives de la Banque de France, Délibérations du Conseil général, 29 April 1869.

26 Ibid., 7 May 1869.

27 CAOM, 80S/124, procès-verbaux du conseil d'administration, 1870–1874. M. Lazhar-Gharbi, op. cit., pp. 34–45. Board of directors' report to the general assembly of shareholders, 27 November 1890.

28 CAOM, 80S/125, 1879. M. Lazhar-Gharbi, op. cit., p. 46.

29 Archives de la Banque de France, Délibérations du Conseil général, 20 December 1877, 17 January 1878.

30 Ibid., 24 January 1880. M. Lazhar-Gharbi, op. cit., p. 4.

31 By way of comparison, the lowest denomination of a *Banque de France* banknote was 50 francs.

146   *Samir Saul*

32 CAOM, 80S/126. M. Lazhar-Gharbi, op. cit., p. 162.
33 M. Lazhar-Gharbi, op. cit., p. 163.
34 Bernard Lavergne, 'La Banque de l'Algérie. Son activité générale et le renouvelle-ment de son privilège,' *Revue d'économie politique*, 5/6, September–December 1918, pp. 523, 525.
35 It was replaced by Crédit foncier d'Algérie et de Tunisie in 1907. See Hubert Bonin, *Un outre-mer bancaire méditerranéen*, op. cit., 2004.
36 Guy Duménil, op. cit., pp. 115–29.
37 Archives de la Banque de France, Délibérations du Conseil général, 22 March 1883.
38 CAOM, 80S/1, 25 November 1897.
39 Henri Garrot, *La Banque de l'Algérie. Ses origines, ses modes d'opérer et ses résultats en Algérie*, Paris, A. Savine, 1892, is a vehement 310-page diatribe, but not without useful information. Among the mildest statements is the charge that the bank acquired land by taking advantage of its privilege to issue banknotes which cost it nothing (p. 292).
40 *Quelques courtes réflexions sur la Banque de France, la Banque de l'Algérie, les Caisses d'épargne*, Paris, Grande Imprimerie, 1891.
41 CAOM, 80S/1, 24 November 1892.
42 Ibid., 25 November 1897.
43 Archives de la Banque de France, Délibérations du Conseil général, 16 and 28 November 1889.
44 CAOM, 80S/180, minutes of the board, circular letter dated 31 October 1897.
45 Ibid., 30 November 1897.
46 CAOM, 80S/131, minutes of the board, 16 March 1899.
47 CAOM, 80S/132, minutes of the board, 4 July 1899. According to article 6 of the bank's statutes, at least one-half of capital and reserves had to be invested in state bonds (*rentes*), a liquid asset.
48 CAOM, 80S/1, 25 November 1897, 15 November 1900; law of 5 July 1900 in Jaïs, pp. 141–5; analysis of law in J. Franconie, 'Transformation des banques coloniales. La Banque d'Algérie,' *Questions diplomatiques et coloniales*, XIII, 1 March 1902, pp. 283–90.
49 CAOM, 80S/181, minutes of the board, 23 March 1901.
50 CAOM, 80S/181, minutes of the board, 18 December 1912.
51 L. de Sarnez, *La Banque d'Algérie contre l'Algérie. Étude documentaire par un com-merçant*, Algiers, Imprimerie Fontana, 1913, pp. 7, 10–11, 33–4, 38.
52 Board of directors' report to the general assembly, 25 November 1926.
53 Pierre Bonifay, pp. 73, 75. *Banque de France* advanced 17.8 billion francs.
54 In fact, the sum paid out was 5.2 million francs in 1919, 8 million in 1921 and 7.8 million in 1927. Lejeune, op. cit., p. 27.
55 Pierre Bonifay, op. cit., pp. 126–54. Martial Douël, *Un siècle de finances coloniales*, Paris, Librairie Félix Alcan, 1930, pp. 640–1. Paul Ernest-Picard, op. cit., pp. 232, 310–11.
56 This assertion was not entirely correct.
57 Jean-Vivien Saint-Germès, op. cit., p. 52. Pierre Bonifay, op. cit., pp. 95–8, 120–5.
58 André Lejeune, op. cit., pp. 22–3. Pierre Bonifay, op. cit., pp. 102–8.
59 CAOM, 80S/185, minutes of the board, 20 May 1924. Guy Duménil, op. cit., pp. 220–52.
60 CAOM, 80S/186, minutes of the board, 11 January 1929, letter from Paul Ernest-Picard, general manager-chairman, to the assistant general manager of the *Mouvement général des fonds* (French Ministry of Finance), 11 January 1929.
61 At least one-third of the total had to be bullion and gold currency.
62 CAOM, 80S/186, minutes of the board, 11 January 1929, draft letter.
63 Ibid., 14 February 1929.
64 Board of directors' report to the general assembly, 28 November 1929.
65 Ibid., 24 November 1938.
66 Archives du ministère de l'Économie et des Finances (EF), B24816; Jean-Vivien Saint-Germès, p. 50.

67 Banque de l'Algérie et de la Tunisie, *Cinquante ans au service de la Tunisie*, Paris, Presses de J.-G. Malochet, 1955, p. 12.
68 Samir Saul, 'La Banque d'État du Maroc et la monnaie sous le protectorat,' in Jacques Marseille (ed.), *La France & l'outre-mer. Les relations économiques & financières entre la France & la France d'outre-mer*, Paris, Publications du Comité pour l'histoire économique & financière de la France, 1998, pp. 389–427. Georges Hatton, *Les enjeux financiers et économiques du Protectorat marocain (1936–1956). Politique publique et investisseurs privés*, Paris, Publications de la Société française d'histoire d'outre-mer, 2009.
69 Samir Saul, op. cit., pp. 401–15. CAOM, 80S/184, minutes of the board, 30 April 1920; 80S/186, minutes of the board, 27 April 1923.
70 Jean-Vivien Saint-Germès, op. cit., pp. 139–49. André Lejeune, op. cit., pp. 31–45. Guy Duménil, op. cit., pp. 85–99.
71 Board of directors' report to the general assembly, 25 November 1937.
72 EF, B24811, Denys Routaboul, assistant general manager, to commissioner of finance, 1 July 1944; handwritten notes.
73 Board of directors' report to the general assembly, 16 April 1942.
74 CAOM, 80D/55, Note sur l'exploitation en Tunisie, 18 November 1954.
75 Archives du ministère des Affaires étrangères (AE), Tunisie 1944–1949, General Mast, Resident General, to Georges Bidault, Minister of Foreign Affairs, 4 May 1945; Mast to the Minister of Finance, 26 March 1946.
76 CAOM, 80D/59, Projet pour un nouveau statut d'émission en Algérie et en Tunisie, n.d.
77 EF, B24802, minutes of the board, 2 July 1948.
78 AE, Tunisie 1944–1949, no. 121, Jean Mons, Resident General, to Ministry of Foreign Affairs, 27 June 1948; Ministry of Foreign Affairs to Mons, 19 July 1948.
79 CAOM, 80D/59, Relevé de la circulation fiduciaire algérienne et tunisienne.
80 AE, Tunisie 1944–1949, no. 121, Mons to Minister of Finance, 20 January 1949 and 14 April 1949; to Minister of Foreign Affairs, 10 June 1949.
81 CAOM, 80S/191, minutes of the board, 20 January 1950.
82 Coincidentally, internal documentation and published annual reports contain even less information about the bank than previously. More and more space is devoted to the Algerian and Tunisian economies.
83 Annual report presented to the president of the Republic by Brunet, chairman-managing director, 1953.
84 EF, B34126, Report on activity in 1948 by Marcel Flouret, governor.
85 EF, B24816.
86 CAOM, 80D/59, Relevé de la circulation fiduciaire algérienne et tunisienne.
87 EF, B24811, list of advances from 26 February 1952 to 14 January 1953.
88 EF, B34126, Rapport sur la Banque de l'Algérie et de la Tunisie (exercices 1949 et 1950) par la Commission de vérification des comptes, p. 8.
89 CAOM, 80D/56, Notes sur les disponibilités métropolitaines de la BAT et fonctionnement du compte du Trésor public, 12 June 1953; EF, B24810, Projet de note sur le régime monétaire de l'Algérie, n.d. [1961].
90 Archives du Crédit lyonnais, DEEF 72958/3.
91 EF, B24802, minutes of the board, 27 May 1955.
92 Ibid., 23 September 1955, 16 December 1955, 23 March 1956.
93 Ibid., 5 April 1957.
94 CAOM, 80D/55, Note remise aux ministères des Finances et des Affaires marocaines et tunisiennes par Jean Watteau [governor of BAT], 1 September 1954; EF, B24813, Jean Denizet to Watteau, 28 May 1956.
95 CAOM, 80S/191, minutes of the board, 7 February and 26 September 1958.
96 Ibid., 26 April 1963.
97 Archives de la Banque de France, 1069200602/18, last meeting of the BAT board, 28 February 1964.

98 Yasuo Gonjo, *Banque coloniale ou banque d'affaires. La Banque de l'Indochine sous la IIIe République*, Paris, Comité pour l'histoire économique & financière de la France, 1993.

99 For comparisons, see Geoffrey Jones et al., *The History of the British Bank of the Middle East*, vol. 1: *Banking and Empire in Iran*; vol. 2: *Banking and Oil*, Cambridge, Cambridge University Press, 1986–1987.

100 See Frank King, *The History of the Hongkong & Shanghai Banking Corporation*, four volumes, Cambridge, Cambridge University Press, 1987–1991; Richard Roberts and David Kynaston, *The Lion Wakes: A Modern History of HSBC*, London, Profile Books, 2015.

8 Parisian banking networks and the empire

Measuring the influence of 'colonial' bankers

Hubert Bonin

A number of economic and overseas historians have reconstituted and analyzed the organization of the networks linking the major players involved in the colonization and the life of the empire. Several smaller, critical books have attempted to define the links between corporate groups, financial companies and banks within the framework of the 'two hundred families' (supposed to control *Banque de France* and the main capitalist connections) and the 'trusts' which were thought to have 'governed' France. The masterful volumes edited by Marxist historian Jean Suret-Canale[1] have amply fulfilled their goal of gathering all the data regarding the implantation of companies in French Africa and detailing the business networks there, as they were attributed hugely powerful of influence, under the guidance of 'imperial banking.'

Still, are we for that matter any closer to apprehending the reality of the business there and that of the City? Does not the simple stating of such an imperial economic 'force' skew the perception of what really happened? It is one thing to weave and maintain networks and quite another to mobilize and turn them into efficient, influential and active entities capable of weighing on the course of history. After the pioneering book by Jacques Marseille, Catherine Hodeir's thesis has dealt exhaustively and richly with the formation of an imperial patronage and its influence on the process of decolonization.[2]

Similarly, our aim here is to weigh the influence wielded by the networks set up by imperial bankers: were they able to use them to influence government decisions? In order to answer this, we have chosen a few case studies which seem to us to be emblematic of the debates that have surrounded the key issues regarding the empire's 'development.' We pretend to no exhaustiveness, and we have restricted ourselves to 'bankers' (credit and asset management), while excluding from our field of study all 'financiers' (managers of investment companies). We outline the complex webs ('cohesive groups' made up of confederations of companies and business hubs) which gathered businessmen and companies around banking centers in order to influence overseas markets and to form 'power bases' within the business, social and political decision-making spheres (for public works concessions, mining and land concessions, etc.). We shall first give an outline of these complex webs before attempting to take a snapshot of their interactions.

The reality of colonial and overseas bankers' networks of influence

We shall start by isolating several 'spheres of influence' which gradually began to exert their power over the imperial, overseas banking business – we do not talk here of the financing of international, trans-oceanic trade in general.

The historic influence of Comptoir national d'escompte de Paris

It was the weight of history that turned *Comptoir national d'escompte de Paris* (CNEP) into the keystone of the banking sphere of influence within the imperial community of interests. When, in 1848, the government wanted to boost the Parisian market's credit rating which had been eroded by a series of crashes and political troubles, the young *Comptoir* found itself entrusted not only with the mission of rebuilding Paris' image and confidence in the region's trade, but also with the job of rediscounting the micro credit systems that the government had set up overseas after the first wave of colonization – mainly the Antilles. It thus assumed the title of 'godfather' to the colonial banks in Martinique, Guadalupe[3] (especially to turn the bond compensations given to those who had lost their 'property' in slaves into cash) and Senegal.[4] This in turn gave it a knowledge capital and a relations capital in the overseas market (sugar, rum, shipping, trade, etc.) and, shall we say, some precedence due to the simple fact that it had appeared earlier on the scene. It was the first to get involved in these imperial business dealings and it sought to make the most of its technical and relational capital in territories acquired during the 'second wave of colonization.'

In contrast, none of the other banks such as *Crédit industriel et commercial*, *Crédit lyonnais* or *Société générale* concerned themselves with the empire[5] before the first four decades of the twentieth century – excepting one that we shall take up later. The unwritten but well-founded custom of keeping 'hunting preserves' seemed to be in force, and CNEP turned into the most important imperial bank, with agencies in Tunisia (where it arranged for several war loans in 1865–1867), in Egypt and in British Oceania.[6] Its influence was particularly strong in major trading and shipping centers in mainland France, and its agencies spearheaded the financing of overseas trade. The bank wove close ties with medium-large enterprises which had their eyes set on overseas markets. In Paris too, it built itself a clientele of small- and medium-sized enterprises involved in import-export or commission sales by offering them FOREX (foreign exchange) and warrant services or documentary credit.

According to us, it is this historical heritage and rooting which explain the CNEP's influence within the colonial networks, symbolized by its vice-president, Émile Mercet (1894–1902, before becoming president). We also find him very much present in numerous other institutions inspired by the imperial economic spirit such as the *Union coloniale* (he was made president at its inception in 1893) where he rubbed shoulders with corporate honchos whom he financed. But he was equally well positioned within the network of the moderate Republicans – being one of the founders (along with Léon Say and Édouard Aynard)[7] of the *Union libérale républicaine*, one of the three organizations formed by the 'progressives,' the right-wing opportunists who made up the base of a moderated majority between 1892 and 1899 (along with Jules Méline), and one of the strongest proponents of free trade. Senator Ernest Denormandie, president of CNEP and one-time governor of *Banque de France* (1879–1880), also contributed to its growing overseas influence as a 'regional establishment' because he was also president of *Banque de l'Indochine* between 1892 and 1902. Much later, the CNEP's overseas clout was revitalized by Henri Bizot: after being assistant general secretary, he won a seat on the house's board and re-planted the flag in several overseas territories: 'After the war, he increased his visits to the *Comptoir*'s strongholds like India and Australia. Promoted as General Manager in 1958 and President in 1964, he toiled to modernize it,'[8] mainly by using his overseas strongholds to weave new commercial networks.

Paribas's colonial combativeness

Though *Banque de Paris et des Pays-Bas*'s core activities were those of a European corporate bank, its directors were not, for that matter, any the less interested by the empire and the opportunities it provided for 'investment companies' (mobilizing capital into investment projects, placement of their securities) and commercial banks (financing the activities of these projects once completed). Paribas gradually began to realize that the empire could turn out to be a 'good business proposition,'[9] that the clearing of 'virgin territories' (mines, trade, finance of infrastructure) could be as attractive as those in Russia and Latin America, and even more so than those in Central or Eastern Europe. An as yet little studied team[10] seemed to have been formed to orient a part of the house's portfolio of strategic activities towards the empire. By leveraging Paribas's status in the Parisian market, the players who were instrumental in introducing it into the economic imperialism that took shape at the turn of the twentieth century also turned into influential agents within relational banking networks as well as in the totality of imperial business affairs. Paribas went hunting for business opportunities: how and where to invest retail (rich families, captains of industry, patrician families) and institutional (e.g. insurance companies) investors' funds. The overseas market provided many new avenues: company shares to be issued, loans for infrastructure projects (to construction and power companies and sometimes to railway companies) and, gradually, to mining and industrial companies that had begun to emerge.

In 1920, Paribas gave a concrete shape to this strategy by setting up a holding subsidiary, *Compagnie générale des colonies*. It enriched its relational and business network by buying stakes in dozens of companies in Madagascar, sub-Saharan Africa and Indochina. In Morocco,[11] Paribas was the lynchpin of the 'Moroccan Consortium'[12] (Paribas, *Crédit lyonnais*, *Société générale*, CNEP, *Crédit industriel et commercial* (CIC), *Crédit algérien* and *Banque française pour le commerce et l'industrie* (BFCI), and later, *Banque nationale de crédit* (BNC),

Société marseillaise de crédit (SMC), *Banque de l'union parisienne* (BUP) and *Banque de l'Indochine*) that was established in 1902 to distribute major business deals according to the sphere of influence, such as for the issue of *Chemins de fer du Maroc* or for public works and electrification projects. It also actively patronized the *Compagnie générale du Maroc*. This overseas business hub retained its importance until as late as 1950–1960,[13] strengthened even further by a growing partnership with the trading company SCOA (Société commerciale de l'Ouest africain). The key man in the 1970s, when this 'economic model' was at its apogee, was Georges Nesterenko,[14] an influential engineer who became president of SCOA and treasurer of the *Société française d'histoire d'outre-mer*. But within Paribas itself, the overseas business was consolidated when Pierre Moussa, who had solid access to overseas business opportunities, was inducted into its board in 1969 (until 1981).[15]

The years 1900–1940 are a little opaque regarding the relative weight of these 'imperial' bankers within Paribas or the importance accorded to them by Finaly.[16] In the 1920s, a number of inter-bank meetings concerning Morocco were chaired by André Laurent-Atthalin, apparently imperial Paribas's godfather,[17] while the chairman (Gaston Griolet, and later Émile Moreau) represented the house on the boards of several colonial companies. In any case, it was Laurent-Atthalin who sat on the *Union coloniale*'s board in the mid-1920s. Managing director of *Compagnie générale des colonies* and *Compagnie générale du Maroc*, vice-president of the State Bank of Morocco and *Banque de Madagascar*, he seems to us to be Paribas's key man in its imperial networks till the beginning of WWII.

The diversification of the Big Banks' sphere of influence

We have long known how Rothschild expanded his business in certain overseas segments such as nickel in New Caledonia,[18] non-ferrous metals in Penarroya and *Société anonyme de gérance & d'armement* (SAGA's) forwarding activities. But we don't find any of the Rothschilds or their representatives in any of the available documents pertaining to the world of overseas Parisian elites. The key figure of the 1950s turns out to be René Fillon, the bank's general secretary who rose to become chairman of Penarroya and even senator in Sudan in 1955. One still needs to determine the team set up by Rothschild in order to stage a comeback in the oil business (given up in Baku at the turn of the century) and to launch itself (with Worms bank) in the financing of overseas oil exploration[19] (Cofirep, Francarep) in direct competition with Paribas-BUP partnership (*Finarep*) in the mid-1950s. It must be added that, apart from its shipping and fuel trading activities, Worms itself was a latecomer in the overseas markets and made its presence felt mainly after the 1940s (control of *Banque industrielle d'Afrique du Nord*, etc.), following the growth of its banking business after 1929.[20]

On the other hand, we also know that several other Big Banks did capture significant positions overseas because, as with Paribas, they too needed to expand their asset management business to help their retail and institutional investors while looking for new overseas markets for their merchant banking activities. Mirabaud was one of the key players in this group, mainly because of the attraction of the mining sector, which had historically become one of the house's main strengths from as early as the end of the nineteenth century (Phosphates of Gafsa, Mokta, Penarroya). Pierre Mirabaud's role in this regard during the inter-war period seems to us to have been decisive as the Mirabauds[21] were influential within *Banque de l'union parisienne* (BUP).[22] They were again in the picture after 1953, when the investment bank absorbed the Mirabaud Bank in Paris, jointly financed various banking companies (*Compagnie algérienne*[23]) and supported the initiatives of a network including the Mirabaud (with Eugène Mirabaud,[24] who presided over *Compagnie algérienne* and *Phosphates de Gafsa*'s board in the 1950s), the Nervo, the Durand-Réville and the Lemaignen. In fact, this move inherited the material and relational capital of the Talabot, as the Nervo were the inheritors. This also explains why it resumed the guardianship of the SCAC, *Compagnie algérienne* (which succeeded *Société générale algérienne*) and Mokta (Algerian iron mines and later also non-ferrous metals). It was strengthened by the links it forged with Optorg, the technological trading company in sub-Saharan Africa, which merged with *Société commerciale du Haut-Ogooué* and *Peyrissac* and which was financed by Durand-Réville and Chavanel. These last two also helped to strengthen the group's links with Bordeaux's trading hub and a section of its business community.

Though we still lack a precise account of this confederation of interests, there is no doubt that a solid, dynamic and lasting (till the 1960s) relational hub had been formed which acted as the spearhead of the imperial banking influence in the Paris market. After being a member of the commission of European communities in charge of African relations between 1958 and 1961, Robert Lemaignen, CEO of Optorg (1962–1969) (a trade house) and SCAC (a transit company), presided over the National Committee of French Africa at the International Chamber of Commerce. This movement also had some modest but possibly active political elements such as Robert Lemoult, CEO of Optorg (1940–1962) and also senator.

Earlier, an informal group of 'imperial' bankers had been formed within BUP when it developed its overseas business independently of this confederation. In fact, BUP had associated itself for a while with *Schneider*'s initiatives in Morocco (*Compagnie marocaine*). Though we lack explicit archival evidence, our investigation has unearthed a key 'imperial' banker, Joseph Courcelle, who represented BUP at *Compagnie générale des colonies*, *Compagnie marocaine*, *Chemins de fer du Maroc*, and *Port de Tanger* as well as *Tramways & éclairage de Shanghai* (until 1937) – the last of which was financed by BUP right from its inception in 1906. Jean Exbrayat, a director and close business associate of the BUP, was president of SCOA – a big trading house in sub-Saharan Africa – which, given its size, worked with several bankers. The rapid growth of the BUP-Mirabaud group's mining business in North Africa (Gafsa), sub-Saharan Africa and non-ferrous metals (Huaron, Mokta; Penarroya, Nickel, following the Rothschild) and the consequent rise in financial investments (invariably crowned with success) explain the direct involvement of its president, Henri Lafond. Coming from an engineering background and being president of the SCAC, he maintained the link between heavy transportation (coal), transit and bank as had been done by the Talabot brothers since the days of the Second Empire.

Still, despite a systematic search of the BUP's archives and the 'imperial' sections of our monograph, we have not been able to identify any group that may be called 'imperial' because the overseas business files were treated like any other project, dependent on the occasions that present themselves, relations forged ad hoc, proposals from *Haute Banque* sister houses (Mallet for *Tramways de Shanghai*, Odier-Bungener for *Compagnie algérienne*), the house's Belgian partners (for the same, for example), or wealthy families (Gradis, Maurel & Prom) that the bank pampered and which subsequently involved it in their projects, etc. Paradoxically, the present stage of our research does not allow us to determine the influence wielded by the directors of *Compagnie algérienne* (the tenth biggest French bank by loan in the inter-war period), while Lucien Bordet (a graduate of the *École polytechnique* and inspector of finance) retained its presidency between 1893 and 1926. The house though was more or less closely supervised by the Mirabaud group, especially by Jean Boissonnas (director of *Compagnie algérienne*, Haut-Ogooué, *Banque de Syrie & du Grand Liban*, etc.), as the Boissonnas branch constituted one of the Boissonnas group's main hubs for several decades.

The emergence of autonomous colonial and imperial banking hubs: Banque de l'Indochine *and* Crédit foncier d'Algérie & de Tunisie

Meanwhile, banks which had hitherto concentrated on overseas territories gradually began to make their banking and relational presence felt on the Paris market. They set themselves up as intermediaries between the Parisian market and the overseas hubs where they were key players. Still, they were dependent on the banking community for loan refinancing and sharing in the issue of securities, and it took several decades for them to establish themselves at the core of the imperial networks – only after they had attained the financial scale and market position which allowed them some measure of autonomous action.

How influential was Crédit foncier d'Algérie & de Tunisie?

Generally unknown till some recent publications,[25] *Crédit foncier d'Algérie & de Tunisie* (CFAT) had quietly turned itself into an important and influential player, especially after the years 1910–1920. Naturally starting with trans-Mediterranean business affairs and west Mediterranean flows, it also turned into one of the main relays of French influence in the north-eastern Mediterranean. We have already shown how this bank, which had been long considered as simply an outgrowth of *Crédit foncier de France* (a large mortgage bank) in Maghreb, transformed itself into a mini power centre. This could happen because, apart from its rapid growth as a trans-Mediterranean commercial bank, it inserted itself into powerful business networks which used it as a financial and banking agent without impinging on its autonomy or the position and influence of some overseas capitalists. In this regard, André Lebon,[26] a former minister of Colonies, became chairman of CFAT (from 1902 to 1937) who was the keystone within his network of influence: president of *Messageries maritimes*, vice-president then president of CFAT, director (and vice-president) of Suez and president of the *Union coloniale* itself. Another fine example is Edmond Philippar[27]; though not particularly well known – being CFAT's chief executive from 1907 to 1935 – he was present in so many business deals, and was so often at the forefront of this trans-Mediterranean expansion, especially east Mediterranean, that he turned into a decisive pillar of influence and treasurer of the *Union coloniale* – though not quite like his president:

> Marshall Lyautey himself decided to recommend Philippar to the rank of Commander of the *Légion d'honneur* in December 1932, because CFAT's boss clearly symbolised the Empire's growing economic power in the Mediterranean, especially Morocco, where he had played, at his scale and in his field, a determining role in agricultural and housing colonisation.[28]

Yet another president of CFAT, Xavier Loisy (1937–1944), was also made treasurer of the *Union coloniale* in the 1930s. CFAT went on to participate in numerous financial operations regarding the Maghreb, less and less as a sidekick to the Big Banks and more and more as a full partner. It tried to short-circuit CNEP in Madagascar by joining hands with Messageries maritimes to set up *Crédit foncier de Madagascar* in 1919. Ultimately, it became one of the major agents responsible for the implantation in the Levant during the inter-war period.

The Banque de l'Indochine's growing importance within the colonial and imperial networks

Meanwhile, over the decades, *Banque de l'Indochine*[29] outgrew its initial function as a monetary and banking tool in South East Asia and became a banking and financial powerhouse – as well established overseas as in mainland France. Our colleagues have already highlighted the extent of its influence in both Indochina and New Caledonia, where its activities of a commercial bank – after the opening of a branch in 1888 – established it as the go-to bank for all local businesses (the industrial and commercial Ballande group, from Bordeaux, trade houses, nickel companies including *Le Nickel*, ship-owners). In the years 1940–1950, it implemented a strategy of asset re-allocation towards both mainland France and Africa, where it wanted to participate in the modernization drive – which had also tempted the Lazard bank to the extent of drawing up plans for taking over *Banque de l'Indochine* in 1954–1955. Meanwhile, the latter roped in CFAT and transferred a big portion of its liquid assets from *Crédit foncier indochinois* to Morocco. By 1958, some 18 per cent of its securities portfolio was invested in Africa (as against only 12 per cent in Asia) and it was still 12 per cent in 1963. This naturally boosted its image as an 'imperial' bank.

The key question lay in the ability of the directors of these two houses to enter into the 'imperial' banking networks, that is to say, of their sphere of influence within the community of businessmen promulgating the imperial economic spirit.

Jean Laurent's disappearance after WWII shook the relational equation, though the managing director François de Flers (1952–1974), who had been with him since 1937, did manage to retain the institution's clout, especially as he was supported by his president, Émile Minost, a former chief of *Crédit foncier égyptien* who knew all the intricacies of overseas business affairs.[30]

The emergence of an ambitious troublemaker: Banque nationale pour le commerce et l'industrie

While its predecessor, BNC, had neglected the overseas market and had battled for over a decade to make a name for itself for reliability and win market share, BNCI (*Banque nationale pour le commerce et l'industrie*) suddenly found itself part of the group of 'imperial' bankers when its managing director, Alfred Pose, unveiled an African deployment policy in Algiers in 1940–1942. BNCI-Afrique was thus created by transforming the little *Banque de l'union nord-africaine* that had been acquired in September 1940. In the years 1950–1960, it was called upon to spread throughout Madagascar, the Antilles and the African shores along the Mediterranean Sea and the Atlantic and the Indian oceans.

The extent of these 'imperial' bankers' influence

Apart from the day-to-day business and some exceptional cases that we shall look into in this second part, we could legitimately ask ourselves how active or present were these 'imperial' bankers within the networks and institutions that were oriented towards the empire, and whether they were part of its economic and political networks. We still lack a systematic review of their activities within these interest groups. Though we are unable to draw up an exhaustive and systematic chart detailing the influence exerted by these 'imperial' bankers, we can present some case studies which could help judge their capacity to intervene, even regarding political issues. It involves not so much the simple recounting of history, but of going direct to the heart of the matter and seeing how business rivals came together to expand or consolidate their relational networks.

The successive 'affairs' of Banque de l'Indochine

The first potential stumbling block was that right from its birth *Banque de l'Indochine* was faced by competition in the form of *Comptoir d'escompte de Paris* (CEP, as CNEP called itself till 1889) which, from as early as 1864, was busy financing colonial banks and had agencies in Cochinchina and branches in several Asian territories (Pondicherry, Calcutta and Bombay, Shanghai and Hong Kong, Yokohama). Naturally it felt that it could play the role of a relay and that of a guardian to any issuing and banking house in Indochina. Unfortunately, despite its strong position as an 'imperial' banker in Paris, its brand image had taken a hit because it was thought to have been overly cautious regarding the granting of loans in Indochina and helping plantations (to which it had refused unguaranteed loans). Could it be that this Franco-international trade bank simply lacked the financial stature to directly assume the responsibility for a new *Banque de l'Indochine*? No wonder then that a rival group came to be formed around CIC, which had strong ties to ports and trading hubs via regional banks that it either financed or represented in Paris. Thus, before creating *Société bordelaise de CIC* in 1880, it joined hands with *Société marseillaise de crédit* and *Société lyonnaise de dépôts* to advance a competing project. It is also true that because the CIC was the British Hongkong & Shanghai Bank's correspondent in Paris, it could use its Catholic contacts to reach out to the reactionary MacMahonian majority which was in power in 1873–1876.

The competition boiled down to these two concurrent projects. But the deal went CEP's way because, at that time, its status and power in the imperial business world was greater than that of the CIC: *'Banque de l'Indochine* is CEP's daughter.'[31] It, along with its allied *Haute Banque* houses (merchant banks Hentsch-Lütscher,[32] Hoskier, Mirabaud-Paccard) and the very young investment bank Paribas (the result of a collaboration among several others), concluded a gentlemen's agreement with CIC in October 1874 regarding the creation of *Banque de l'Indochine*. Édouard Hentsch, chairman of CEP and a director at Paribas, was made chairman while Pierre Girod, director at CEP, was made director here too. The latter and CIC took 8,000 shares each, while *Société générale* and *Crédit lyonnais* kept away from the project and the capital, and CEP handed over several of its Asian branches to the new bank.

The question of the renewal of the *Banque de l'Indochine*'s concession in Tonkin became a major issue for these 'imperial' bankers. *Société générale*, which had by then acquired a solid international stature, wanted a piece of the Asian pie and proposed setting up a rival investment bank in Tonkin. Two of its bosses, chairman Edward Blount and head manager Octave Homberg approached the government, especially the foreign affairs and finance ministers, in 1887. They insisted on the necessity of eliminating any kind of monopoly by the CEP, proposing instead to set up a bank which would be open to all – what would have already been the case with *Banque de l'Indochine* if *Société générale* and *Crédit lyonnais* had agreed to collaborate:

> These gentlemen [Émile Flourens, Minister of Foreign Affairs in 1888–1889, and Maurice Rouvier, Finance Minister] did not hide that fact that we had, in *Banque de l'Indochine*, a formidable rival who, taking advantage of a sudden increase in its social capital, has asked via the intermediation of Comptoir d'escompte de Paris, for an extension of its privileges at Annam and Tonkin. In this situation, *Société générale* and *Comptoir d'escompte de Paris* are diametrically opposed, with *Comptoir d'escompte de Paris* wanting no help and *Société générale* proposing to conduct the operation with all credit establishments [...]. Any operation in Tonkin will depend on the bank which will provide the funds, with all adjudication, private or public, being influenced by forex issues. It is thus evident that if *Comptoir d'escompte de Paris* succeeds in extending the *Banque de l'Indochine*'s rights in Annam and Tonkin,

only those establishments which would have its support would be able to submit tenders [for the potential contracts and concessions in these countries]. It would amount to a monopoly granted to *Banque de l'Indochine* for all major projects in Tonkin. On the other hand, *Société générale* will take help from all quarters and proposes to establish *Banque privilégiée du Tonkin* with the support of all the big credit establishments, thus opening the door to the best deals.[33]

Société générale pointed to the necessity of maintaining an open field for the allocation of the future contracts and concessions which would result from the development of these territories: here too it remained loyal to the course set by its modernist and Saint-Simonian founders. Meanwhile, it tried to bring aboard the businessman Récopé, who had all sorts of projects regarding Indochina. In fact, it would seem that the government used Société générale and Récopé to put pressure on *Banque de l'Indochine* to increase the number of services that it would have to provide.[34] Negotiations were also underway between Homberg, CEO of Société générale, and Stanislas Simon, chairman and manager of *Banque de l'Indochine* (along with Édouard Hentsch, chairman of CEP). They toyed with the idea of doubling the *Banque de l'Indochine*'s capital, of which half would be reserved for Société générale (and its allies), which would give it control over one-fourth of the total capital.

Ultimately, Société générale lost out to *Banque de l'Indochine* and CEP because it was seen in the political circles as leaning too far right relative to the moderate Republican majority,[35] which CNEP courted successfully. In 1887, it abandoned its own project to gather the financing circle for *Banque de l'Indochine*. In February 1888, the *Banque de l'Indochine*'s rights were extended to Annam and Tonkin (as well as New Caledonia). Meanwhile, its directors agreed to include Société générale in the issuing bank's capital and in the community of French banks which had turned *Banque de l'Indochine* into a sort of local representative, their ambassador not only in Indochina but also in South East Asia and China (against the powerful British Hongkong & Shanghai Bank). Its capital was increased from 8 million to 12 million francs in July 1888 (2 million to 3 million in paid-up capital). Société générale should have got half, but the shareholders refused to cede their subscription rights, and it could subscribe to only 3,720 shares of the 8,000 issued on this occasion, which gave it 15.5 per cent of the capital for a total of 744,000 francs (as only one-fourth of the nominal value of 125 francs was paid, over a share premium of 75 francs). Société générale won a seat on the board, given to its director Homberg, while Paribas (one seat), CIC (three seats) and CEP (four seats) retained their positions among the 11 board members.

But after the fall of CEP, the Société générale's influence grew as it was now one of the three establishments which financed the *Banque de l'Indochine*. Along with CIC and Paribas, it received an additional seat on the board (occupied by Hubert Henrotte, a member of its own board) as well as a spot in a five-member committee (completed by two *Banque de l'Indochine* directors) charged with executive supervision. Finally, Homberg was made board secretary. Of course, the rebirth of CEP (as CNEP) some months later meant that a place had to be made for it on the *Banque de l'Indochine*'s Board (May 1890), and it even attained to the presidency in 1892. Homberg remained board secretary, and *Société générale* became a major stakeholder in the *Banque de l'Indochine*'s business affairs and conduct, representing French banks in Asia, with *Crédit lyonnais* also joining in 1896. It also participated in the banking pool which refinanced *Banque de l'Indochine* in Paris and the guarantee of the credits of acceptance it received in London.

Sometime later, the balance of power was shaken for a third time when the *Banque de l'Indochine*'s Asian strategy itself was called into question: should its issuing concession be renewed? How to improve the specifications? Meanwhile, *Crédit lyonnais*, which had launched branches in India in 1894–1895 and had established itself in Egypt, also turned into an 'imperial' bank and wanted to participate in Chinese and Indochinese business. CEP had lost some of its financing and relational power when it collapsed in 1889; the new CNEP was nowhere as strong, especially as several of its close banking houses had also been swept away by the crash (Hentsch) and it had to abandon its role of guardian. The reduction in the CNEP's capacity to influence and the fact that it had to restructure its network within the power circles, coupled with the increase in the number of participants, changed the inter-bank balance of power. Still, the prospects of divided French interests in Asia being pitted against the power of British banking[36] led to the formulation of a new consensus regarding *Banque de l'Indochine*. The issuing concession was renewed in 1895–1896 on condition of an expansion policy in the rest of Asia; it was an implicit contract between the French houses, turning it into the national business community's 'local establishment' in Asia, especially as it took over the CNEP's Hong Kong agency, and *Crédit lyonnais* stopped all direct activity in Asia and entered its board of directors.

This more or less confirmed its independence from its erstwhile godfather who had now to give it its freedom so that it could become a center of influence in its own right within the 'imperial' banking group. At the same time, CNEP's disappearance from Asia did not, for that matter, let other bankers succeed in short-circuiting *Banque de l'Indochine*, either in 1887–1888 or 1894–1895. Over the years, an Indochinese-Asian pressure group was formed to quash any budding desire in Parisian banks to act directly in Asia (like *Deutsche Bank* with *Deutsche Asiatische Bank*). By the turn of the century, it was strong enough to become one of the flag-bearers of the imperial economic spirit – before, as we shall see later, falling victim in its turn to a competitive offensive.

The crisis faced by Banque industrielle de Chine

The affair of *Banque industrielle de Chine* (BIDC) is too well known[37] to warrant further clarification. The attempt to set up a mixed bank, at once a commercial and investment bank endowed with a large share portfolio, officially in China to complement, but in reality to rival, the *Banque de l'Indochine*, resulted in a managerial nightmare wherein the risk management was such that it left the bank teetering on the brink on numerous occasions – just before WWI and later, in the early 1920s. But Paris was familiar with the advent of such entities which, in the name of modernist expansionism, confused the banking business with speculative investing in times of economic boom and served as a caution against belliger-ent wheeling and dealing. Be that as it may, this example takes place in 1923 with the collapse of BIDC. Everyone knows that Paribas used its influence to expand its imperial reach in Asia. At the same time, it was unthinkable that, for the sake of French interests on the international scene, BIDC would be allowed to completely disappear, especially when the nation faced such strong British and Japanese competition.

We have a magnificent case study of Paribas deploying its entire arsenal of contacts in favour of its 'imperial banking' strategy: mobilizing the press and its networks within the Finance and Foreign Affairs ministries, etc. It was a fight between two banking spheres of influence.[38] On one side, the Finance Ministry and the Treasury were against the bailing out of the BIDC. To this camp also belonged *Banque de l'Indochine*, shored up by Finance Minister Paul Doumer, who had been governor of Indochina when Paribas had balked at co-financing the *Chemin de fer du Yunnan*. Among those in favour of the rescue was the Ministry of Foreign Affairs, the Minister Louis Loucheur, Paribas and other influential entities in the Far East. Finally, the refusal by the Big Banks, Rothschild and the *Comité des forges* (metallurgists' association) to get involved led to the collapse of BIDC in July 1921. It was 'a war of banks: Indochina against Paribas [...]. No one doubted that at the bottom of its heart, the *Banque de l'Indochine* must have felt some satisfaction at the fall of a rival whose audacity and conceit had been so irritating and whose competiveness and entrepreneurial spirit so disturbing.'[39]

After the dust settled, business resumed gradually: BIDC's healthy assets were taken over by Paribas and transformed into, first, *Société française de gérance de la BIDC* and finally, *Banque franco-chinoise pour le commerce et l'industrie* (BFC). The success of this discreet coalition was exemplified by the composition BFC's board[40]: several Paribas executives rubbed shoulders with a representative of *Banque nationale de crédit* (the establishment which had played the role of spoilsport among the big banking names) and several former senior officials from the ministries of Finance and Foreign Affairs, including a former ambassador to Japan who was also a CFAT director – completing the network that Paribas had been weaving for the past half-century. It would seem then that it was possible for France to get a bigger slice of the Chinese eco-nomic boom and contain the British and American offensives (especially with merchant banker Jean Monnet). This study serves to confirm Paribas's entry into the group of 'imperial' bankers: after Morocco and Madagascar, the invest-ment bank added (much more modestly) Indochinese and Chinese banking and trading hubs to its portfolio (while by and large letting *Banque de l'Indochine* assume leadership in Indochina).

Issuing banks in the Maghreb

The geopolitical, administrative and economic development of several regions in the Maghreb sometimes led to some competitive friction between banking houses which were keen to get themselves privileged positions on the money market.

The rush for Tunisia (from 1881 to 1904)

The historical rooting of *Banque de l'Algérie*[41] (established in August 1851) justified its abstention from any particular interest group. Due to the region's relatively large economic strength and its own legitimacy (the result of good governance), it became a centre of influence in its own right – a fact that historians have not yet fully appreciated. Still, the fact that senior officials were sometimes 'exiled' to its administration (due to political reversals) meant that its stature was perhaps due more to the outgrowth of the central administration than to any self-created sphere of influence. Moreover, having the status of a colony, it was close to the Finance Ministry.

Gradually, the growth in its activities and knowledge portfolio and its financial solidity turned it into a mini sphere of influence, with some clear maneuvering room or, at the least, the capacity to promote its own interests within the state's economic apparatus. It is true that it was supported more and more by the layers of European capitalism which were multiplying in Algeria's regional capitals. Be that as it may, our colleague Lazar Mohamed Gharbi[42] has clearly shown how its management and administration succeeded in quashing a project for the creation of a money issuing institution in the newly formed Tunisian protectorate. To begin with, in 1881–1884, it put the brakes on any initiatives coming from mainland France or the Tunisian trading sector; then, in 1884, it proposed expanding its issuing privileges into Tunisia. It formed a mini pressure group by joining hands with East Algerian businesses and the network that had been formed around the *Bône-Guelma* railway company. There did not seem to be too much of a fight as the state's economic apparatus and the political majority agreed that the 'development' of the new protectorate required a rigorous framework and that the Tunisian money market needed the support of a solid institution. Thus, the views of the Finance Ministry (Joseph Caillaux) prevailed over the 'autonomous' Ministry of Foreign Affairs (Théophile Delcassé) and the law of July 1900 paved the way for the creation of *Banque de l'Algérie* in Tunisia, which extended its issuing privileges in 1904 – before changing its name to *Banque de l'Algérie et de Tunisie* in 1948.

The rush for Morocco: the creation of Banque d'État du Maroc

Everyone knows of the banking and financial battles that raged in Morocco and the resulting strongholds that were erected there over the years. The bigger fights concerned the creation of an issuing bank when the French protectorate came to be recognized by the international community. Though the young BUP could not, by itself, challenge Paribas, CIC (which supported *Banque commerciale du Maroc* and various commercial interests), BUP (allied with Schneider and its *Compagnie marocaine* – a holding company that supervised trade and public works companies) and groups such as Hersent or Gradis, could hinder Paribas's growth. It could well be that the notable absence of the three big credit establishments left the field open for Paribas, as together, they could have formed a decisive power block. It is also evident that the investment bank's financing power was the most suited to the massive loan requirements of a region in the throes of an intense and rapid development.[43]

Finally and most importantly, the authorities (especially the Ministry of Foreign Affairs, with Delcassé) thought that in the international situation then prevailing, it was the only establishment which could adequately represent French power in the face of the German financing might threatening Morocco. What was needed was a European bank, solidly established in Belgian, Dutch, Italian and Spanish relational networks, which could hide the French influence on the new issuing bank to be established – as the other countries needed to take a large block to counter the French presence. Attempts by other banking spheres were brushed aside. The BAO's ideas seem scarcely credible – but it could have been CNEP pushing from behind – like in the case of the *Banque de l'Algérie* which was supported by the business community of Oran.[44] And we know how *Banque d'État du Maroc* was created under Paribas' patronage after the conference of Jazira.

Banque de l'Algérie *versus Paribas:* the question of the State Bank of Morocco (1919–1925)

After some 15 years of consolidation, *Banque d'État du Maroc* found itself once again at the heart of in inter-bank rivalry regarding the controlling stake and the renewal of its issuance privilege. The protectorate's monetary difficulties in 1919 pushed people to reconsider Paribas's strategic position: an influential group advocated that *Banque de l'Algérie* assume the privilege – which would make it the Maghreb's main central bank, especially as the aid given to the Moroccan currency during the crisis led to the injection of Algerian Francs into Morocco. This group, which united the *Banque de l'Algérie*'s management with the Ministry of Finance, wanted a monetary rationalization which would facilitate pooling their resources to support the currency in Morocco with the backing of a more solid establishment.[45] But in opposition, a coalition was formed which united the Moroccan authorities (who did not want Algeria to interfere in the protectorate's economic life), the Ministry of Foreign Affairs and Paribas. In the meantime, French authorities agreed to let the investment bank take over the Russian, Swedish and German shares in *Banque d'État du Maroc* (1919–1920), increasing its power. Though *Banque de l'Algérie* conceded priority to its sister concern regarding the establishment of the new Moroccan franc (March 1920), it pushed the spread of Algerian francs and its own interests in Morocco.

Finally, the fight was won by the autonomous group: 'The battle proved too costly for *Banque de l'Algérie*. In 1923, its governor, Moreau, began negotiations for an armistice between the two establishments.' *Banque du Maroc* received several assurances from the authorities which guaranteed its autonomy and its modus operandi and 'in early 1925, an agreement was reached with the *Banque de l'Algérie* which put an end to the hostilities,'[46] signaling a de facto victory for the group led by Paribas.[47] Henceforth, along with the investment holding *Compagnie générale du Maroc*, *Banque d'État du Maroc*[48] would become one of Paribas's main weapons in the protectorate, opening the doors to pertinent information and profitable joint financing. 'Banque de Paris et des Pays-Bas is the undisputed leader of all the groups active in Morocco. In fact, along with our State Bank, Compagnie générale du Maroc and the Omnium nord-africain, it controls most of the important sectors of the economy.'[49]

Issuing banks in French West Africa, Lebanon and Madagascar

At the same time, several other overseas territories also turned into mini battle-fields for banks wanting to dominate the local money market.

Was Afrique occidentale française *a banking battleground (1901)?*

The creation of the FWA (French West-Africa, the institution of *Afrique occidentale française*, managing French western sub-Saharan Africa), the economic emergence of the central African colonies and the establishment of a banking architecture capable of consolidating the maturing economic system raised questions regarding the *Banque du Sénégal*'s status. Since 1853, its conduct had been the result of a subtle balance between the CNEP's management, Girondin interests (with 73 per cent of the capital) in the house's business community (especially behind the Maurel, such as Émile Maurel[50]) and interest groups from Marseille. When *Banque du Sénégal* spread its activities into the *Afrique occidentale française*, the latter mobilized to break this half-century-old balance and to affirm the Phocaean city's trade and shipping power.

Could CNEP play its card in all this? As we have said, history explains why it was the 'colonial' banks' point man in Paris. Despite the setbacks of 1889, it had retained its mediating and refinancing capacity and it was natural that it found itself topping the list when it came to deciding the fate of the old *Banque du Sénégal* regarding the deploying of French economic and political interests along the west coast of Africa. The historical coalition of trade interests, headed by Émile Maurel, seemed to have been in favour of *Banque du Sénégal* – a long-time partner. But the economic problems of 1889–1899 had affected trade and weakened *Banque du Sénégal*. CNEP itself was just limping back to normalcy after its crash of 1889. Thus, compromises had to be made between the partners in the creation of a new French bank in sub-Saharan Africa. It has to be noted though that they were helped by the absence of the other big Parisian banks, which apparently were reluctant to pump money into the region, while Paribas, *Compagnie algérienne-Mirabaud* and CFAT were concentrating on the opportunities offered by the Maghreb. Meanwhile, despite its problems, CNEP continued to be a stabilizing agent in the colonial banking sector, whose fragility was due, in part, to the lack of a sufficiently large financial capacity in markets that were not only delicate but marked by profound developmental inequalities and, on the other, the volatility of FOREX and commodity prices on the world's markets.[51] This led the public authorities to retain their confidence in CNEP – whose directors also happened to be well entrenched within the 'colonial party.'

Meanwhile, realizing that a relative weakening of its rival-partners limited its scope of action, the Marseille interest group pushed for the creation of a second issuance bank in which they would have the controlling majority as the traditional trading houses of Bordeaux were hardly active outside Guinea and were practically non-existent in Ivory Coast and Dahomey.

> In February 1900, Augustin Féraud, the architect of the Marseille offensive [president of the Chamber of Commerce, vice-president of Société marseillaise de crédit and CNEP], began negotiations with [Henri] Nouvion and [Émile] Mercet, directors of Banque du Sénégal and CNEP [respectively]. The negotiations proved rather difficult because his proposal – of founding an establishment of two million francs with 60 percent of the shares reserved for Bordeaux, 20 percent for CNEP and 20 percent for the Marseille coalition [Mante-Borelli-Régis, *Compagnie française de l'Afrique occidentale* (CFAO), Cyprien-Fabre, SMC] – was met by fierce resistance from Nouvion who wanted to retain his autonomy by completely removing the CNEP and reducing Marseille's share.[52]

Meanwhile, the Girondists hunkered down around Maurel, and we still do not know the part played by the government in these debates. Finally, the lion's share in the new BAO, established in 1901, went to Bordeaux and the Marseille camp's offensive seemed to have been negated. The Girondin (*Maurel frères*, Maurel & Prom) and Parisian (CNEP) hubs came to an understanding with Marseille, with the SMC, Mante & Borelli, *Compagnie française de l'Afrique occidentale* (CFAO) and Cyprien Fabre, joining the project which culminated in the creation of *Banque de l'Afrique occidentale* (BAO) in 1901.[53] It would seem that there was no conflict regarding this between the 'imperial' bankers – but access to new archives (CNEP?) would allow us to better determine their real interaction on this occasion. Girondin traders continued to maintain their influence during the inter-war period via Lucien Maurel (also vice-president of the *Union coloniale*) and Gaston Gradis – both directors of the BAO.

Paribas in the French Levant (1923–1924)

It came as no surprise that when the Ottoman Empire collapsed, the Imperial Ottoman Bank's agencies in what became the French *Levant*, passed under the tutelage of a new establishment controlled by Paribas. In fact, the investment bank included *Banque impériale ottoman* (BIO) in its sphere of influence and, in 1923–1925, took control of this budding commercial bank. The positions thus acquired led logically to the creation of *Banque de Syrie et du Grand Liban* (BSGL) in 1921, which acted as Paribas's quasi-subsidiary. Paribas' initiatives were amply rewarded when the issuing privilege for the two territories was granted to BSGL in 1924. Meanwhile, its competitors were not sitting idle. An alliance between CFAT and Société générale (which had come close when the former bought over *Banque de Salonique* from the latter) resulted in the establishment of *Banque française de Syrie*.

Paribas in Madagascar (1924–1926)

The growth of the Madagascan economy and the multitude of players on the commercial banking market necessitated the creation of an issuing and refinancing institute to stabilize the credit situation in the Big Island. A rivalry thus sprang up between CNEP (the Big Island's 'natural' bank,[54] which had established offices in Tamatave and Tananarive as early as the nineteenth century, provided liquidity to the local colonial business community and had proposed the creation of an issuing bank in 1895) and Paribas, which wanted to make the most of its experience in the management of overseas issuing banks and of banks in developing countries, especially in Central and Balkan Europe. The latter had already prepared a project along these lines in November 1922.[55] Political historians have emphasized the political aspect of the concession: Paribas's pressure group turned towards partisan and parliamentary hubs with the house's directors choosing, by and large, to support the left majority in 1924–1926, without taking part in the 'wall of money.' Not surprisingly, the Édouard Herriot government granted it the *Banque de Madagascar*'s concession on 28 November 1924.

The agreement was signed on 18 December,[56] the bill tabled in the House on 19 December and passed on 22 December 1925 – whatever the difficulties faced by the Left through all this time. While the positive effects of activating the political network is undeniable, we must also note that Paribas was behind *Crédit foncier de Madagascar* and that its subsidiary, *Compagnie générale des colonies*, had undertaken to support several Franco-Madagascan companies (*Compagnie lyonnaise de Madagascar*, etc.). Paribas's profile of an investment bank, due to its co-financing capacity and the ability to mobilize investors in mainland France, was deemed more pertinent than the CNEP's profile of a simple commercial bank. Paribas was well and truly the victor, retaining 20 per cent of the capital (15 per cent directly) and partnering its former rival for 10 per cent.

The rescue and control of overseas interests in the 1930s

The balance between the growing influence of the state in the overseas mixed economy and the prosperity of the imperial interest hubs was confirmed by the choices made following the crash of the early 1930s. The state's economic apparatus would support the 'imperial' banking movement if it would also act in the general interest, and its support increasingly took the form of counterparties. A fine example can be found in sub-Saharan Africa, when two of the three big establishments, *Banque française de l'Afrique* (BFA) and *Banque commerciale africaine* (BCA) found themselves on the brink. BFA was bailed out by the BAO and its partners (who had to wait to recover their loans). BAO dug deep into its pockets to advance a loan to the state so that it could guarantee BFA's deposits and at the same time extended loans to various other local governments to help them tide over the cash crunch caused by the BFA's fall. Meanwhile, BFA was bailed out by BUP. Though BUP thus confirmed its presence in sub-Saharan Africa (links with SCOA, Gradis and Maurel & Prom; investments in various plantation companies), it had to pay the price by giving subsidies to BCA which it had helped create in 1924 with Belgian investors (from the SGB group), *Banque transatlantique* and CCF.

It was the government which asked BUP to reestablish confidence by refinancing its subsidiary: 'I would have you know the main reasons why bailing out BCA would be in the general interest.'[57] Once it had been refinance and re-capitalized by BUP, BCA could resume its activities, gradually recoup its debts and clear its liabilities. In 1941, BAO took over from BUP and became a majority shareholder of BCA. It thus eliminated two dangerous competitors by gradually including them in its sphere of influence. But it paid the price by having to come to a compromise with the government which wanted to stabilize the money market in Africa and by, if absolutely required, consolidating BAO's oligopolistic position.

Saving the banking empire in the 1950s and 1960s?

The school of thought that we will call 'economism' spread over numerous business communities when, for several years, the notions of modernization and assimilation seemed to dominate the reorganization of the overseas territories in the best interests of preserving the positions captured in these countries.[58] There is no doubt that men at the heart of banking and financial circles played a major role: Robert Lemaignen[59] (*'Les liaisons intérieures de l'Union française'*) and Luc Durand-Réville[60] (*'L'Afrique équatoriale'*) participated in the key publication of 1953, *La France d'outre-mer. Sa situation actuelle*, which by and large symbolized the apogee of the imperial economic spirit[61] just prior to the independence movements. The fact was that the African empire, along with mainland France (and certain hubs in Europe such as Geneva) was one of the destinations for the funds being repatriated from Indochina. Morocco and sub-Saharan Africa were especially important in this redeployment, which required a certain overseas institutional stability.

Does that mean therefore that the 'imperial' bankers were part of the 'hard' pressure group which resisted the movement for autonomy and independence in these overseas territories?[62] We have been able to identify some such actors within the UPANG (Private Union to aid General de Gaulle's National Action) which was created in November 1949–January 1950 to collect funds from big donors, including the business community, to co-finance the RPF.[63] Though one of the CNEP's bosses (Henri Bizot) was an active participant, and the secretary general of the Rothschild bank, René Fillon, was the treasurer, the overseas community was thinly represented – despite the fact that both these houses had major overseas interests. Even the fact of Mme Eugénie Félix-Éboué-Tell – the widow of an ex-Governor of Equatorial (Central) Africa and Gaullist during WWII – taking up its presidency is not enough for us to say that 'the bank' supported the RPF because it foresaw a firm overseas policy[64] and seemed opposed to the 'empire destroyers.'

At the same time, we have unearthed names like Luc Durand-Réville (senator and also director of an overseas trading group), Henri Vézia (one of Bordeaux's big traders), Henri Borgeaud (Algerian trader and industrialist), Pierre and Rémy Lebon (heirs to the Lebon group) and Edme Campenon (public works: Campenon-Bernard). Because of Campenon-Bernard and Durand-Réville, one could argue that BUP was active and influential in this Gaullist world – and it is true that the general's brother was also a director in the years 1930–1940. Nevertheless, it would be wrong to conclude that the 'colonial' bank supported the RPF. It was simply one factor among others, and we shall certainly find such 'imperial' bankers among the *Mouvement républicain populaire* (MRP), *Centre national des indépendants et paysans* (CNIP), even radicals.

We did not find any evidence that the directors of either *Compagnie algérienne* or CFAT were involved in the anti-independence movement. Though a month-by-month monitoring of the latter's directors reveals that they were dismayed by the turn of events and that they continued to believe in the future of an Algeria and a Morocco within France (they increased their investments in all their regional branches), there is not a shred of archival evidence to show that they participated in any way in any pressure group resisting the political authority. Let us also not forget that the president of BUP, Henri Lafond, a hard-core 'imperial' banker, was himself assassinated by the *Organisation de l'armée secrète* (OAS) in 1963 because he refused to support the cause of a French Algeria.

In any case, should we accept the contentions made, even by some academic analysts, regarding the state's dependence vis-à-vis financial power-brokers? We rather think that France's colonial policy was not formed at the stock market – to parody de Gaulle – and the supposed tendency of 'imperial' bankers, financiers and businessmen in general to use their networks of influence to weigh on overseas policy does not seem to us to be strong enough to have actually done so in a long term – but that is all that we dare say. Elsewhere, the government's authority too did not weigh on every case: a decree of July 1942 transferred the BAO's privileges in French (freed) sub-Saharan Africa to *Caisse centrale de la France libre* established in December 1941. Moreover, the decision regarding the BAO's fate did not favour the 'imperial' bankers: when BAO lost its issuing privileges in the sub-Saharan Africa in October 1955 and turned into an ordinary commercial bank, *Banque de l'Indochine* let it be known that it was very interested in taking over this new BAO. Unfortunately, its negotiations with CIC fell through, and the government imposed its own choice: the shares held by the central and territorial governments were ceded to a banking pool (CNEP, CCF, *Compagnie algérienne*, Rothschild, *Union européenne industrielle et financière, Banque belge d'Afrique*), with the injunction to sell them on the market.[65] The 'imperial' bankers could do nothing against the power of the public authorities.

On the contrary, it would seem that the corpus of ideas known as 'economism,' which prevailed in certain business communities to favour big investment in the colonies to stir up development and welfare as a substitute to independence, aimed not so much at substituting development with investments in independence, but rather at ensuring a smooth transition from empire to independence in order to preserve company interests and, especially, to stimulate investments. This led to the creation of a 'joint venture' between businessmen and bankers to push for a development that would make the most of all present and future assets.

To us, BUP seemed to be oriented to this end, in both the Maghreb as well as sub-Saharan Africa,[66] as a linchpin for such trends and influential groups connecting 'imperial banking' and firms. We also see the same tendency in the way the financial groups which were linked to the big investment banks restructured their investments – every one of them succeeded in reshaping their positions by leveraging the 'soft' transitions, especially in Morocco and sub-Saharan Africa (excepting Guinea).[67] Does that justify Beau de Loménie's booklet *L'Algérie trahie par l'argent*?[68] Especially when Daniel Lefeuvre has shown how many banks and business confederations believed until the end that they would be able to develop investment projects in the wake of the Constantine Plan, set up in 1960 to modernize colonial Algeria.[69]

Conclusion: did the government arbitrate between rival colonial banking spheres?

In the course of the capitalist battles between colonial business hubs, each supported by its network of institutional relations (especially within the government apparatus) and their 'webs' of economic interest, rivalries between spheres of influence were formed to consolidate each hub's firepower. The 'imperial' banking networks faced each other within this liberal economy, open to the free play of different interest groups. Though both CNEP and Paribas succeeded in capturing business opportunities within the colonial economy, the former's sphere of influence remained stable while that of the latter grew significantly between 1907 (Morocco) and 1925 (Madagascar). CNEP took up the financing of 'colonial' banks, *Banque de l'Indochine* and BAO, while Paribas scored points in Morocco (in 1907 and in 1925) and in the Levant.

Meanwhile, new forces emerged, overseas banks which gradually gained autonomy, built themselves their own spheres of influence and especially, in the context of this study, federated a 'web' of business hubs: *Banque de l'Indochine* thus won its battle against CIC, *Crédit lyonnais* and *Société générale* (to spread across Tonkin and become the French local establishment oriented towards Asia) and pushed back Paribas, which wanted to save BIDC. Similarly, *Banque de l'Algérie* succeeded in gaining advantage in Tunisia, though it was prevented from sliding towards Morocco. Finally, CFAT and BUP turned into powerful hubs, but they did not take part in the institutional inter-bank battles, preferring to concentrate on the unceasing war being fought in the overseas money markets.

Be that as it may, despite all the friction between the various government agencies (especially between the departments of Foreign Affairs and Finance) and the recurrent outbreaks of corruption, we do not think that France was a 'banana republic.' The checks and balances in place and the airing of influential rivalries by the press which was often aware of the interest groups, were effective counters, not to mention the intrinsic qualities of the higher civil servants themselves. The state's imperial economic apparatus took a more concrete shape during the inter-war period – whether it be specialized departments in the ministries of the Interior (Algeria), Foreign Affairs (protectorates) or Colonies – and came to challenge the government's traditional departments (Commerce, Finance). Numerous case studies show that the state had some real margin for maneuvering and that the decision-makers could impose their choice on the 'money powers.' Bit by bit, government interventionism gained ground in people's minds, especially when it took the form of a mixed economy (like the *Caisses de Crédit Agricole* in Algeria and Madagascar).

Thus, the government was very much involved at the creation of *Banque de Madagascar*: it was a shareholder, held seats on the board and had a clear say in the administration. The renewal of the BAO's issuing privilege in 1927 (voted through the National Assembly on 21 February 1928, through the Senate on 25 January 1929; promulgated in January 1929, implemented in February) confirmed this tendency towards a mixed economy, with the state taking 28 per cent,[70] appointing the managing director and holding three seats on the board. The agreement of June 1931 (followed by the law of April 1932) increased the state's hold by allowing it to increase its share to 32 per cent in exchange for letting the BAO rescue its finances which had been compromised by the bailing out of *Banque française de l'Afrique* – especially to counter the threat posed by the growth of *Banque belge d'Afrique*.

Meanwhile, though on one hand the powerful *Banque de l'Indochine* succeeded in dashing the government's hope of increasing its control on the bank in 1924–1926, with even the idea of creating a new issuing bank, the negotiations of 1929 concluded in the bank having to concede to the requirements of the state – even as Poincaré's right-wing government was in power. Though its issuing concession was renewed for 25 years by the law of 1931, it had to concede one-fifth of its capital to the state (which ensued half of the increase in capital from 75 million to 120 million francs), six of the board's twenty and two of the executive committee's six seats, and the power to nominate the president (though the house retained its prerogative to nominate the managing director). This development was capped in 1940 when the president took on the mantle of managing director and the state's hold turned decisive.

We are of the opinion that it would be wrong to believe that the state was no more than a puppet in the hands of 'imperial' bankers. Its role of a referee gradually turned into a clear responsibility regarding the conduct of banking operations or, at the very least, towards a relative control over these operations, in the monitoring of margins and especially, in the promulgation of new contract clauses for the concessions granted for the development of new activities and implantations and to decrease the price of the transactions made with the state itself.[71]

Notes

1 Jean Suret-Canale, *Afrique et Capitaux* (two volumes), Paris, L'arbre verdoyant, 1987.
2 Jacques Marseille, *Empire colonial et capitalisme français. Histoire d'un divorce*, Paris, Albin Michel, 1984. Catherine Hodeir, *Stratégies d'empire. Le grand patronat colonial face à la décolonisation (1945–1962)*, Paris, Belin, 2003.
3 Alain Buffon, *Monnaie et crédit en économie coloniale. Contribution à l'histoire économique de la Guadeloupe, 1635–1919*, Société d'histoire de la Guadeloupe, 1979.
4 *Banque de La Martinique, Banque de La Guadeloupe, Banque de La Réunion*, in 1853; *Banque de la Guyane, Banque du Sénégal*, in 1855.
5 Hubert Bonin, 'L'outre-mer, marché pour la banque commerciale (1876–1985)?,' in Jacques Marseille (ed.), *La France & l'outre-mer* (proceedings of the conference of November 1996; *Les relations économiques & financières entre la France & la France d'outre-mer*), Paris, Comité pour l'histoire économique & financière de la France, 1998, pp. 437–83.
6 Hubert Bonin, 'Le Comptoir national d'escompte de Paris, une banque impériale (1848–1940),' *Revue française d'histoire d'outre-mer*, 78(293), 1991, pp. 477–97. Hubert Bonin, 'The French banks in the Pacific area (1860–1945),' in Olive Checkland, Shizuya Nishimura and Norio Tamaki (eds), *Pacific banking (1859–1959). East meets West* (proceedings of the Tokyo conference in 1993), London, MacMillan; New York, St Martin's Press, 1994, pp. 61–74.
7 Gilles Le Béguec, 'L'exemple des républicains modérés (1888–1903)', in Sylvie Guillaume (ed.), *Les élites fins de siècles, XIXᵉ–XXᵉ siècles*, Pessac, Publications de la Maison des sciences de l'homme d'Aquitaine, 1992, pp. 141–56. About Mercet, see Christophe Charle, *Les élites de la République, 1880–1900*, Paris, Fayard, 1987, pp. 167–8.
8 Félix Torres, *Banquiers d'avenir. Des Comptoirs d'escompte à la naissance de BNP Paribas*, Paris, Albin Michel, 2000.
9 We have borrowed this expression from Jacques Marseille, when he talked of the empire as 'good business' for a small number of enterprises.
10 Éric Bussière, *Paribas, l'Europe et le monde, 1872–1992*, Antwerp, Fonds Mercator, 1992.
11 See Georges Hatton, *Les enjeux financiers et économiques du protectorat marocain (1936–1954). Politique publique et investisseurs privés*, Paris, Publications de la SFHOM, 2009.
12 See File of the State Bank of Morocco, Archives of CIC, box 34, years 1920s–1930s.
13 'La Banque de Paris et des Pays-Bas,' in *La France et les trusts*, spécial *Économie et politique*, 5/6, 1954, pp. 73–7 (revue proche du PFC).
14 Hubert Bonin, 'La SFHOM et les milieux d'affaires ultramarins: Georges Nesterenko trésorier,' in Hubert Bonin, Bernard Droz and Josette Rivallain (eds), *Cent ans d'histoire des outre-mers. SFHOM, 1912–2012*, Paris, Publications de la SFHOM, 2013, pp. 333–55.
15 Moussa had been Chief of staff to a Minister of Overseas France, director of economic affairs at the Ministry of Overseas France and director of the World Bank's Africa Department in 1962–4.
16 Éric Bussière, *Horace Finaly, banquier, 1871–1945*, Paris, Fayard, 1996.
17 Ibid., p. 264.
18 Yves Bencivengo, 'Les réseaux d'influence de la banque Rothschild: l'exemple de la société Le Nickel en Nouvelle-Calédonie (1880–1914),' in Hubert Bonin, Jean-François Klein and Catherine Hodeir (eds), *L'esprit économique impérial (1830–1970). Groupes de pression & réseaux du patronat colonial en France & dans l'empire*, Paris, Publications de la SFHOM, 2008, pp. 429–45; Yann Bencivengo, Nickel. La naissance de l'industrie calédonienne, Tours, Presses universitaires François-Rabelais, series 'Perspectives historiques', 2014.
19 'Eldorado ou Panama?,' in Henri Coston, *La Haute Banque et les trusts. Les financiers qui mènent le monde*, Paris, La Librairie française, 1960, pp. 368–80.

20 *Un centenaire, 1848–1948. Worms & Cie*, Paris, Worms, 1948. The bank established itself in Algiers and Casablanca in 1945–1946.

21 Isabelle Chancelier, *Messieurs Mirabaud et Cie. D'Aigues-Vives à Paris, via Genève et Milan*, Paris, Éditions familiales, 2001.

22 Hubert Bonin, *La Banque de l'union parisienne (1874/1904–1974). De l'Europe aux outre-mers*, Paris, Publications de la SFHOM, 2011.

23 Hubert Bonin, 'La Compagnie algérienne levier de la colonisation et prospère grâce à elle (1865–1939),' *Revue française d'histoire d'outre-mer*, 328/329, second term 2000, pp. 209–30. Hubert Bonin, 'Une histoire bancaire transméditerranéenne: la Compagnie algérienne, d'un ultime apogée au repli (1945–1970),' in Daniel Lefeuvre et al. (eds), *La Guerre d'Algérie au miroir des décolonisations françaises* (in honor of Charles-Robert Ageron), Paris, Publications de la Société française d'histoire d'outre-mer, 2000, pp. 151–76 (second edition in 2005).

24 Cf. 'Famille Mirabaud,' in Henri Coston, *Le retour des '200 familles'*, Paris, La librairie française, 1960, p. 38.

25 Hubert Bonin, *Un outre-mer bancaire méditerranéen. Le Crédit foncier d'Algérie & de Tunisie (1880–1997)*, Paris, Publications of Société française d'histoire d'outre-mer, 2004. Hubert Bonin, 'Une banque française maître d'oeuvre d'un outre-mer levantin: le Crédit foncier d'Algérie & de Tunisie, du Maghreb à la Méditerranée orientale (1919–1970),' in *Outre-Mers. Revue d'histoire*, 91(342–3), 2004, pp. 239–72.

26 Joël Dubos, *André Lebon. Un homme d'affaires en République (1858–1938)*, Rennes, Presses universitaires de Rennes, 2003.

27 Hubert Bonin, *CFAT*, op. cit., pp. 212–13.

28 Ibid., p. 213.

29 Marc Meuleau, *Des pionniers en Extrême-Orient. La Banque de l'Indochine, 1875–1975*, Paris, Fayard, 1990. Yasuo Gonjo, *Banque coloniale ou banque d'affaires. La Banque de l'Indochine sous la IIIᵉ République*, Paris, Publications du Comité pour l'histoire économique & financière de la France, 1993.

30 'La Banque de l'Indochine,' in *La France et les trusts*, 1954, pp. 77–80.

31 Marc Meuleau, *La Banque de l'Indochine*, op. cit.: all this was inspired by M. Meuleau's book.

32 Robert Hentsch, *Hentsch. Banquiers à Genève et à Paris au XIXᵉ siècle*, Paris, self-published, 1996. Robert Hentsch, *De mère en fille. Histoire des familles Hoskier, Appert, Giroud, Hentsch*, Paris, self-published, 1997.

33 Minutes of the *Société générale*'s board, 9 August 1887. Cf. Hubert Bonin, *Histoire de la Société générale. I. 1864–1890. Naissance d'une banque*, Geneva, Droz, 2006.

34 Minutes of the *Société générale*'s board, 18 October 1887. Marc Meuleau, *Des pionniers en Extrême-Orient*, especially pp. 139–41, where one can find details regarding the *Société générale*.

35 Hubert Bonin, *Histoire de la Société générale*, op. cit.

36 Hubert Bonin, 'The French banks in the Pacific area (1860–1945),' in Olive Checkland, Shizuya Nishimura and Norio Tamaki (eds), *Pacific Banking (1859–1959). East Meets West*, London, MacMillan; New York, St Martin's Press, 1994, pp. 61–74. Hubert Bonin, 'L'activité des banques françaises dans l'Asie du Pacifique des années 1860 aux années 1940,' *Revue française d'histoire d'outre-mer*, 1994, 81(305), pp. 401–25. Hubert Bonin, 'Les banquiers français à Shanghai dans les années 1860–1940,' in: *Le Paris de l'Orient. Présence française à Shanghai, 1849–1946*, Musée Albert Kahn, Boulogne/Seine, 2002, pp. 113–19. E. W. Edwards, 'The origins of British financial co-operation with France in China, 1906–1961,' *English Historical Review*, LXXXVI, 1971, pp. 285–317. E. W. Edwards, 'British policy in China, 1913–1914. Rivalry with France in the Yangtze Valley,' *Journal of Oriental Studies*, 40, 1977, pp. 20–36.

37 Jean-Noël Jeanneney, 'La Banque industrielle de Chine et la chute des frères Berthelot (1921–1923),' in J.-N. Jeanneney, *L'argent caché. Milieux d'affaires et pouvoirs politiques dans la France du XXᵉ siècle*, Paris, Fayard, 1981, pp. 131–91.

38 Ibid., pp. 150–1.

39 Ibid., p. 173 and 180.

40 'La Banque franco-chinoise pour le commerce et l'industrie,' *L'Illustration économique et financière. Nos possessions coloniales: l'Indochine*, 15, 1925, p. 71.

41 *Banque de l'Algérie et de la Tunisie, Cinquante ans au service de la Tunisie*, Paris, Banque de l'Algérie et de la Tunisie, 1955. Mohamed Lazhar Gharbi, *Le capital français, à la traîne. Ébauche d'un réseau bancaire au Maghreb colonial (1847–1914)*, Tunis, Université de la Manouba, 2003.

42 Mohamed Lazhar-Gharbi, 'La Tunisie et la Banque de l'Algérie, 1881–1903: divergence d'intérêts ou les paradoxes d'une relation,' in *Le capital français à la traîne. Ébauche d'un réseau bancaire au Maghreb colonial, 1847–1914*, Tunis, Faculté des lettres Manouba, 2003, pp. 287–311. See Samir Saul's chapter in this very book.

43 Jean-Claude Allain, 'Les emprunts d'État marocains,' in Charles-Robert Ageron (ed.), *Les chemins de la décolonisation de l'empire colonial, 1936–1956*, Paris, Institut d'histoire du temps présent & Éditions du CNRS, 1986, pp. 131–45. Pierre Guillen, 'Les investissements français au Maroc de 1912 à 1939,' in Maurice Lévy-Leboyer (ed.), *La position internationale de la France*, Paris, EHESS, 1977, pp. 399–412.

44 Mohamed Lazhar Gharbi, op. cit., pp. 472–8.

45 See Éric Bussière, *Horace Finaly, banquier, 1871–1945*, Paris, Fayard, 1996, pp. 147–52.

46 Ibid., p. 152.

47 For the entire file, cf. Mohamed Lazhar Gharbi, op. cit., pp. 461–96.

48 Samir Saul, 'La Banque d'État du Maroc et la monnaie sous le protectorat,' in Jacques Marseille (ed.), *La France & l'outre-mer. Les relations économiques & financières entre la France & la France d'outre-mer*), Paris, Publication of the *Comité pour l'histoire économique & financière de la France*, 1998, pp. 389–427.

49 Edmond Spitzer, director of *Banque d'État du Maroc*, in Michel Poniatowski, *Mémoires*, Paris, Plon/Le Rocher, 1997, p. 243.

50 Yves Péhaut, 'Le réseau d'influence bordelais: la "doyenne" Maurel & Prom jusqu'en 1914,' in Hubert Bonin, Jean-François Klein and Catherine Hodeir (eds), *L'esprit économique impérial (1830–1970). Groupes de pression & réseaux du patronat colonial en France & dans l'empire*, Paris, Publications de la SFHOM, 2008, pp. 225–37.

51 Cf. Christian Schnakenbourg, 'La Banque de la Guadeloupe et la crise de change, 1895–1904,' *Bulletin de la Société d'histoire de la Guadeloupe*, (87–90), 1991, pp. 31–95. Suite, ibid., 104–5, 1995, pp. 3–100.

52 Xavier Daumalin, *Marseille et l'Ouest africain*, Marseille, Publications of the *Chambre de commerce et d'industrie Marseille-Provence*, 1992, pp. 226–7.

53 Yves Ekoué Amaïzo, *Naissance d'une banque de la zone franc, 1841–1901. La Banque du Sénégal*, Paris, L'Harmattan, 2001. Jacques Alibert, *De la vie coloniale au défi international. Banque du Sénégal, Banque de l'Afrique occidentale, B.I.A.O. 130 ans de banque en Afrique*, Paris, Chotard, 1983.

54 Louis-Bernard Rakotomanga et al., *Madagascar, cent ans d'expériences bancaires, 1866–1986*, Antananarivo, Bankin'ny Tantsaha Mpamokatra, 1987.

55 Minutes of Paribas's board, 21 November 1922.

56 Ibid., 2 and 18 December 1924.

57 *Banque commerciale africaine* file, archives of the BUP, 45A.654, minutes of the meeting with the minister, the AOF's governor general, the managing director of the flow of funds, the BUP's managing director and under-secretary of state to the minister of Colonies, 19 October 1931, two days after the bank closed its counters. After the meeting, the BUP-*Banque transtlantique-Paribas-Crédit lyonnais* group rediscounted 29 million francs in bills, BAO for 70 million. The dead liabilities amounted to 100 million in December 1931.

58 See Jacques Marseille, *Empire colonial*, op. cit.

59 Regarding Lemaignen and Durand-Réville, we have based ourselves on Catherine Hodeir's fine analyses, *Stratégies d'empire*, op. cit., Paris, Belin, 2003, pp. 216–21.

60 Also see Luc Durand-Réville, 'Les conditions de l'essor économique des colonies françaises d'Afrique subsaharienne,' *Marchés coloniaux du monde*, 19, March 1946, pp. 265–8.

61 Hubert Bonin, 'La perception de la puissance de la France impériale,' in Hubert Bonin, 'Les milieux d'affaires et la perception de la puissance française au tournant des années 1960,' *Relations internationales*, 57, spring 1989, pp. 49–76.

62 See Catherine Hodeir, 'Jouer Maroc, jouer Tunisie? Le grand patronat colonial français entre pari et réalisme (1945–1956),' in Hubert Bonin, Jean-François Klein and Catherine Hodeir (eds), *L'esprit économique impérial (1830–1970). Groupes de pression & réseaux du patronat colonial en France & dans l'empire*, Paris, Publications de la SFHOM, 2008, pp. 599–614.

63 H. Bonin, 'Le financement du RPF,' in Fondation Charles de Gaulle-Université de Bordeaux 3, *De Gaulle et le RPF, 1947–1955*, Paris, Armand Colin, 1998, pp. 78–88.

64 The board included Henri Fouques-Duparc, senator-mayor of Oran, deputed in 1951; Yves Perrussel, lawyer, mayor of Tunis; and Jacques Foccart.

65 Jacques Alibert, op. cit.

66 Cf. Luc Durand-Réville, 'La décolonisation et ses conséquennces sur les investissements privés français', *Revue politique et parlementaire*, 717, November 1961, pp. 17–24.

67 Cf. Jean Suret-Canale, 'Les banques d'affaires et l'outre-mer dans les années 1950–1980,' in *La France et l'outre-mer. Un siècle de relations monétaires et financières*, Paris, CHEFF, 1998, pp. 485–95.

68 Emmanuel Beau de Loménie, *L'Algérie trahie par l'argent*, Paris, 1957.

69 'Industrialisation et grand capital,' in Daniel Lefeuvre, *Chère Algérie, 1930–1962*, Paris, SFHOM Publications, pp. 327–9.

70 Jacques Alibert, op. cit.

71 We thank the WordPro business unit in Pondicherry (India) for translating our French version into that chapter.

9 Concluding remarks

Colonial banking, imperial banking, overseas banking, imperialist banking: convergences, osmoses and differentiation

Hubert Bonin

Though several books (think of A. S. Baster or G. Jones), articles and chapters have recounted and analyzed colonial banking history, it still remains difficult to specify the true 'nature' of a 'colonial bank.' No doubt that all of them were 'overseas banks,' with several even being 'international(-ized) banks,' but our main purpose is to initiate a discussion regarding the definitions of 'colonial' versus 'imperial.'

From colonial banking ...

Colonial banks seem to be readily definable – supported by the state, these banks were established in European colonies (we are not talking here of the Russian/Soviet or Chinese empires) and enjoyed several 'privileges' such as the power to issue banknotes and manage the military and Treasury accounts. Some of them were merely banks of issue and rediscounts, like *Bank of Algeria* (a study by S. Saul appears in this volume), *Banque de l'Indochine* in Indochina, *Banque d'Afrique occidentale*, HSBC in Hong Kong, *Bank of Taiwan* in Japanese Taiwan and the two banks in Spanish Cuba and Puerto Rico (the last two being the subject of the analysis presented in this volume by P. Martin-Acena and I. Rodan de Montaud). They were set up to accompany the economic development of their colonies, their businessmen and their wholesale trade, maritime and insurance services, the agro-business, industrial firms and individual entrepreneurs.

These banks were used to subject the people and wealth of the colonies to the interests of the metropolis, either as conduits to the latter or as levers for export of commodities towards other countries (like Indochinese rice to Hong Kong for *Banque de l'Indochine*). In any case, they could not be limited to merely colonial functions i.e., between the metropolis and its colonies, because they were also used by foreign companies to penetrate the territory. It was extremely rare that territories, even those proclaimed as '*preserves*,' were really isolated and prevented from having exchanges with other nearby territories (for example, French sub-Saharan Africa was opened to Belgian and British firms like the *Unilever* affiliates). Thus, colonial banks also practiced international banking.

Colonial banking naturally implied a strong commitment by the state to protect the interests of its colonial banks, especially when they were banks of issue. The state encouraged the founding of banks in the Dutch Indies, French Africa and Indochina. But this did not mean the institution of a monopoly. Though *Banque de l'Indochine, Société générale* and *Banque de l'Afrique occidentale* dominated their respective spheres of influence, it was because of a co-operative agreement between the French banks, and competition was rife in South Africa, Algeria, Tunisia, Morocco and the British colonies. The richer the colony, the greater was the competition.

The fact that sometimes a monopoly was applied meant that metropolitan banks used it as a correspondent, and competition for the distribution of credits to firms was harsh. Some metropolitan bankers were much more involved in banking to the companies active overseas. The scramble was at its maximum in the port cities of the metropolis which were used as hubs for cash and FOREX operations, and for credit connections. The extent of the competition could be used as a tool to measure the development of colonial economies. The Dutch Indies were also penetrated by Chinese, Japanese and American banks, and colonial banking did not encourage a monopolistic way of life.

One issue to be kept in mind was the difference between metropolitan banks directly or indirectly (via affiliates or sponsored establishments) active in the colonies on one side, and banks founded by local business communities, on the other side. Examples may be found in South Africa (the *Boers'* banks), Australia and New Zealand, Canada and India, with local banks set up by powerful business dynasties. They were colonial in the sense that they worked under the rules of the colony (or dominion), but they were also somewhat 'independent' as they were managed and owned by 'nationals,' sometimes with 'nationalist' mindsets. This mixture characterized these territories and favoured the rapid development of local banking systems after independence (especially in Canada, Australia and New Zealand and, to a lesser extent, Brazil).

In the latter case, as recounted by C. G. Guimarães, Brazilian-Portuguese interests developed their own banking institutions in the form of 'colonial banks.' These institutions also associated themselves with British businessmen, traders and bankers to establish transatlantic connections via new banks, whether 'colonial' like the Brazilian-Portuguese ones, or 'imperial' – the face of British business thalassocracy. This latter dominated from the independence of Brazil until the First World War, as 'henceforth, imperial banking mixed Brazilian and British business communities through clearing operations, trade finance and issues on the London market'. Co-operative forms of banking capitalism favoured such an 'imperial banking' modus operandi for mutual benefit, with Brazilian businessmen and bankers profiting from the transatlantic skill spill-over.

A last sign of a special 'colonial' status borne by 'colonial banking' was its outcome alone – the very closing of the curtain over so many years of colonial business abroad! When the knell of independence rang out, the sheer number of colonial banks that were nationalized showed the extent of the colonial system which had to be destroyed by the new nationalistic Third World powers – as has been described in several chapters here. Very few 'colonial banks' escaped this fate – only those which had anticipated the decolonization and had diversified their assets either to the metropolis (*Crédit foncier d'Algérie & de Tunisie* and *Compagnie algérienne*), to other colonies (*Banque de l'Indochine*) or internationally. Some of them accumulated financial assets which transformed them into holding companies that were easily repatriated and merged with other holdings, as in the case of the erstwhile *Banque d'Etat du Maroc*.

… Jumping over imperialism …

Why should we use the words 'imperial banking' instead of focusing on colonial banking? Imperialist issues suffice to define the other ways of spreading overseas. For instance, from its sole role as a local bank in Hong Kong, HSBC positioned itself as a major Chinese and South East Asian institution, active in the city ports and concessions in China and with its fingers in French Indochina. Everywhere it epitomized and complemented British thalassocracy and could be perceived as a lever for British imperialism,[1] if we understand imperialism as a Marxian force mixing banking, industry, trade and public influence to sustain powerful economies abroad. Outside the grip of colonial powers, 'imperialist banks' asserted their multi-faceted action overseas, in both the less common unconquered countries like China and in those that attained independence, like Brazil.

Moreover, capitalist 'groups' sketched the outlines of a strong and pervasive influence in all colonial territories and those independent countries that were considered to be fit targets for the export of capital, equipment, consumer goods and trade. Such French interests have been analyzed regarding Morocco, Algeria and Indochina as well as several territories in Asia and Latin America, whatever their political status: imperialist processes had gathered momentum. But contemporary experts speak of overseas 'imperial interests' and 'imperial standing,' only touching to some extent the reality of true imperialism. 'Imperial' was often a disguise for 'imperialist,'[2] but far more discreet and 'elegant.' Today, the word 'imperialist' has almost disappeared from the academic field, except within the remnants of Marxist theory. I must admit that I have myself worked with leftists for the sake of pluralism.[3] 'Imperial'[4] did prevail, but its ambiguity remains a source of debate.

Using 'imperial' instead of 'imperialist,' without depriving it of the latter's connotations,[5] might seem more appropriate in the case of the areas dealt with in this book. 'Co-operative' capitalism took shape, with 'imperial committees' formed for each continent (*Comité français de l'Asie*, etc.), pressure groups, specialized publications and books, committees of parliamentary representatives promoting rules favourable to colonization and overseas trade and cartels and 'agreements' to mobilize banks and finance, notably on the occasion of the issuing of bonds by colonial authorities or corporations.

... To imperial banking

This leads us to using the term 'imperial banking' for denoting the activities either of those banks that were active in the colonies or those banks and banking groups which had a presence in the colonies or in independent countries abroad. HSBC was no doubt the epitome of imperial banking, but *Nederlandsche Handel-Maatschappij* (NHM) was no laggard either, extending its network from its core Dutch Indies to the whole of East Asia in the 1900s. Imperial banking spread from one colony to other colonies or to neighbouring independent countries. Dutch and British banks rushed to cater to Dutch-origin and British-origin (and British-controlled) people and business communities in South Africa and neighbouring colonies, which led S. Jones to entitle his book *The Great Imperial Banks*.

Money and banking empires spread over several statutes and types of territories. The capital of experience and the art of risk management acquired thanks to colonial banking were mobilized to new port cities and market-places, where FOREX, discounting, trade finance and wholesale banking could be practiced. *Crédit foncier d'Algérie & de Tunisie*, ever at the service of French interests and of foreign clients, covered Algeria, Tunisia and, in the interwar period, the Middle East, Salonica and Libya. It was a double company with, on one side, its core colony (Algeria) and the entire East-Mediterranean trade (both connected through Marseille), and on the other, French and foreign business. When it practiced imperial banking, it evolved within and through an open market economy, as was the case with *Banque de l'Indochine*, the *Chartered Bank of India, Australia & China*, HSBC or Bank of London & Latin America (BOLSA), which inserted themselves into pockets of developing economy in Asia and Latin America.

Barclays itself exemplified this strategy, which was crowned by the creation of Barclays DCO in 1925 – DCO standing for 'Dominions, Colonies and Overseas,' thus comprehensively summing up our entire present analysis! It acquired (rescued) the National Bank of South Africa. From its origin, the latter was a government-privileged bank in Transvaal, established with German, British and Dutch capital. *Nederlandsche Bank voor Zuid-Afrika* (NBvZA) in 1925 merged with another Dutch bank, the Transvaal Commercial Bank. In South Africa itself, NBvZA changed its name into NBSA in 1951; a holding company was then continuing NBvZA in Amsterdam, and had brought its South African business in a separate South African bank called NBSA, in which the parent company still held 75 per cent (later reduced, and ultimately sold). But NBvZA itself changed its name in 1954 after a merger in the Netherlands and became Nederlandse Overzee Bank. The move from 'colonial banking' to 'imperial banking' with some kind of 'confederal' influence and operations had been thus more and more intensive.

Imperial banking was obvious when British interests set up the *Imperial Bank of Persia*, because, besides the name itself, it proclaimed the inclusion of Persia (and Iran) within the British imperial/imperialist grip. Should we stick to our expression 'imperial banking' in the case of Latin America? We know that Lloyd chose to focus on Latin America and controlled BOLSA. Earlier, *Deutsche Bank* had established *Deutsche Überseeische Bank* and *Deutsch-Asiatich Bank. Hollandsche Bank voor Zuid-Amerika* (*Bancolanda*, HBvZA) was founded in Amsterdam in 1914 by *Rotterdamsche Bankvereeniging*. HBvZA turned to *Hollandsche Bank-Unie* (Holland Banking Union, HBU) in 1933 after the purchase of an affiliate in Istanbul and the take-over of *Hollandsche Bank voor West-Indië* in 1935, joining the bunch of imperial banks active in colonies and independent states, plural overseas banking, mixing portfolios of talents and influences.

Does this mean that we can say that the experience of British overseas banking was very different from that of continental Europe? The British system relied almost exclusively on 'standalone banks,' colonial banks active solely overseas and the multi-territorial imperial banking as practiced by Barclays DCO and Lloyds (with its affiliate BOLSA). Continental Europe, on the other hand, seemed to favour a process whereby metropolitan banks expanded their operations abroad, mainly in the colonies, but also on other statutory territories, like China. The question boils down to 'varieties' of business models and banking micro-systems.

In terms of range of operations and geographical scope, HSBC's example epitomizes the arguments of our book, as it brings in the issue of what exactly is a colonial or imperial bank. HSBC was formed at the initiative of Thomas Sunderland[6] and started its activities in the British colony of Hong Kong and in the newly opened ports along the Chinese coast. It succeeded in resisting catastrophes and in grappling with its intense risks, conversely with the Oriental Bank,[7] which collapsed in 1884. HSBC later expanded, especially after WWII, acquiring Mercantile Bank and British Bank of the Middle East, which had established themselves in India and in the Middle East, respectively.[8] Mercantile Bank started as a local Indian bank, Mercantile Bank of Bombay, in 1853. In 1858, it became a freestanding bank under the name of the Mercantile Bank of India, London & China, but returned to its earlier status as Mercantile Bank of India in 1893, although it continued some activity in the Far East until the post-WWII years. It was finally acquired by HSBC in 1959. The British Bank of the Middle East was created in 1887 as the Imperial Bank of Persia. It extended its activities to the Middle East in general, before its acquisition by HSBC in 1959. HSBC lost all its operations in Iran after the fall of the monarchy in 1979, and its assets went to the nationalized Tejerat Bank. We see how HSBC went from being merely a 'colonial bank' to an 'imperial bank': it first entered neighbouring China (in competition with *Banque de l'Indochine, Yokohama Specie Bank, Deutsche-Asiatich Bank* and *Citibank*), and later it spread itself all over the regions under British influence, like Persia and India. It stuck to its legacy of 'imperial Britain' before finally joining the 'transnational banking' scene in the 1970s.[9]

Whatever the business model or area chosen by these banks, they were all confronted by the need to acquire and consolidate their skills portfolio to tackle the heightened risks of being abroad, in foreign port cities, market-places and countries where 'the civilization of (sound) banking' had yet to be rooted. The danger for imperial banking was to cede to imperial pressure groups and forget sound banking management. So many chapters and monographs dedicated to colonial and imperial banks talk of the over-support brought to some sectors, companies and interests groups through credit lines and even the issue of securities, without an adequate scrutiny of the balance-sheets. No wonder that many clients turned out to be 'bad risks' and had to be relegated and finally disposed off as bad assets at the expense of profitability. Let us not forget the collapse of *Barings* in 1890 and its support of Argentine securities for the sake of British imperial influence in the area. We all know of the British and French banks which had to contend with terrible assets in Asia!

What was undeniable was the business connection between the major European banking hubs – before the advent of New York – and the colonial or economic empires overseas. The mainland banking hubs became more and more committed to imperial banking. They acted as European hubs for managing correspondence banking, clearing, FOREX, treasury flow, cash management and transfers and refinancing, as backup lenders to colonial and imperial banks. Imperial banks flourished in London, Paris, Berlin, Brussels and Amsterdam, before the rise of New York from the 1900s–1910s. Apart from those embedded in overseas territories, even the ones in the mainland became more and more involved in colonial and imperial banking, thus adopting the skills and taking on the guise of veritable 'imperial banks.'

Is the present regional transnational banking a new form of imperial banking?

The conversion of a few colonial banks into imperial banks helped them to resist the tempests of decolonization. Some South African banks attained a 'southern and eastern African' scope after joining multi-nationalized groups. Barclays was first, followed by Standard Chartered. G. Verhoef has recounted how Nedbank achieved a 'continental approach to banking in South Africa.' They all succeeded in getting some South African legitimacy by converting from 'colonial' to 'imperial' banking, that is, by submitting to local regulation: NBvZA changed its name to Netherlands Bank of South Africa (NBSA) in 1951 when a South African holding company was formed and incorporated in South Africa. ABN (now *Algemene Bank Nederland-Amsterdam Rotterdam Bank* (ABN-AMRO)) inherited the Latin American stake of Dutch banks after an amalgamation towards the end of the 1960s. Standard Chartered itself integrated experience, corporate cultures and skill portfolios from Africa and Asia and developed an autonomous, implicit but pervasive and substantial form of imperial banking on these two emerging continents by adding a subtle British influence to the many Asian and African stake-holders.

The present power of Standard Chartered and HSBC is an expression of this legacy of colonial banking: widened at first to a form of imperial banking (from the 1910s to the 1950s) spread across colonized territories or those controlled by imperialist powers, they then turned to the independent states, using transnational paths of overseas imperial banking in Asia and elsewhere.[10] They had no political power, only delocalized sources of influence – far from the traditional British thalassocracy. In that regard, the latter's legacy could well be those very mini-systems of 'imperial banking' which have continued over the past 150 years or so. British imperial banking mixed colonial banking and imperial banking because 'colonial banks' spread their activities across the entire region of their original action and then proceeded to other continents, for example when Chartered merged with Standard to form Standard Chartered.

N. Valerio and T. Tjipilica told us that *Banco Africano de Investimentos* had spread its network to South Africa, Portugal and Cape Verde, with connections via joint ventures to Brazil and São Tomé and Príncipe. One could say that such an array of participations transformed the Angolan mother company into an 'imperial bank,' practicing imperial banking across borders. The new powerful countries like South Africa, Nigeria, Angola, and, northwards, Morocco (with *Attijariwafa Bank* – the result of a merger between two banks in 2008 mainly through *Wafabank*, the result of a nationalization of a French affiliate in Morocco in 1964), Gabon (with BGFI) and even Togo (with the *Ecobank* group, starting in 1985) were able to foster 'pan African' banks along the same 'imperial banking' lines that were used by European banks active in the colonies and elsewhere.

Meanwhile, terms like 'pan-African' and 'transnational' have replaced the now old-fashioned 'imperial.' A few, rapidly growing, independent, former Third World countries have committed themselves to the shaping of a globalized inter-dependent economy on the African scale, and it is the same with Latin America, with the 'economic colonization' of the less strong by the more powerful economies.

Notes

1   See D. McLean, 'International banking and its political implications: The Hong-Kong & Shanghai Banking Corporation and the Imperial Bank of Persia, 1889–1914,' in Frank King (ed.), *Eastern Banking*, London, Athlone Press, 1983.
2   See: Leonard Woolf, *Empire and Commerce in Africa: A Study in Economic Imperialism*, London, 1920; reedition, London, George Allen & Unwin, 1968. John Gallagher & Ronald Robinson, 'The imperialism of free trade,' *Economic History Review*, vol. 6, 1953, pp. 1–15; reedited in A. G. L. Shaw (ed.), *Great Britain and the Colonies, 1820–1850*, London, Methuen, 1970; David Kenneth Fieldhouse, '"Imperialism": A historiographical revision', *Economic History Review*, 14, 1961, pp. 187–209. Ralph A. Austen, *Modern Imperialism: Western Overseas Expansion and its Aftermath, 1776–1965*, Lexington, Mass., Heath, 1969.
3   See Hubert Bonin and Michel Cahen (eds), *Négoce blanc en Afrique noire. Le commerce de longue distance en Afrique subsaharienne du XVIIIe au XXe siècles*, Paris, Publications de la Société française d'histoire d'outre-mer, 2001. Hubert Bonin, 'Banques et outre-mer; Bordeaux; Chambres de commerce; Charles-Roux; Compagnies de navigation; Conférences économiques; Douanes; Huileries; Investissements; Lobby colonial; Marseille (le port colonial); Monnaie outre-mer; Plan; Planification; Préférence impériale; Suez,,' in Claude Liauzu (ed.), *Dictionnaire de la colonisation française*, Paris, Larousse, 2007. And some leftist authors in: Hubert Bonin, Jean-François Klein and Catherine Hodeir (eds), *L'esprit économique impérial (1830–1970). Groupes de pression & réseaux du patronat colonial en France & dans l'empire*, Paris, Publications de la SFHOM, 2008.
4   For instance: Anthony Gerald Hopkins, 'Imperial business in Africa. Part I: Sources,' *Journal of African History*, LVII(1), 1976, pp. 29–48. 'Imperial business in Africa. Part II: Interpretations,' *Journal of African History*, LVII(2), 1976, pp. 267–90.

5 A perfect example might be: Ronald Robinson, 'Perspectives on imperial history: Imperial theory and the questional imperialism after empire,' *Journal of Imperial and Commonwealth History*, 12(2), 1984, pp. 42–54.

6 David Kynaston and Richard Roberts, *The Lion Wakes: A Modern History of HSBC*, London, Profile Books, 2015. Also see the whole collection of books on HSBC published by Frank King.

7 'The failure of the Oriental Bank Corporation,' *The Economist*, 10 May 1884, p. 567. John McGuire, 'The rise and fall of the Oriental Bank in the nineteenth century: A product of the transformation that occurred in the world economy or the result of its own management?,' working paper, Canberra, 2004.

8 On the evolution of the Hongkong & Shanghai Banking Corporation, see Frank King, *The History of the Hong Kong & Shanghai Banking Corporation*, Cambridge, Cambridge University Press (4 volumes), 1987–1991. Also see the respective website.

9 David Kyaston and Richard Roberts, op. cit., 2015.

10 Geoffrey Jones (ed.), *Banks as Multinationals*, London, Routledge, 1990. Geoffrey Jones, *British Multinational Banking, 1830–1990*, Oxford, Clarendon Press, 1993. Shizuya Nishimura, Toshio Suzuki and Ranald Michie (eds), *The Origins of International Banking in Asia. The Nineteenth and Twentieth Centuries*, Oxford, Oxford University Press, 2012.

Hubert Bonin's publications about overseas history

'Les offensives d'Unilever et de ses ancêtres sur la chasse gardée commerciale française et franco-africaine (1890–1940)', in Jean Batou, Frédérique Beauvois, Thomas David, Mathieu Humbert and Claude Lutzelschwab (eds), *Deux mondes, une planète. Mélanges offerts à Bouda Etemad*. Lausanne: Éditions d'en bas, 2015, pp. 211–28.

Hubert Bonin, Bernard Droz and Josette Rivallain (eds), *Cent ans d'histoire des outre-mers. SFHOM, 1912–2012*. Paris: Publications de la SFHOM, 2013, p. 664.

'Commémorer le centenaire de la SFHOM: défis et enjeux', *Outre-Mers. Revue d'histoire*, n°spécial *Cent ans d'histoire des outre-mers. SFHOM*, 1912–2012, 2nd semester 2012, no. 376/377, pp. 13–42.

'La SFHOM et les milieux d'affaires ultramarins: Georges Nesterenko trésorier', *Outre-Mers. Revue d'histoire*, n°spécial *Cent ans d'histoire des outre-mers. SFHOM*, 1912–2012, 2nd semester 2012, no. 376/377, pp. 333–55.

'The complementarities between merchant shipping and ancillary activities: The case of two French firms, SCAC and SAGA (1880s–1990s)', *International Journal of Maritime History*, volume XXIII, no. 1, June 2011, pp. 95–114.

'La perception des risques du nationalisme anti-impérial et de l'indépendance: trois compagnies africaines dans les années 1940–1910', *Outre-Mers. Revue d'histoire*, n°spécial *Cinquante ans d'indépendances africaines*, 2nd semester 2010, pp. 37–62.

'Introduction. La maturation d'une historiographie'; 'Des outre-mers tripolaires: Suez et CFAO', in Hubert Bonin, Christophe Bouneau and Hervé Joly (eds), *Les entreprises et l'outre-mer français pendant la Seconde Guerre mondiale*. Pessac: Maison des sciences de l'homme d'Aquitaine, 2010, pp. 11–24; 79–98.

'Bordeaux et la traite des noirs', in *Les tabous de Bordeaux*. Bordeaux: Le Festin, 2010, pp. 13–23.

History of the Suez Canal Company, 1858–1960. Between Controversy and Utility. Geneva: Droz, 2010.

'Les banques et l'Algérie coloniale: mise en valeur impériale ou exploitation impérialiste?', *Outre-Mers. Revue d'histoire*, tome 97, no. 362–3, June 2009, pp. 213–26.

'Compagnie algérienne', 'Banque de l'Algérie', 'Crédit foncier d'Algérie & de Tunisie', 'Grands chantiers (BTP)', 'Centrales et réseaux électriques', 'Chemins de fer', 'Compagnies de négoce', 'Compagnies de transit', 'Compagnies maritimes', 'Compagnies foncières de colonisation', 'Hydrocarbures (pétrole et gaz)', 'Marseille et l'Algérie', 'Mines', 'Plans de modernisation', in Jeannine Verdès-Leroux (eds), *L'Algérie et la France*. Paris: Robert Laffont-Bouquins, 2009.

'Marcher sur deux jambes: les dualismes du négoce girondin sur la Côte occidentale d'Afrique au début du XIXᵉ siècle', in René Favier, Gérard Gayot, Jean-François

Klein, Didier Terrier and Denis Woronoff (eds), *L'industrie et ses patrons, XVIe-XXe siècles. Mélanges offerts à Serge Chassagne*. Valenciennes: Presses universitaires de Valenciennes, 2009, pp. 207–17.

Hubert Bonin and Bruno Marnot, 'The international scope of Bordeaux port: Logistics, economic effects and business cycles in the nineteenth and twentieth centuries', in Tapio Bergholm, Lewis Fisher and Elisabetta Tonizzi (eds), *Making Global and Local Connections: Historical Perspectives on Ports, Research in Maritime History*, no. 35, autumn 2007, pp. 1–22.

CFAO (1887–2007). *La réinvention permanente d'une entreprise de commerce outre-mer.* Paris: Publications de la SFHOM, 2008, p. 768.

Hubert Bonin, Jean-François Klein and Catherine Hodeir (eds), *L'esprit économique impérial (1830–1970). Groupes de pression & réseaux du patronat colonial en France & dans l'empire*. Paris: Publications de la SFHOM, 2008, p. 950.

'Les réseaux bancaires parisiens et l'empire: comment mesurer la capacité d'influence des "banquiers impériaux?,"' in Hubert Bonin, Jean-François Klein and Catherine Hodeir (eds), *L'esprit économique impérial (1830–1970). Groupes de pression & réseaux du patronat colonial en France & dans l'empire*. Paris: Publications de la SFHOM, 2008, pp. 447–72.

'La construction d'un système socio-mental impérial par le monde des affaires ultramarin girondin (des années 1890 aux années 1950)', in Hubert Bonin, Jean-François Klein and Catherine Hodeir (eds), *L'esprit économique impérial (1830–1970). Groupes de pression & réseaux du patronat colonial en France & dans l'empire*. Paris: Publications de la SFHOM, 2008, pp. 243–74.

'Un gouverneur face aux enjeux du développement: Éboué et le monde des affaires en AEF en 1942 (commentaires de la lettre d'Éboué du 18 juillet 1942)', in Josette Rivallain and Hélène d'Almeida-Topor (eds), *Éboué, soixante ans après*. Paris: Publications de la SFHOM, 2008, pp. 402–8.

'Les banquiers', in Jean-Pierre Rioux (ed.), *Dictionnaire de la France coloniale*. Paris: Flammarion, 2007, pp. 563–8; 'Les ports', Ibidem, pp. 533–8.

'Banques et outre-mer; Bordeaux; Chambres de commerce; Charles-Roux; Compagnies de navigation; Conférences économiques; Douanes; Huileries; Investissements; Lobby colonial; Marseille (le port colonial); Monnaie outre-mer; Plan; Planification; Préférence impériale; Suez', in Claude Liauzu (ed.), *Dictionnaire de la colonisation française*. Paris: Larousse, 2007.

'L'outre-mer dans la stratégie des milieux d'affaires français: le point sur les débats et l'historiographie', in 'Missions en Afrique orientale (XVIIe–XXe siècles). Ambivalences de rencontres', *Histoire & missions chrétiennes*, no. 4, December 2007, Karthala, pp. 141–50.

'Empire, French: 1815–Present'; 'Ghana'; 'Senegambia', in John McCusker et al. (eds), *History of World Trade since 1450* (two volumes), Farmington Hills, MI, Thomson-Gale, 2005.

'The Compagnie du canal de Suez and Transit Shipping, 1900–1956', *International Journal of Maritime History*, volume XVII, no. 2, December 2005, pp. 87–112.

Un outre-mer bancaire méditerranéen. Histoire du Crédit foncier d'Algérie & de Tunisie (1880–1997). Paris: Publications de la Société française d'histoire d'outre-mer, 2004; Rev. edition in 2010, p. 370.

'Une banque française maître d'oeuvre d'un outre-mer levantin: le Crédit foncier d'Algérie & de Tunisie, du Maghreb à la Méditerranée orientale (1919–1970)', *Outre-Mers. Revue d'histoire*, premier semestre 2004, tome 91, no. 342–3, pp. 239–72.

'Un outre-mer bancaire en Orient méditerranéen: des banques françaises marraines de la Banque de Salonique (de 1907 à la Seconde Guerre mondiale)', *Revue historique*, CCCV/3, November 2003, pp. 268–302.

'Des négociants français à l'assaut des places fortes commerciales britanniques: CFAO et SCOA en Afrique occidentale anglaise puis anglophone', in Hubert Bonin and Michel Cahen (eds), *Négoce blanc en Afrique noire. Le commerce de longue distance en Afrique subsaharienne du XVIIIe au XXe siècles*. Paris: Publications de la Société française d'histoire d'outre-mer. Paris, 2001 [actes du colloque de septembre 1999 à l'Institut d'études politiques de Bordeaux], pp. 147–69, 422.

'La Compagnie algérienne levier de la colonisation et prospère grâce à elle (1865–1939)', *Revue française d'histoire d'outre-mer*, 2nd semester 2000, no. 328–9, pp. 209–30.

'Une histoire bancaire transméditerranéenne: la Compagnie algérienne, d'un ultime apogée au repli (1945–1970)', in Daniel Lefeuvre et al. (eds), *La Guerre d'Algérie au miroir des décolonisations françaises* (En l'honneur de Charles-Robert Ageron). Paris: Publications de la Société française d'histoire d'outre-mer, 2000, pp. 151–76 (2nd edition in 2005).

'L'outre-mer, marché pour la banque commerciale (1876–1985)?', in Jacques Marseille (ed.), *La France & l'outre-mer* (actes du colloque de novembre 1996; *Les relations économiques & financières entre la France & la France d'outre-mer*). Paris: Comité pour l'histoire économique & financière de la France, 1998, pp. 437–83.

'Le Comptoir national d'escompte de Paris, une banque impériale (1848–1940)', *Revue française d'histoire d'outre-mer*, tome 78, no. 293, 1991, pp. 477–97.

'Suez et le commerce international (1957–1987)', in François Crouzet (ed.), *Le négoce international, XIIIe–XXe siècles*. Paris: Économica, 1989 (actes du colloque de Paris de l'Association française des historiens économistes, 1988).

Suez. Du canal à la finance (1858–1987). Paris: Économica, 1987, p. 673.

C.F.A.O. (Compagnie française de l'Afrique occidentale). Cent ans de compétition (1887–1987). Paris: Économica, 1987, p. 560.

Index

For Product Safety Concerns and Information please contact our EU
representative GPSR@taylorandfrancis.com Taylor & Francis Verlag GmbH,
Kaufingerstraße 24, 80331 München, Germany

Printed and bound by CPI Group (UK) Ltd, Croydon, CR0 4YY
08/05/2025
01864536-0002